ENCOUNTERS WITH GOD IN MEDIEVAL AND EARLY MODERN ENGLISH POETRY

To Noel Rowe

and

in memory of my father

Robert Julian Clutterbuck

22.3.1916–25.3.2000

He alone is the true atheist to whom the predicates of the Divine Being – for example, love, wisdom, justice – are nothing; not he to whom merely the subject of those predicates is nothing.

Ludwig Feuerbach

Encounters with God in Medieval and Early Modern English Poetry

CHARLOTTE CLUTTERBUCK
Abbotsleigh School, Australia

Routledge
Taylor & Francis Group

LONDON AND NEW YORK

First published 2005 by Ashgate Publishing

Published 2017 by Routledge
2 Park Square, Milton Park, Abingdon, Oxfordshire OX14 4RN
711 Third Avenue, New York, NY 10017, USA

First issued in paperback 2017

Routledge is an imprint of the Taylor & Francis Group, an informa business

British Library Cataloguing in Publication Data
Clutterbuck, Charlotte
  Encounters with God in medieval and early modern English poetry
  1. Langland, Williams, 1330?-1400?. Piers Plowman 2. Donne, John, 1572-1631 3.
  Milton, John, 1608-1674. Paradise lost 4. English poetry – Middle English, 1100-1500 –
  History and criticism 5. English poetry – Early modern, 1500-1700 – History and
  criticism 6. God in literature 7. Spirituality in literature
  I. Title
  821.1'00938231

Library of Congress Cataloging-in-Publication Data
Clutterbuck, Charlotte.
  Encounters with God in medieval and early modern English poetry / Charlotte
  Clutterbuck.
      p. cm
  Includes bibliographical references (p.   ) and index.
  ISBN 0-7546-5270-X (alk. paper)
   1. Christian poetry, English (Old) – History and criticism. 2. Christian poetry, English
(Middle) – History and criticism. 3. Christian poetry, English – Early modern, 1500-1700 –
History and criticism. 4. Christianity and literature – England. 5. God in literature.
 I. Title.

  PR508.C65C58 2004
  811.009'3823–dc22

                                                                            2004027889

ISBN 13: 978-1-138-26483-0 (pbk)
ISBN 13: 978-0-7546-5270-0 (hbk)

Contents

Acknowledgments

I would like to thank The Pierpont Morgan Library, New York, for permission to reproduce the Crucifixion from the *Gospels of the Countess Judith* (MS M.709, f.1v.); the Bibliothèque Nationale de France, for permission to reproduce the Lamentation, *Grandes Heures de Rohan*, (Latin 9471, Folio 135); A.V.C. Schmidt for permission to quote from *Piers Plowman: A Parallel-Text Edition of the A, B, C, and Z Versions*;[1] the Estate of Sir Herbert Grierson for permission to quote from *John Donne: Poetical Works*;[2] and to Longman for permission to quote from John Milton's *Paradise Lost*.[3]

This book is the result of more than thirty years of interest in religious art and literature, and it is difficult to be sure that I will thank everyone who has helped me along the way. Acknowledgements

Firstly, I would like to thank my parents, Suzanne and the late Robert Clutterbuck, for their constant practical, emotional, and financial support without which my education would not have been possible.

Next, I thank my husband, Bob Moen: for going to England with me so that I could study at Oxford University; for supporting me and our children financially for many of their early years; for sharing my love of words and paintings; for building me a study to work in; and for much patience and much proof-reading. Our children, John and Jocelyn, have always shared our love of words and literature (especially Dickens), and I thank them for many meals cooked, for proof-reading, and most of all for listening sympathetically to my disasters and occasional triumphs along the way. Thanks are also due to my family: Victoria, Harriet, and Lucinda Clutterbuck, and Dorothy Sutherland for emotional support. Especial thanks to my cousin Jocelyn Walmesley-White for her enthusiasm, insight, and suggestions, and to her sister Judith Beale who would have loved to see the book if she had lived long enough. Special thanks to my friends Jillian Anderson, Elizabeth Boothby, Felicity Bremner, Jo Crooks, Susan Moore, Jennifer Rose, Averil Treloar, and Gillian Wait for their help, support, and enthusiasm at various stages of this project.

My initial love of religious art and literature germinated at the University of Sydney in the 1970s. I am forever grateful to the past and present staff and students of its English Department who have taught me or learned with me over many years: especially Peter Barrat, Peter Collins, Edina Eisikovits, Helen Fulton, Joanna Jaaniste, Denise Lyell, Gary Simes, Barry Spurr, Diane Speed, Russell Stendel, Betsy Taylor, and the late Leslie Rogers and Frederick May. In particular,

---

[1] *The Vision of Piers Plowman: A Complete Edition of the B-Text* (London, 1978).

[2] *John Donne: Poetical Works*, ed. Herbert Grierson, (London, 1967).

[3] *Paradise Lost*, ed. Alastair Fowler (London, 1968).

Stephen Knight inspired my initial passion for medieval literature with his lectures on Chaucer and Malory, disabused me of my post-Romantic notions, supervised my MA thesis, and told me to learn to type – all invaluable lessons. The late Bernard Martin deepened my knowledge and enthusiasm with his seminars on *Troilus and Crisseyde* and his astonishing generosity in always treating me as an equal in discussions both inside and outside the classroom. Raymond Misson first introduced me to *Piers Plowman* with a breathless enthusiasm which taught me a lot about how to teach and instilled a life long love of the poem.

The project really began to take shape when I attended the first International Conference of the Society for Religion, Literature and the Arts in 1994, and I thank Michael Griffiths for his work on the conferences that provided me with a forum for sharing ideas. Thanks to James Tulip for encouraging me to commence the doctoral thesis that led to this book. Thanks also to John Murray, Francis Moloney, and Mary Dove for their encouragement. A special mention goes to the late Bill Jobling, who supervised the thesis all too briefly before his sudden death, but who encouraged me to undertake my rather unwieldy task with the motto *solvitur scribendi*, which I found a great comfort as I struggled to grasp the material.

At critical points in a difficult journey, Jenny Gribble and David Jasper came to my rescue: without them, I might have abandoned the whole project in despair; I offer them my heartfelt thanks.

I also wish to express my appreciation to all the staff of Ashgate who have assisted me with professionalism and warmth, in particular Erika Gaffney, whose sympathetic, prompt, and efficient efforts enabled me to bring the book into publishable shape.

Above all, my thanks go to Noel Rowe, who supervised the last stages of my doctoral thesis: for his firmness in pointing out pitfalls; for his companionship; but most of all, for liberating me to find the full extent of what I wanted to say.

List of Illustrations

List of Abbreviations

AUMLA	*Journal of the Australasian Modern Language Association*
EETS	Early English Text Society
ELN	*English Language Notes*
ES	*English Studies*
JDJ	*John Donne Journal*
MÆ	*Medium Ævum*
MiltonQ	*Milton Quarterly*
MiltonS	*Milton Studies*
OED	*Oxford English Dictionary*
RES	*Review of English Studies*
SEL	*Studies in English Literature*
SP	*Studies in Philology*
ST	*Summa Theologica*
YLS	*Yearbook of Langland Studies*

Introduction

Gramer, the grounde of al, bigileth nouthe childrene:
For is noon nouthe, hoso nymeth hede,
That can versifye vayre or formalliche endite
Ne can construe kyndeliche that poetes made.
                            William Langland, *Piers Plowman*, C.XVII.107-10

So of hol herte cometh hope, and hardy relacioun
Seketh and seweth his 'sustantif' savacioun –
That is God, the ground of al, a graciouse 'antecedent'.
                            Piers Plowman, C.III.351-3

In *Piers Plowman*, William Langland sees grammar as 'the grounde of al', because it is through grammar that educated men can understand the Christian faith, instruct the unlearned laity, and thus maintain the 'love-knotte' of the Holy Church (C.XVII.107-31). Grammar is 'the grounde of al' because it helps the believer to understand and relate to 'God, the ground of al'. The unchanging and fundamental grammatical relationships of adjective and noun provide one of Langland's most powerful metaphors for the ideal or 'true' relationship between God and the man who relates to him with a 'hol herte' (C.III.343-406). This book explores how poets use language (particularly grammar) to explore their relationship with God and create a sense that the poet, and often the reader as well, are encountering God through the medium of the poem.

One possible purpose of religious poetry in the Judaeo-Christian tradition is to convey this sense of encounter with God, either through the poet's persona, as in Dante's *Divine Comedy*, or through a character, as in the Book of Job. Indeed, C.S. Lewis implies that this is *the* paramount purpose of religious poetry when he says of *Paradise Lost* that

> ... in some very important sense it is not a religious poem... in the religious life man faces God and God faces man. But in the epic it is feigned, for the moment, that we, as readers, can step aside and see the faces of both God and man in profile...[1]

The purpose of this book is to examine how four English poems or groups of poems – the anonymous medieval Crucifixion lyrics, William Langland's *Piers*

---

[1] *A Preface to Paradise Lost* (London, 1960), pp.132-3.

Plowman, John Donne's Divine Poems, and John Milton's *Paradise Lost* – use language to construct this sense of encounter with God.

These particular poems are the only major English poems that combine two key factors. First, they all use a stable persona to depict an individual encounter with God. Secondly, they take a *public* approach to encounter: the climaxes of these poems depict one or more of the central moments of salvation history. The Crucifixion lyrics, of course, focus on the Crucifixion; the climax of *Piers Plowman* depicts the Easter sequence from the Passion to Pentecost; Donne's Divine Poems meditate on the Incarnation, the Crucifixion, and Judgement; the action of *Paradise Lost* centres on the Fall. In all of these poems there is a strong sense of God speaking or acting in these key moments of salvation history, even when, as in Donne's poems, his response is seen as desired rather than actual.[2]

By contrast, both George Herbert and Gerard Manley Hopkins use a persona who encounters his 'Lord' *privately*, in nature, in his study, or in his heart, rather than in the Christian story. Although there are brief references to the Crucifixion in poems such as Herbert's 'Redemption' and Hopkins' 'The Wreck of the Deutschland', it is not, on the whole, the narrative focus of their poems.[3] Conversely, T.S. Eliot depicts key aspects of salvation history in several of his poems, but uses shifting, fragmentary voices[4] rather than a stable persona.

Despite the differences in their style, Herbert and Hopkins are fairly close to each other in depicting a private and intimate relationship between the persona and God with all its struggles and celebrations. However, because the lyricists, Langland, Donne and Milton engage with the more public face of Christian history, it is possible to trace a development in the way that they represent God. They all present radically different pictures of the relationship between the persona and God. These poems span a period of some four centuries bisected by the Protestant Reformation. The Crucifixion lyrics were written at the height of the Catholic Middle Ages, sometimes called the age of Faith. *Piers Plowman* is marked by the social and religious conflicts of the pre-Reformation period. Donne lived at the height of the English Reformation, and Milton towards its end. As the unity of Latin Christendom, expressed in the institution of the Catholic Church, broke down into conflict and division, the accompanying changes in poetic encounter form a distinct narrative.

This narrative of poetic encounter has two key threads. First, the anonymous meditator of the medieval lyrics gives way to the highly individual personae of Langland, Donne and Milton. Secondly, the lyrics, as love poems,

---

[2] Mary Clement Davlin points out that this is true of *Piers Plowman*, *Paradise Lost* and *Paradise Regained*, but argues that most religious *lyric* poets concentrate more on their own 'prayer, longing, repentance, suffering or joy, than on the nature of God': *The Place of God in* Piers Plowman *and Medieval Art* (Aldershot and Burlington, 2001), p.1. This may be true of Herbert and Hopkins, but the medieval Crucifixion lyrics do construct a voice for Christ, and although Donne's Divine Poems do not construct a voice for God, they are very much concerned with his nature and the mysteries of faith.

[3] Herbert's 'The Sacrifice' is an exception to this rule, but it is a monologue spoken by Christ and there is no persona who experiences encounter within this particular poem.

[4] Helen Gardner, *The Composition of 'Four Quartets'* (London, 1978), p.29.

focus on the loving figure of the crucified Christ. Langland, Donne and Milton, however, also represent God's more complex, awesome, even frightening aspects – depicting him as Creator, Trinity, Paraclete, or Judge, as well as loving Redeemer.

These changes are reflected in the poets' language choices, particularly in their use of *tenses*. At the time when the lyrics were written, Catholic theology insisted on the real presence of the historical Christ in the Eucharist, and thinkers such as John of Fécamp and St Anselm instilled a loving devotion to the humanity of Christ.[5] Thus the lyrics tend to use the *present tense* to express confidence in the presence of the historical Christ with all the marks of his human suffering. One of Langland's purposes, however, was to address the moral and religious problems leading up to the Reformation. He uses the *past tense* to set the story of Redemption at a distance from the corruption of fourteenth-century society. Donne was born a Catholic, but, due to the pressures of the English Reformation, he apostatized. His Divine Poems often use imperatives and interrogatives to depict his persona's anxious desire for God to save him in the *immediate future*. Milton, writing from within the iconoclastic Protestant tradition, struggled to avoid the idolatrous implications of writing in fallen language.[6] He uses the temporal dislocations of the epic to suggest the loss of direct encounter with God by depicting it as occurring only in the *distant past* or the *distant future*.

However, these poems are all alike in depicting the moment of encounter itself as occurring outside the historical periods in which they were written, conveying the timeless relevance of salvation history. Therefore, this is not a historical study. Jacques Derrida argues that modern European historians fail to understand the true connection between history and responsibility, 'losing themselves in the details. For at the heart of this history there is... an abyss that resists totalizing summary.'[7] Derrida defines *responsabilité* as 'the call to explain oneself [*répondre de soi*]... to respond to the other and answer for oneself before the other.'[8] When Paul Ricoeur discusses this abyss at the heart of human experience, he does so in terms of language:

> How can the positive quality of the verbs 'to have taken place', 'to occur', 'to be', be reconciled with the negativity of the adverbs 'no longer', 'not yet', 'not always'... How can time exist if the past is no longer, the future is not yet, and the present is not always... the absence of eternity... is felt at the heart of temporal experience... permeated through and through with negativity... raised to the level of a lamentation.[9]

My interest is in the *response* of the poetic persona who struggles to find God in this abyss, and my analysis will focus on language – on *how* poets 'speak' to God in a particular period – rather than on the historical details of that period.

---

[5] See Rachel Fulton, *From Judgement to Passion* (New York, 2002), pp.80-89; 140-192.
[6] Christopher Ricks, *Milton's Grand Style* (Oxford, 1963), p.109.
[7] Jacques Derrida, *The Gift of Death*, tr. David Wills (Chicago and London, 1995), p.4.
[8] Derrida, p.3.
[9] Paul Ricoeur, *Time and Narrative*, tr. Kathleen McLaughlin and David Pellauer (Chicago and London, 1984) Vol. I, pp.7, 26, following Augustine, *Confessions*, XI.14.

Even the most detailed historical study can never fully recreate the individual poet's 'temporal experience'. Indeed, the historical approach to literature can create problems, particularly in a work as long and complex as *Piers Plowman*. Concentrating on the details of the specific historical issues and controversies that form the background to a poem can make it hard to focus sufficient attention on its language and narrative structure – on the *meaning* of the poem as a whole. Brian Cummings criticizes the historicism of recent literary study for seeing religion in literature as an ideological construct. He argues the need for literary study 'to reassert its primary burden in the examination of language'.[10]

The linguistic approach allows a deeper engagement with 'the absence of eternity', the 'lamentation' that is found in the poems I am considering. Although Cummings seems to suggest otherwise,[11] I believe that the language of religious poetry can achieve a transcendence that allows it to speak with almost unabated force to the modern reader. As David Patterson remarks, religious literature tries to hear God's call and respond: 'The word or spirit that descends from the divine spirit – from language – voices the affirmation and is the vessel of presence.' He sees literary interpretation as 'not so much a reaction *to* the text as a relation *with* the text'.[12] Similarly, Joseph S. Wittig says that *Piers Plowman*,

> so densely concerned... with damning the wrong and praising the right... demands active participation by the reader – who must wrestle with associations, effect connections often merely implicit, fill in with specific villains the blanks offered by derogatory but general diction, and decide, finally, what it means "for me".[13]

This study has grown out of my wrestling to decide what these poems mean for me, a meaning I have found through focusing mainly on their language, listening, as well as I can, to what they are saying to readers of a later century. In doing so, to borrow from Wittig again, 'my "agenda" – my preoccupations and suppositions – reflects my own cultural formation'.[14] I hope I write as a serious student of literature and language, but I also write as a Catholic with ecumenical sympathies who has always tried to follow Donne's injunction to:

> ...doubt wisely; in strange way
> To stand inquiring right, is not to stray;
> To sleepe, or run wrong, is On a huge hill,
> Cragged, and steep, Truth stands, and hee that will
> Reach her, about must, and about must goe;
> And what the hills suddennes resists, winne so.

Satyre III, 77-82

---

[10] Brian Cummings, *The Literary Culture of the Reformation* (Oxford, 2002), pp.12-13.
[11] Cummings, pp.12-13.
[12] David Patterson, *The Affirming Flame* (Norman, 1988), pp.10, 14-15.
[13] Joseph S. Wittig, '"Culture Wars" and the Persona in *Piers Plowman*', *YLS*, 15 (2001), 167-95 (p.167).
[14] Wittig, '"Culture Wars"', p.184.

The 'lamentation', the anguish felt at the absence of the eternal, is a key theme of this book, since it provides the grounds for encounter. Paul Ricoeur and Theodore Jennings argue that encounter is the fundamental condition of the human soul, and that when this condition is disrupted by sin, this breakdown of relationship paradoxically brings the soul closer to the terrible otherness of God as a Thou, a lover.[15]

In discussing the nature of anguish, I have drawn on Ricoeur's essay 'True and False Anguish', which identifies five types of anguish: the fear of death; the fear of psychic disintegration; the fear that history is meaningless; the anguish of guilt; and the fear that God may be malevolent.[16] In examining the way in which poets express this anguish, I have developed Jennings's discussion of the characteristics of the two main ways of talking to God – praise-prayer and plea-prayer.

The main linguistic focus of this book is on the nature of dialogue with God in religious poetry. This area has been neglected by grammarians[17] and is often overlooked in studies of literary style.[18] More recently, however, Cummings, although he concentrates mainly on prose writers, has offered some very interesting insights into the language of the Reformation and what he calls 'this neglected hinterland of grammar. The inclinations and deviations by which a sentence moves'.[19]

---

[15] Ricoeur, *The Symbolism of Evil*, Tr. Emerson Buchanan (Boston, 1969), pp.50-69. Jennings, *Beyond Theism* (New York, Oxford, 1985), pp.93-113.

[16] Ricoeur, *History and Truth* (Evanston, Illinois, 1965), pp.287-304.

[17] Most confine their discussion to secular, non-literary texts. See, for example, M.A.K. Halliday, 'Language as Code and Language as Behaviour' in *The Semiotics of Culture and Language*, ed. Robin P. Fawcett, et al. (London, 1984), I.3-35; E. Giachin and S. McGlashan, 'Spoken Language Dialogue Systems', in *Corpus Based Method in Language and Speech Processing*, ed. Steve Young and Gerrit Bloothooft (Dordrecht, Netherlands, 1997), pp.69-117; John Haynes, *Introducing Stylistics* (London, 1989); Teun A. Van Dijk, *Handbook of Discourse Analysis: Volume 3* (London, 1985). Rosemary Huisman, however, makes some interesting observations on Browning's use of the second person in 'Who Speaks for Whom?', *AUMLA*, 7 (1989) 64-87. Scholars who discuss religious language tend to talk theoretically, offering little linguistic analysis of specific texts: for example, Jennings, Patterson, John Macquarrie's *God-Talk* (London, 1967) and Dan Stiver's *The Philosophy of Religious Language* (Cambridge, Massachusetts and Oxford, 1996).

[18] Dennis Freeborn's *Style*, (Basingstoke and London, 1996) offers no analysis of direct address in poetry. Ronald Carter is more concerned with levels of formality than with how dialogue works: *Investigating English Discourse* (London and New York, 1997). Mary Louise Pratt focuses more on the relationships between spoken and literary narratives than on dialogue as such: *Towards a Speech Act Theory* (Bloomington and London, 1977). Michael Toolan takes most of his examples from secular prose texts: *Language and Literature* (London, 1998). In *Transforming Words* (Bern, 1999) J.P. van Noppen discusses some features of Wesleyan hymns, but none of these are common in the poems I am discussing. William J. Samarin's *Language in Religious Practice* (Rowley, Massachusetts, 1976) is anthropological rather than linguistic. Peter Donovan's *Religious Language* (London, 1976) is more concerned with the purpose of religious language than the grammar.

[19] Cummings, p.11.

I have found that traditional grammatical distinctions are most pertinent to my argument:[20] distinctions between nouns and modifiers; between tenses; between persons; between transitive and intransitive verbs; between subject and object; between active and passive voice; between abstract and concrete language; between main and subordinate clauses. However, I also draw on the work of the functional grammarian, M.A.K. Halliday. His analysis of the differences between speech and writing[21] applies to the differences between poetic dialogue and narrative. His distinction between the giving and the demand functions of dialogue is also particularly useful to my discussion.[22]

Michael Macovski suggests that New Criticism concerned itself with lyric forms, while structuralists, deconstructionists and historicists are concerned with narrative texts. This book lies somewhere between the two. I am concerned both with 'the lexical ambiguities of lyric language' and with 'the *aporia* that belie narratives of ostensible linearity and sequence'.[23] This book examines the Crucifixion lyrics and Donne's Divine Poems on the one hand, and the extended narratives of *Piers Plowman* and *Paradise Lost* on the other. But the distinction between the lyric and the narrative approaches is somewhat artificial: even a short lyric about anguish often has a simple embedded story. At the same time, even the complex narratives of Langland and Milton use lyrical techniques to convey the intensity of moments of encounter at the climaxes of their narratives. This book aims to explore the ways in which poetic narrative and language intertwine to create the sense of a poetic encounter that momentarily bridges the abyss between the soul and God.

---

[20] My main reference is Sidney Greenbaum, *The Oxford English Grammar* (Oxford, 1996).

[21] Halliday, *Spoken and Written Language* (Deakin, Victoria, 1985).

[22] Halliday, *An Introduction to Functional Grammar*, 2nd edn (London, Melbourne, Auckland, 1994), pp.68-71.

[23] Michael Macovski, *Dialogue and Critical Discourse* (New York and Oxford, 1997), Introduction, p.3.

Chapter 1

Speaking across the Gap: The Language of Encounter with the Divine

My soul is also sore vexed: but thou, O Lord, how long?
Return, O Lord, deliver my soul: O save me for thy mercies' sake.

Psalm 6:3-4

1. Encounter, anguish, and dialogue with God

The primary meaning of the transitive verb 'encounter' suggests conflict, difficulty, and a meeting with the unexpected:

'To meet as an adversary, to confront in battle' (*OED* 1);
To go counter to, oppose, thwart; to contest, dispute (*OED* 2)
Meet, fall in with...*esp.* casually (*OED* 4).
To meet with, experience (difficulties, opposition etc.) (*OED* 5).

To talk of the 'encounter' between God and the soul in Christian poetry is thus to suggest some kind of struggle, the possibility of defeat or surrender. It is a term that is appropriate for Jacob's wrestling with the angel or Job's final capitulation to God. It acknowledges that God is far beyond the capacity of the soul to know, and that, since the time of primal innocence when God walked in the Garden of Eden (Gen. 3:8), God has not been accessible to any simple meeting with the seeking soul. It is in this sense that I use the term in this book.

According to Paul Ricoeur, encounter with God is the fundamental condition of the human soul, 'a preliminary dimension of encounter and dialogue... an utterance of God and an utterance of man'. Sin, however, ruptures this dialogue: it violates the personal bond with God, and leads to 'the absence and silence of God, corresponding to the vain and hollow existence of man.' For a fallen people, God can no longer be seen purely in his gentle aspect, and Ricoeur speaks of the trauma experienced by the chosen people when their sins called down on them the 'fury' of Old Testament prophecies of destruction, and the God who begot his people became a wrathful, threatening Enemy.[1]

Yet, according to Ricoeur, sin does not completely destroy the relationship between God and the sinner, making God 'the Wholly Other'. Paradoxically, it is

---

[1] Ricoeur, *The Symbolism of Evil*, pp.50-4.

in the sense of division from God, in confessing its sin to God, that the soul is closest to God:

> ... the sinner discovers that its separation from God is still a relation... In the movement of the invocation the sinner becomes fully the subject of sin, at the same time as the terrible God of destruction becomes the supreme Thou.[2]

Similarly, Theodore Jennings suggests that 'the breakdown of the regular patterns of life and experience' cause the structures that try to 'domesticate and control the other' to collapse. This can lead not only to a terror of obliteration by God, but also to an epiphany, 'the inbreaking of radiance, light, illumination... astonishment and delight.' He argues that division from God allows the soul to become fully aware of God as other, beyond human control, and thus as a 'Thou', a lover.[3] John D. Caputo also speaks of 'the incoming of the *tout autre*' as an 'excess or breach that exceeds and shocks our expectation'.[4] Thus the abyss of sin enables the soul to perceive God's true otherness in his anger and absence, his capacity for destruction as well as creation. Sin is the very thing that allows, even forces, the soul to approach God as a lover, a 'Thou', in the intimacy of dialogue.

This intimate encounter with God as a lover requires the individual soul to experience God as an individual. In speaking of this encounter, I will often use the term 'Man': it is the only English word that functions as a name for the human race; it enables the human race to be represented as an individual who can meet God one-to-one, in a way that is impossible for a collective, gender-neutral term like 'humanity'; it is also the term that is used by most of the authors I am discussing. I will also follow these authors in using male pronouns for God.

2. Avoiding idolatry: varieties of religious language

When trying to convey a sense of encounter between Man and God, poets have to struggle with the problem that the finite human mind cannot apprehend God's true nature, and thus human language is inadequate to the task of talking about God's essence. Christian writers have traditionally distinguished two basic ways of talking about God, the *via negativa* and the *via positiva*. The negative way focuses on the things that God is not. As R.S. Thomas puts it in 'Via Negativa',

> ... God is that great absence
> In our lives, the empty silence
> Within, the place where we go
> Seeking, not in hope to
> Arrive or find.[5]

---

[2] Ricoeur, *The Symbolism of Evil*, p.69.
[3] Jennings, pp.93-5, 113.
[4] John D. Caputo, *The Prayers and Tears of Jacques Derrida* (Bloomington and Indianapolis, 1997) p.22.
[5] R.S. Thomas, *Collected Poems* (London, 1993), p.220.

One problem with the negative way is that its proponents deny that it is possible to communicate meaningfully about their experience, and thus 'the only consistent response would simply be to be silent and not say or write anything'.[6] Indeed, as John Macquarrie notes, knowledge obtained through the negative way is vacuous on its own.[7] In order to praise God, or obey God, or write a narrative about God, one has to say what he is or what he does or says, which throws the poet back on the *via positiva*.[8]

On the other hand, using the positive way, trying to express what God is or does or says, creates enormous problems for poets and visual artists. The Jewish tradition prohibits images of God, and early Christian art is also reluctant to portray God for fear of idolatry.[9] However, as T.R. Wright observes, the Jewish refusal to speak God's name recognizes that language can also be idolatrous.[10] Stiver also warns of the dangers of idolatry in language, noting that in writing about God language is stretched 'to its breaking point – and perhaps beyond'.[11]

Kevin Hart argues that with the Fall, 'Language, too, has fallen... By dint of Adam's sin... God is for us an *absent* presence... the Fall introduced a gap between man and God, words and objects'.[12] However, stretching language beyond the literal, even breaking it, allows a writer to avoid idolatry by writing in the gaps. This can be achieved by the use of metaphor, hyperbole, parable,[13] and paradox.[14] Indeed, Patterson sees the gaps in language as being the ultimate expression of religion:

> Viewing the Word as spirit or along spiritual lines, I place myself forever on the threshold, at the critical *zero* point, where I encounter the *not yet* of the process of becoming. This is where religious longing is transformed into literary text. Thus... religion, language, and literature merge to form... a single event: the creation of meaning through affirmation.[15]

To some extent, poets can avoid the problem of talking about God's essence by talking, not about what God *is*, but about what he *does*, speaking about him in terms of verbs rather than nouns and adjectives. Indeed, the usual nominal attributes of God – power, wisdom, and love – do not relate to things at all. Like

---

[6] Stiver, p.18. Caputo suggests that 'the effect of negative theology is always so verbal and verbose' because it is 'an event *within* language' (pp.11-12, 32).

[7] *God-Talk* (London, 1967) pp.26-7.

[8] Kevin Hart, *The Trespass of the Sign* (Cambridge, 1989) p.6.

[9] Michael Camille, *The Gothic Idol* (Cambridge, 1989).

[10] T.R. Wright, *Theology and Literature* (Oxford, 1988), pp.18-19.

[11] Stiver, p.19.

[12] Hart, pp.6-7. In *The Dark Interval* (Allen, Texas, 1975), John Dominic Crossan argues that God 'is either inside language and in that case... an idol; or he is outside language, and there is nothing out there but silence'; for him, transcendental experience of God 'is found only at the edge of language and the limit of story' (pp.44-5). For Jennings, 'the irruption of or encounter with "otherness"... both shatters and founds our language' (p.166).

[13] Wright, pp.18-19.

[14] Macquarrie, *God-Talk*, pp.31, 213.

[15] Patterson, pp.14-15.

many abstract terms, they express in noun form something that can only exist in the real world in the verbal form of powerful, wise, and loving actions.[16] Macquarrie says that God 'must be described in verbs rather than in nouns, for he is sharing, coming, even suffering, then overcoming'.[17] In the Old Testament, God uses a verb to name himself: 'I am that I am,' he tells Moses (Exod. 3:14).[18] In the New Testament too, the divine is presented as active: in Greek, *Logos* means 'the word by which the inward thought is expressed',[19] which the Vulgate translates into Latin as *Verbum*, a word, or verb.[20] The Gospel narratives do not describe Christ as a man, a noun (they give no physical image of him at all), but relate what he did and said.

This stress on verbs also applies to Christian teaching. As Ricoeur says of the story of the Good Samaritan, Christ's doctrine centres on verbs or events, not on nouns or objects:

> Jesus answered that the neighbour is not a social object but a behaviour in the first person. Being a neighbour lies in the habit of making oneself available... The story relates a series of *events*: a chain of unsuccessful encounters and a successful encounter... the story... turns into a command: 'Go and do likewise' ... a pattern for action.[21]

He also points out that Christ's Judgement prophecy (Matt. 25) insists upon actions,[22] and suggests that this verbal quality is the essence of the Image of God in Man:

> ... what should happen... if we should see the image of God not as an imposed mark but as the striking power of human creativity; if we treat it not as the residual trace of a craftsman who has abandoned his work to the ravages of time, but as a continuous act in the creative movement of history and duration?[23]

Thus the relationship of God and Man is not static, but dynamic, based on their actions and interactions in the world of time.

When attempting to express this interaction with God, poets have two main language choices. Jennings identifies these two main forms of religious language: doxological, or *praise*, in which the speaker 'stands in plenitude'; and

---

[16] John Coulson, *Religion and Imagination* (Oxford, 1981), pp.93-5.

[17] Macquarrie, *The Humility of God* (London, 1978), pp.79-80; see also Anthony Thiselton, *New Horizons in Hermeneutics* (Grand Rapids, Michigan, 1992), p.569.

[18] Macquarrie notes that the Hebrew verb is dynamic, more like 'to become' than 'to be', and that some scholars even take the verb in the sense of 'I cause to be' or 'I bring to pass': *Principles of Christian Theology* (London, 1966), p.180.

[19] *A Lexicon Abridged from Liddell and Scott's Greek-English Lexicon* (Oxford, 1949).

[20] For the links between action and the words for 'verb' in several languages see Jacob L. Mey, *Pragmatics* (Oxford and Cambridge, Massachussetts, 1993), p.133.

[21] Ricoeur, 'The Socius and the Neighbour', in *History and Truth*, p.99.

[22] Ricoeur, *History and Truth*, p.100.

[23] Ricoeur, 'The Image of God and the Epic of Man', *History and Truth,* pp.110-11.

oralogical, or *prayer*, in which 'the speaker stands empty and in need'.[24] Although the sense of God's presence finds expression in praise, while the sense of his absence informs prayer, the two types of discourse are intimately connected:

> ... this absence is not simply absolute. The longing, yearning, opening, and orienting of existence qualifies this absence as a 'no longer present' or a 'not-yet present'. Thus presence is... the shadow of the absence which gives rise to prayer... Prayer is the articulation of the absence of that for which it yearns. Praise is the articulation of the presence of that for which prayer asks.[25]

Jennings's term 'prayer' is ambiguous, since the word is commonly used for both praise and pleas. I will use the term 'plea' in my own discussion of these two types of language. Praise-poems express joy and adoration, exalting God through pouring out to him a sense of spiritual fullness. Plea-poems express need, anguish and suffering, and implore God to fill a deep emptiness in the speaker. This chapter will discuss the grammatical and narrative differences between praise-poems and plea-poems. It will seek to show that the anguish at the heart of plea-poems enables them to write in the 'gaps' of language, conveying the sense of encounter with a God who is fundamentally 'Other'.

3. Praise-poems: contemplation of the eternal

Jennings observes that little critical attention has been given to the language of praise and plea-prayer. His own analysis is theoretical, giving no examples of praise and plea in action.[26] He does, however, identify some key differences between the two. He observes that praise, as the articulation of God's presence, minimizes contrast and separation:

> Whereas the language of prayer emphasizes the contrast or opposition of the identity of speaker and hearer (sin–grace, need–fullness) the language of praise anticipates and articulates the collapse of this separation and alienation and alterity.[27]

Praise is thus a joyful mode that celebrates God's presence with confidence and certainty.

It is quite hard to find poems that do express only praise, with no sense of doubt, sin, enemies or griefs to be overcome. As George Herbert suggests in 'Praise (III)', a prayer that is based on praise alone soon exhausts its possibilities, requiring a measure of anguish to replenish it:

---

[24] Jennings, p.189.

[25] Jennings, p.188.

[26] Jennings, pp.186-208. Patterson similarly claims that 'the reader's task is not the appreciation of beauty or form, but the achievement of presence' (p.25).

[27] Jennings, pp.194-5.

> Lord, I will mean and speak thy praise,
> Thy praise alone.
> My busie heart shall spin it all my dayes:
> And when it stops for want of store,
> Then I will wring it with a sigh or grone,
> That thou mayst yet have more...[28]

Lacking the conflict and anguish of plea-poems, pure praise-poems cannot sustain a narrative. When happiness is achieved, as D.A. Miller argues, narrative ends:

> The narrative of happiness is inevitably frustrated by the fact that only insufficiencies, defaults, deferrals, can be 'told'... To designate the presence of what is sought or prized is to signal the termination of narrative – or at least, the displacement of narrative onto other concerns.[29]

Praise poems thus tend to be short, descriptive poems.

The following discussion will focus largely on the language of the Psalms. As a key part of the Christian liturgy, they would have been familiar to all the English poets whom I will be discussing in detail. Moreover, the Psalms provide a number of pure praise-poems, numerous plea-poems, and poems with a mixture of praise and plea. It is thus possible to make almost all the points I wish to make about the nature of poetic dialogue with God by referring to a single, cohesive body of poetry and without pre-empting my detailed analysis of individual English poets. I will quote from the Authorized Version because it is roughly contemporaneous with two of the poets, Donne and Milton.

Fewer than one tenth of the Psalms are focused entirely on praise, and these are all short (ten verses or less), for example:

> The Lord reigneth, he is clothed with majesty; the Lord is clothed with strength, wherewith he hath girded himself: the world also is stablished, that it cannot be moved.
> Thy throne is established of old: thou art from everlasting.
> The floods have lifted up, O Lord, the floods have lifted up their voice; the floods lift up their waves.
> The Lord on high is mightier than the noise of many waters, yea than the mighty waves of the sea.
> Thy testimonies are very sure: holiness becometh thine house, O Lord, forever.
>
> Psalm 93[30]

There is no story here, no sense of passing time or chain of events; the poem is written in a uniform present.

---

[28] *The Poems of George Herbert*, ed. Helen Gardner (London, 1961).

[29] D.A. Miller,, *Narrative and its Discontents* (Princeton, 1981), p.3.

[30] The Authorized Version (London and New York, 1957). Other pure praise Psalms are 8, 24, 98, 99, 100, 111, 113, 114, 117, 138, 146, 148, and 150.

Psalm 93 avoids the idolatry of attempting to name or quantify God's attributes directly by speaking figuratively and comparatively: God is clothed with majesty and strength; he is mightier than the waves. However, as I suggested earlier, the Bible tends to favour verbs when describing God, and many psalms do this, for example Psalm 29:

> Give unto the Lord, O ye mighty, give unto the Lord glory and strength.
> Give unto the Lord the glory due unto his name; worship the Lord in the beauty of holiness.
> The voice of the Lord is upon the waters: the God of glory thundereth: the Lord is upon many waters.
> The voice of the Lord is powerful; the voice of the Lord is full of majesty.
> The voice of the Lord breaketh the cedars; yea, the Lord breaketh the cedars of Lebanon.
> He maketh them also to skip like a calf; Lebanon and Sirion like a young unicorn.
> The voice of the Lord divideth the flames of fire.
> The voice of the Lord shaketh the wilderness; the Lord shaketh the wilderness of Kadesh.
> The voice of the Lord maketh the hinds to calve, and discovereth the forests: and in his temple doth everyone speak of his glory.
> The Lord sitteth upon the flood; yea, the Lord sitteth King for ever.
> The Lord will give strength unto his people; the Lord will bless his people with peace.

The first two verses here relate to the action of the worshippers, and say nothing specific about God's nature. The rest of the psalm presents a vigorous picture of God thundering, breaking cedars, dividing flames, shaking the wilderness, making hinds calve, and sitting on the flood, giving strength and blessings to his people.

These very verbs, however, direct the content of the poem outwards from God onto the objects of the verbs: the narrative direction of a praise-poem can shift away from God, out into a world remade by his creative love. Thus Psalm 104 starts with descriptions of God's actions, covering himself with light, stretching out the heavens, laying the beams of his chambers in the waters, and walking upon the wings of the wind (1-7), but then the creatures who benefit from his actions take over the centre of the stage:

> He causeth the grass to grow for the cattle, and herb for the service of man: that he may bring forth food out of the earth;
> And wine that maketh glad the heart of man, and oil to make his face to shine, and bread which strengtheneth man's heart.
> The trees of the Lord are full of sap; the cedars of Lebanon, which he hath planted;
> Where the birds make their nests: as for the stork, the fir trees are her house.
> The high hills are a refuge for the wild goats; and the rocks for the conies.

Psalm 104:14-18

God himself is sometimes curiously absent from the lexis of a praise-poem: the two psalms just quoted celebrate God's presence within creation, but their actual words focus far more on various aspects of creation than they do on God. Gerard Manley Hopkins partially avoids this problem in 'Pied Beauty' by making the wonders of creation grammatically dependent upon his opening injunction to glorify God:

> Glory be to God for dappled things -
> For skies of couple-colour as a brinded cow;
> For rose-moles all in stipple upon trout that swim;
> Fresh-firecoal chestnut-falls; finches' wings;
> Landscape plotted and pieced – fold, fallow, and plough;
> And áll trádes, their gear and tackle and trim.
>
> All things counter, original, spare, strange;
> Whatever is fickle, freckled (who knows how?)
> With swift, slow; sweet, sour; adazzle, dim;
> He fathers-forth whose beauty is past change:
> Praise him.[31]

The central reality of the poem, expressed in the only main-clause indicative verb, is God's fathering-forth. Nevertheless, it is the creatures that dominate the content of the poem. God keeps still: he is the object of 'Glory be' and 'Praise'; his beauty is 'past change', and therefore indescribable; his fathering-forth can only be seen in his creatures. Hopkins avoids the possible vacuity of the negative way by allying it to positive descriptions of God's creation.

Another feature of praise-poetry is that the speaker is also often absent from the text of the poem. Most of the examples I have given so far are written in a mixture of the third person (describing God's acts) and the second (commanding the worshipper to praise him). Apart from Herbert, who expressed a tinge of anguish mixed with his praise, the individual voice of the speaker is largely silent, content with the status quo and thus not making demands on his own behalf.

Another feature of praise-poetry is its use of declarative sentences: in the Psalms I have quoted, *all* the verbs with God as their subject are in declarative sentences – they make positive assertions about God. Praise-poems thus express certainty and assurance. As such, their narrative possibilities are reduced: as Anthony Thiselton notes, assertions or descriptions simply reflect the existing state of affairs in the world, whereas commands (or imperatives) and promises intend to change the world.[32]

Imperatives in praise-poems are usually directed, not to God, but to those who should be praising him:

---

[31] *The Poems of Gerard Manley Hopkins*, 4th edn, ed. W.H. Gardner and N.H. MacKenzie (Oxford, 1970), pp.69-70.
[32] Thiselton, p.296.

Praise ye the Lord. Praise God in his sanctuary: praise him in the
firmament of his power.

Praise him for his mighty acts: praise him according to his excellent
greatness.

Praise him with the sound of the trumpet: praise him with the psaltery
and harp.

Praise him with the timbrel and dance: praise him with stringed
instruments and organs.

Praise him upon the loud cymbals: praise him upon the high sounding
cymbals.

Let everything that hath breath praise the Lord. Praise ye the Lord.

Psalm 150

This psalm says almost nothing about God: it attributes power and greatness and
'mighty acts' to him, but it does not say what these acts might be. Apart from the
qualifying clause 'that hath breath', there is only one verb in the psalm, 'praise'.
This is repeated thirteen times: it is the worshippers who are the subject of this
verb, and God is the object. The worshippers have no identity in the poem beyond
their duty of praise.

Pure praise-poems thus tend to be short, confident, descriptive poems.
They have a limited range of participants (God, creation, and the worshipper) and
while God can perform a range of creative actions in them, the worshipper is
usually allowed only one act – praise. They are centred on God (and his creation)
rather than on the speaker, or even the worshipper, and express the actuality of
God's presence in the present tense and the indicative mood. In his *Confessions*, St
Augustine connected the present tense with eternity, 'which is supreme over time
because it is a never-ending present'.[33] Praise-poems concern what Ricoeur has
called 'the celebration of the absolute' or the eternal.[34]

4. Plea-poems: change and narrative

It is by stretching language, by writing in the gaps, that a religious poet can avoid
idolatry when talking of God. Although praise-poems may stretch language by
metaphor and hyperbole, they have a limited capacity for writing in the gaps: using
the present tense and declarative sentences to celebrate God's presence, they
cannot represent him as 'an absent presence'. Praise-poems express certainty and
confidence in God and his creation. As Jennings points out, this certainty risks
becoming too conservative – 'merely the sanctification of the status quo or the
privileging of one's own status'. Praise on its own prevents that rupturing of
structures that Jennings sees as the prerequisite for encounter: it needs to be
counterbalanced by 'the articulation of absence, lack, and yearning as prayer'.[35]
Caputo too speaks of the dangers of certainty. He says that prayer cannot be

---

[33] St Augustine, *Confessions*, XI.13, tr. R.S. Pine-Coffin (London, 1961), p.263.

[34] Ricoeur, *Time and Narrative*, p.28.

[35] Jennings, pp.93-5, 195.

fulfilled or it becomes union and is replaced by presence.[36] He warns against negative theology's tendency towards a 'dangerous triumphalism' that can 'shatter faith and turn it into union', claiming a closure and an access to 'the Heart of Truth' that 'spells trouble... exclusion... spills blood'.[37]

By its nature, plea-poetry avoids this triumphalism and closure. Plea-poems express a desire for an absent God who has not yet answered their pleas. They thus enact their own limitations. Praise-poems, with their lack of conflict, their satisfaction with the status quo, and their focus on God's eternal presence, cannot sustain a narrative. Plea-poems, seeking through conflict and anguish to change the status quo, can. While praise-poems celebrate God's eternal presence, plea-poems range from the past or present situation to the future, expressing the need for and the possibility of a change that will occur only with God's help. Plea-poems avoid closure, tending to the type of open-ended narratives that end with a continuing tension rather than a sense of satisfaction:[38]

> O Lord God of my salvation, I have cried day and night before thee:
> Let my prayer come before thee: incline thine ear unto my cry;
> For my soul is full of troubles: and my life draweth nigh unto the grave...
> Thou hast laid me in the lowest pit, in darkness, in the deeps.
> Thy wrath lieth hard upon me, and thou hast afflicted me with all thy waves. Selah.
> Thou hast put away mine acquaintance far from me; thou hast made me an abomination unto them: I am shut up, and I cannot come forth...
> Wilt thou shew wonders to the dead? shall the dead arise and praise thee? Selah.
> Shall thy lovingkindness be declared in the grave? or thy faithfulness in destruction?
> Shall thy wonders be known in the dark? and thy righteousness in the land of forgetfulness?
>
> Psalm 88:1-3, 6-8, 10-12

This Psalm ends with question rather than closure, with a continuing desire for full encounter with a still distant God. Another common way of avoiding closure is by using the future tense to depict a desired state of affairs that does not yet exist:

> Hear my cry, O God; attend unto my prayer.
> From the end of the earth will I cry unto thee, when my heart is overwhelmed: lead me to the rock that is higher than I.
> For thou hast been a shelter for me, and a strong tower from the enemy.
> I will abide in thy tabernacle for ever: I will trust in the covert of thy wings. Selah.
>
> Psalm 61:1-4

---

[36] Caputo, p.40.
[37] Caputo, pp.6, 71.
[38] For this kind of narrative closure see Pratt, p.59.

The imperatives that seek to change the world are now directed to God instead of to the believer as the poet sketches a story of what he wishes to happen: he is in present difficulties and needs God's help, but because of God's past support, he trusts that God will help him again in the future.

The speaker, the 'I', is often absent from the text of praise-poems. They can be addressed to a nebulous plural 'you', a set of worshippers who are only allowed one activity – praise. In a plea-poem, the speaker is usually present, loudly vociferating his problems and performing a range of actions to capture God's attention. Depending on how one reads the tone of such a poem, there is a kind of glorious or desperate presumption, as the individual, made powerfully present in the first person pronouns, attempts to force the eternal God to act within the world of time.

One distinctive feature of God in the Judaeo-Christian tradition is that he does speak and act in the world of time: this is particularly so in the Incarnation – 'the point of intersection of the timeless with time' as T.S. Eliot has it.[39] As Ricoeur argues, time and narrative are interdependent:

> The world unfolded by every narrative work is always a temporal world... time becomes human time to the extent that it is organized after the manner of a narrative; narrative, in turn, is meaningful to the extent that it portrays... temporal experience.[40]

Judaeo-Christian narrative tends towards linear progression:[41] the stories, parables, and histories of the Old Testament and Gospels for the most part follow a simple linear structure; so do the medieval cycle plays, *The Divine Comedy*, *Piers Plowman*, and *Pilgrim's Progress*. A linear narrative allows the author to create a sense that the drama of the spiritual quest – progress, backsliding, further progress, and final resolution – is happening 'now', and to involve the reader in that drama. Even in shorter religious poems, there is often a strong sense of a simple story.[42] A coherent narrative structure within a poem satisfies some deep need in the writer and reader, particularly when coping with anguish, as Ricoeur notes:

> We tell stories because in the last analysis human lives need and merit being narrated. This remark takes on its full force when we refer to the necessity to save the history of the defeated and the lost. The whole history of suffering cries out for vengeance and calls for narrative.[43]

Narrative is intimately concerned with anguish because, as Ricoeur points out, meditating on time causes the human heart to feel uncertainty, or 'the sorrow of the finite':

---

[39] T.S. Eliot, 'Dry Salvages' V *Collected Poems* (London, 1963), p.212.
[40] Ricoeur, *Time and Narrative*, p.3.
[41] S.W. Sykes 'The Role of Story in the Christian Religion', *Literature and Theology*, 1 (1987), 16-26.
[42] Louis Martz, *The Poetry of Meditation* (New Haven, 1962), pp.38-9.
[43] Ricoeur, *Time and Narrative*, p.75.

> How can the positive quality of the verbs 'to have taken place', 'to occur', 'to be', be reconciled with the negativity of the adverbs 'no longer', 'not yet', 'not always'... How can time exist if the past is no longer, the future is not yet, and the present is not always... the absence of eternity... is felt at the heart of temporal experience... raised to the level of a lamentation.[44]

Through their use of temporal narrative, plea-poems express both the longing for God's presence and the sense that this presence is 'no longer' or 'not yet': this creates a gap in the language. They make use of the *via positiva* to express what it is that they long for and the *via negativa* to express its absence. Through their anguish at God's absence, their uncertainty as to when and if he will come, they avoid, to a large extent, the idolatry of language.

In this book, I use 'plea' to mean the expression of anguish at God's absence and need for his presence. Sometimes the plea-poet uses a short lyric form to express with intensity his longing for God; sometimes he uses an extensive narrative to explore the difficulties of the soul's journey towards God. Both types of poem display the features of plea: they are driven by an anguished sense of God's absence and a desire for his presence; they are concerned with time rather than eternity; and they seek a change in the present state of affairs. It is poems of this type that are the subject of this book.

5. Anguish and the narrative drive towards encounter

In his essay, 'True and False Anguish', Ricoeur describes five levels of anguish: fear of death; fear of psychic disintegration; the possibility that history is meaningless; the anguish of guilt or sin; and the ultimate, metaphysical anguish – the possibility that God is not good. Ricoeur argues that one must confront each anguish in order to transcend it. However, transcending one anguish leads directly to the next. One can resolve one's fear of death by discovering that reasons for living are more important than life itself, and can 'become reasons for dying'. However, this search for meaning, with its inner conflicts, leads to psychic anguish – the fear of insanity, alienation, and lack of purpose. Resolving this anguish through 'communal and personal' work, one becomes involved in the world of history, only to awaken the fear that history might be unreasonable and meaningless. One can transcend this fear by accepting that history is a result of human free will and choice, but this leads to the anguish of guilt and responsibility for the evils of history: this anguish can be resolved through repentance for one's own sins. This, however, leads to the final anguish: the realization that humanity is not responsible for all the evil in the world. The problem of innocent suffering forces one to ask if the world is ruled by chaos or a malign God.[45]

According to Ricoeur, the final anguish deepens all the others: 'this anguish, seeping back from the summit of anguish towards its base, appears to

---

[44] Ricoeur, *Time and Narrative*, pp.7, 26-8 , following Augustine, *Confessions*, XI.14.
[45] Ricoeur, *History and Truth*, pp.287-304.

recapitulate all the degrees of it.' The fear that God is malevolent makes him appear responsible for human sin and guilt, for the chaos of history, for the consequent lack of purpose in lives, and for the 'apparent nonsense' of the proposition that Man 'who determines the meaning of things... *must* die'. There are no final answers to this problem: all one can attain is a 'timid' hope that remains close to despair and anguish. However, as in the case of Job, meditation on suffering can open one up to an encounter with the living God.[46]

Ricoeur observes that these anguishes are not equally valid for all times: the anguish of death may be stronger or weaker according to the importance given to individual life; the anguish of psychic alienation is strongest in 'civilized societies, those best protected against danger and during peacetime'.[47] I am not convinced that the anguishes necessarily follow the order that Ricoeur suggests: many poets never directly confront the anguish of history, for example. Moreover, in many of the poems I am considering, it would not be accurate to say that concern over innocent suffering leads the poet to fear that God may be malevolent: these poems are too conscious of human sinfulness for them to have much sense of innocent suffering. Instead, the persona may express doubt that he can be saved by God's goodness and mercy, and fear lest he (and others) may be damned by God's justice. Whatever form this anguish takes, it is the anguish that *questions* God's goodness, his presence, or his very existence: for convenience, I will refer to it as 'the anguish of doubt'.

Despite these reservations, I have found Ricoeur's discussion a useful tool for analysing Christian plea-poems. Every seeking Christian soul must confront its own mortality, its individual psyche, its role in history, its responsibility for the evil in the world, and the possibility that God may be angry or distant. Within the Christian tradition, these anguishes are resolved through Christ: Christ endures the agony of death and makes eternal life possible; he restores psychic health, or the image of God in the soul; his life and death give meaning to history and release humanity from guilt; finally, in his dying cry of abandonment as he dies, and in the Resurrection, he confronts and negates the possibility of God's absence. In wrestling with these anguishes, the Christian poet opens his poem to an encounter with God.[48]

I have suggested already that praise-poems can tend to move away from God towards a creation renewed by his love. Conversely, poems that deal with the negative emotions involved in human anguish are likely to begin in the world and move towards God: it is the pressures of life in the world that cause anguish or suffering, and that suffering can drive the individual to seek God. Sometimes the story of the poet's struggle with anguish takes the form of a long narrative that leads to encounter with God. Thus Dante's *Divine Comedy* starts with the poet

---

[46] Ricoeur, *History and Truth*, pp.302-4.

[47] Ricoeur, *History and Truth*, p.292.

[48] Martz argues that the aim of Ignatian meditative poetry is to enable the soul 'to speak with God... and to hear God speak to man' (*The Poetry of Meditation*, p.36).

struggling through a dark wood, feeling a fear that is as bitter as death;[49] after a long journey through Hell, Purgatory, and Paradise, the poet's persona finally rises to the encounter with God that ends the poem. Similarly, William Langland's *Piers Plowman* moves from a vision of the corruption of the world, through a series of anguished questions to a variety of guides, until at the climax of the poem, the Dreamer encounters Christ at the Harrowing of Hell. The same sense of movement from worldliness and alienation towards God is also apparent in Donne's 'Goodfriday, 1613. Riding Westward'. At the moment of encounter, however, these poems all change from the narrative mode to the mode of dialogue: Dante addresses the 'Light Eternal' (*Paradiso*, XXXIII.124); Christ addresses Lucifer (and, as I shall suggest, the Dreamer) in *Piers Plowman* C.XX; and Donne suddenly moves from the third person to address Christ directly at the end of his poem (line 35). In *Paradise Lost* Milton also (as I shall demonstrate) includes two brief moments when his persona is in direct dialogue with God.

6. Encounter and the characteristics of plea-dialogue

There has been very little written on the grammatical features of plea-dialogue, but an understanding of these features and how they differ from the features of narrative is crucial to my examination of plea-poems. The major differences between narrative and dialogue are, as I shall argue, that narrative tends to use the third person, the past tense, the indicative mood, and the giving function of dialogue. On the other hand, Dialogue naturally favours the second person. It also favours either the present tense, or what I term the 'urgent-future' tense, which is expressed in the imperatives and interrogatives that are common in the demand function of dialogue.

Narrative and dialogue embody the two basic forms of language which Martin Buber has called the I-It and the I-You. The I-It is concerned with 'goal directed verbs... activities that have something for their object. I perceive something... I want something....' The I-You, however, is concerned with relationships:

> Whoever says You does not have something for his object. For wherever there is something there is also another something, every It borders on other Its; It is only by virtue of bordering on others. But where You is said, there is no something. You has no borders. Whoever says You does not have something; he has nothing. But he stands in relation.[50]

---

[49] *Inferno*, 1-9, in *The Divine Comedy of Dante Alighieri*, ed. and tr. John Sinclair, 3 vols. (London, Oxford, New York, 1971).

[50] Martin Buber, *I and Thou*, tr. Walter Kaufmann (New York, 1970), pp.54-5. See also Emile Benveniste, *Problems in General Linguistics*, tr. Mary Elizabeth Meek (Coral Gables, Florida, 1971), pp.197-204.

Similarly, M.A.K. Halliday says that the two main 'purposes' of language are '(i) to understand the environment (ideational [or reflective]), and (ii) to act on the others in it (interpersonal).'[51]

In practice, it is hard to separate the two forms. Even when writing in the third person, a poet is always conveying his or her own ideas (there is always an 'I') to an audience (there is always a 'you'). Conversely, it is rare for dialogue to be totally focused upon the I and the You: if the dialogue is to have any context or content, it must soon talk about other people or things.[52] Other nouns become participants[53] in the action, and nouns other than names are always in the third person. These other nouns inevitably attract some of the attention away from the You and onto themselves. There is a tendency, as I have already noted, for this to occur in praise-poems:

> How amiable are thy tabernacles, O Lord of hosts!
> My soul longeth, yea, even fainteth for the courts of the Lord: my heart and my flesh crieth out for the living God.
> Yea, the sparrow hath found an house, and the swallow a nest for herself, where she may lay her young, even thine altars, O Lord of hosts, my King, and my God.
>
> Psalm 84:1-3

In this passage the reader's attention is divided between the poet's devotion to the Lord and the touching picture of the birds building on the Lord's altars.

Although the two basic forms are often intertwined, the distinction between the two is of critical importance. The strength of the third-person mode is that it is able to state the connections between a number of people and things: it gives a fuller picture of the world as a whole; it is, as Halliday's terms 'reflective' and 'ideational' suggest, useful for reflecting on the meaning of things and ideas.

When using the third person, the 'I' who is writing the text is often suppressed. This has the effect of distancing the narrator from the action;[54] it can give objectivity and perspective. Because of this, narrative writing tends to be less full of emotion than the more subjective dialogue form; it favours the indicative mood, representing its content as facts rather than possibilities.[55] Since it is not possible to relate a story before it has happened (at least in the imagination), the narrative form also tends to favour the past tense. This further increases the sense

---

[51] Halliday, *An Introduction*, p.xiii. In *Cohesion in English* (London, 1976), Halliday and Ruqaiya Hasan argue that the third person refers to items *within* a text, while first and second person refer to the interpersonal situation *outside* the text, pp.31-57.

[52] Halliday notes that the ideational function provides most of language's content (*An Introduction*, p.106); see also Dick Leith and George Myerson, *The Power of Address* (London and New York, 1989), p.xii.

[53] For Halliday's discussion of participants, see *An Introduction*, pp.107-13.

[54] See Edward L. Smith, Jr. 'Achieving Impact through the Interpersonal Component', in *Functional Approaches to Writing*, ed. Barbara Couture, (London, 1986), pp.111-12.

[55] Northrop Frye argues that descriptive narrative is concerned with 'objective truth'. See *Words with Power* (San Diego, 1992), p.5.

of perspective: as Helen Gardner says of George Herbert, 'by describing it as it was, rather than by trying to render it as it is, [he] can keep that tone of "humble sobriety" that convinces us of the truth of what he tells us.'[56]

On the other hand, since the You of dialogue is present (even if only to the writer's mind), focused dialogue tends to use the present tense. This gives a sense of dramatic immediacy,[57] and as I noted earlier, suggests eternity. As Buber says, the I-You is eternal, while the I-It is caught in time:

> When I confront a human being as my You and speak the basic word I-You to him... He is no longer He or She, limited by other Hes and Shes, a dot in the world grid of space and time... Neighbourless and seamless he is You and fills the firmament... if we place a You in time and space he becomes a He or She or It, no longer my You.[58]

Consequently, 'I-You can only be spoken with one's whole being... I-It can never be spoken with one's whole being.'[59] True dialogue, focused exclusively on the I-You, is thus more intimate than the I-It, and suggests a state of affairs beyond time.

In a plea-poem, the I-It and the I-You are both present. In *The Divine Comedy* and *Piers Plowman*, the personae ask continual questions about God and other matters throughout their lengthy narratives, but are, like Job, silenced when the moment of divine revelation answers their questions. In lyric poems such as the Psalms or Donne's sonnets, however, the narrative is brief, and the personae tend to speak more directly to God: the moment of dialogue or encounter with God can take up the whole of the poem.[60] But in both cases there are aspects of both narrative and dialogic encounter: plea-poems, short or long, construct narratives that deal with the temporality of the human experience of God; plea-poems, short or long, also have moments of dialogue that allow access to his eternal aspects.

Because of its intimacy and tight focus, the I-You of dialogue tends to be more dynamic than the I-It of narrative. Narrative has a strong interest in the people, things, and places that form the subjects, objects, and settings of the action. In this, narrative is like writing, which, as Halliday observes, favours noun groups or *things* and thus has 'density of substance'. Dialogue or speech has more verbs and thus more *movement* or action.[61]

Halliday does not offer a reason for the greater dynamism of speech. I suggest two reasons for the dynamism of dialogue in plea-poetry: first, it tends to use pronouns and names rather than common nouns; second, it tends to use the demand function of dialogue and thus often uses the imperative mood.

---

[56] Gardner, *Religion and Literature* (London, 1971), p.189.
[57] At a narrative's climax the 'historic present' is often used to give this sense of immediacy.
[58] Buber, p.59.
[59] Buber, p.54.
[60] Most of these poems are monologues in the sense that God does not speak in them, but as Paul Friedrich says, their deep structure is dialogic, since they attempt 'to engage someone else, an interlocutor'. See 'Dialogue in Lyric Narrative', in Macovski, pp.79-98 (p.79).
[61] Halliday, *Spoken and Written Language*, p.87.

When dialogue is focused upon the interlocutor it uses personal pronouns and names rather than nouns. Names are like pronouns in that they can be used for direct address and do not generally attract adjectives, articles, and possessive pronouns in the way that nouns do. Both as subject and as object of a sentence, the pronoun (or name) stands alone.[62] Thus, using names and personal pronouns means that clauses tend to be shorter, giving a higher proportion of verbs and more sense of movement: dialogue tends to have a lower lexical density or a higher lexical dynamism than narrative.[63] Moreover, personal pronouns are often suppressed, either by ellipsis, or because dialogue tends to use imperatives. This further reduces the number of words per clause and consequently increases the dynamism.

These points are illustrated in Milton's invocation to the Spirit at the start of *Paradise Lost*. Verbs (including participles) – are in italics; nouns are in bold type; names and pronouns that function as subject or object are underlined, with ellipted pronouns in square brackets:

And chiefly thou O Spirit, that *dost prefer*
Before all **temples** the upright **heart** and pure,
Instruct me, for thou *know'st*; thou from the **first**
Wast present, and with mighty **wings** *outspread*
Dove-like [thou] *sat'st brooding* on the vast **abyss**
And [thou] *madest* it pregnant: what in me *is* dark
[Do thou] *Illumine*, what *is low*[Do thou] *raise* and[Do thou] *support;*

                      I.17-23

That to the **heighth** of this great **argument**
I *may assert* eternal **providence**,
And [I may] *justify* the **ways** of God to **men**.
[Do thou] *Say* first, for heaven *hides* nothing from thy **view**
Nor the deep **tract** of hell, [Do thou]*say* first what **cause**
Moved our grand **parents** in that happy **state**,
Favoured of heaven so highly, *to fall off*
From their **creator**, and *transgress* his **will**
For one **restraint**, **lords** of the **world** besides?
Who first *seduced* them to that foul **revolt**?
The infernal **serpent**; he it *was* whose **guile**
Stirred up with **envy** and **revenge**, *deceived*
The **mother** of mankind, what **time** his **pride**
Had cast him out of heaven…

                      I.24-37

The first seven lines are a direct dialogue with the Spirit. There are twice as many pronouns/names (ten) as nouns (five), and if the five ellipted pronouns were included, there would be three times as many pronouns/names as nouns. These

---

[62] Halliday and Hasan, p.45.

[63] Halliday defines lexical density as the number of lexical items in proportion to the total number of items (lexical and grammatical) per clause (*Spoken and Written Language*, pp.61-75). In demonstrating the pace of a passage, it is more effective to calculate lexical dynamism by taking the number of finite verbs and participles (or verbal adjectives) as a percentage of the total word count.

lines move quickly: there are 11 verbs in 55 words (20 percent); the Spirit is the subject of all of these except 'is' (1.23).

In the following fourteen lines, Milton talks about his subject in the third person, and the grammatical patterns are reversed. There are roughly half as many pronouns/names (11, plus three ellipted pronouns) as there are nouns (23). The proportion of verbs (14 in 108 words) drops markedly (13 per cent). Thus a poem that speaks *to* God in the second person may tend to stress God's actions, while one that speaks *about* God in the third person may also tend to stress the things which God is like, or the things on which God acts, or the effects of his actions on his creatures. As Caputo says, prayer speaks to God, praise about God.[64]

The second reason for the dynamism of plea-dialogue is its use of the demand function of dialogue. According to Halliday, the two fundamental types of dialogue are 'giving' and 'demanding'; these functions are 'interacts' in which the speaker invites the listener to respond in 'an exchange in which giving implies receiving and demanding implies giving in response'.[65] Thus dialogue involves two people in a grammatical relationship in which each speech (except perhaps the final one) implies a future response from the interlocutor. This aspect of dialogue increases its forward impulse and dynamism.

It seems to me that the sense of an expected response is much stronger in the demand function than in the giving function. In the giving function, the speaker relates information that already exists in the past or the present. Even if a statement relates to a future event, this event is already known or decided upon in the present: 'the sun will rise at 6.00 a.m.' or 'I will leave for London tonight'. Giving information involves using the indicative mood to relate facts. In many cases, it is possible for the conversation to conclude as soon as the information is given, or merely with a terminating remark such as 'thank-you'.

However, in demand function, the conversation could not possibly end there. The interrogatives and imperatives that express demands initiate an ongoing movement into the *immediate future*: the speaker expects a response. Even if the response is silence, this continues the conversation by rejecting the demand. The forward impulse of demand function can also increase further when the speaker promises to engage in future action if the demand is met:

> Deliver me from bloodguiltiness, O God, thou God of my salvation: and
> my tongue shall sing aloud of thy righteousness.
> O Lord, open thou my lips; and my mouth shall shew forth thy praise.
> Psalm 51:14-15

This immediate future is based on questions, imperatives, requests, and promises. There is an uncertainty about it because it is possible to ask questions that have no answers,[66] to give commands that will be not be obeyed, to make requests that are

---

[64] Caputo, p.38.
[65] Halliday, *An Introduction*, pp.68-71.
[66] John Lyons, *Semantics* (Cambridge, 1977), II.755.

rejected, and promises that will not be fulfilled. This immediate future is very different from the indicative future tense.

In C.S. Lewis's *The Screwtape Letters*, Screwtape advises Wormwood to get his victims 'away from the eternal, and from the Present' and to make them live in the Future because

> ... thought about the Future inflames hope and fear. Also, it is unknown to them, so that in making them think about it we make them think unrealities. In a word, the Future is, of all things, the thing *least like* eternity. It is the most completely temporal part of time for the Past is frozen and no longer flows, and the Present is all lit up with eternal rays.[67]

Lewis argues elsewhere that the last two books of *Paradise Lost* are an artistic failure because they are 'an untransmuted lump of futurity'.[68] Too much use of the future tense can indeed weaken poetry. The compound verbs reduce the verbal dynamism, as in this prophecy from *Paradise Lost*:

> Then all thy saints assembled, thou *shalt judge*
> Bad men and angels, they arraigned *shall sink*
> Beneath thy sentence; hell her numbers full,
> Thenceforth *shall be forever shut*. Mean while
> The world *shall burn*, and from her ashes *spring*
> New heaven and earth, wherein the just *shall dwell*.

III.330-5

Only one of these six verbs ellipses the auxiliary; thus of the 48 words in this passage, five (or over ten per cent) are repetitions of the auxiliary 'shall'. The compound verb form, if maintained for long, can render a passage wordy and dull.

Although predictions and prophecies can be deceptive, as in *Macbeth*, they express a conviction that the predicted events will actually occur: they use the indicative mood to *narrate* the future as a series of facts. However, the demand function of dialogue *requests* the interlocutor to act: it expresses the future largely through imperatives and interrogatives. The demand function does not express certainty, so much as an urgent hope of changing the situation.[69] Perhaps the most marked example of this in English poetry is Donne's Sonnet XIV:

> *Batter* my heart, three person'd God; for you
> As yet but *knocke, breathe, shine*, and *seeke to mend*;
> That I may *rise*, and *stand, o'erthrow* mee, 'and *bend*
> Your force, to *breake, blowe, burn* and *make* me new.
> I, like an usurpt towne, to'another due,

---

[67] Lewis, *The Screwtape Letters* (Glasgow, 1977), p.77.

[68] Lewis, *A Preface to Paradise Lost*, p.129. I will discuss this issue in Chapter 5.

[69] Edward Smith notes that imperatives and interrogatives compel a response from the reader (pp.112-13); Mey, that *directives* aim to change the world (p.132). The term 'directive' covers both pleas and commands: see François Recanati, *Meaning and Force* (Cambridge, 1987), p.161.

> *Labour to 'admit* you, but Oh, to no end,
> *Reason* your viceroy in mee, mee *should defend,*
> But *is captiv'd,* and *proves* weake or untrue.
> Yet dearely'I *love* you,'and *would be loved* faine,
> But *am betroth'd* unto your enemie:
> *Divorce* mee, *'untie,* or *breake* that knot againe,
> *Take* mee to you, *imprison* mee, for I
> Except you'*enthrall* mee, never *shall be* free,
> Nor ever chast, except you *ravish* mee.

Here the subject is usually suppressed, and the seven imperatives are 'bald' rather than polite (Donne does not say 'please').[70] The verbs are simple rather than compound, and there are thirty in 112 words (27 per cent). Thus Donne's imperatives (and the other verbs that depend on them) create a very high degree of lexical dynamism. The purpose of demand is not merely linguistically dynamic, it is also functionally dynamic: as Thiselton notes, commands (or imperatives) and promises intend to change the world.[71]

Imperatives, like names, are a primary feature of interpersonal language as Jennings observes:

> Very early in our education in language we hear words of command: Come. Go. Stop. Don't. We enter into the world of language by being addressed by another. The word of address gives to even our inarticulate behaviour the character of an answer or response, of obedience and revolt.[72]

The imperatives of plea-poetry create far more syntactic tension than do the indicatives of praise-poetry. Whereas the indicative mood aims to express truths, imperatives are neither true nor false, but can only be obeyed or disobeyed.[73]

Moreover, the imperative mood can be used to express three different speech acts: command, plea, and invitation, depending on the tone and circumstances. Command and plea are diametrically opposed. As Pratt notes, in command the speaker is in authority, but in plea the listener is.[74] In plea-imperatives, the speaker has no authority over the listener, and thus no certainty that the request will be granted: the desired future is far less certain than the future implied by command-imperatives.

Plea-imperatives do not predict a temporal future. Rather they refer to what I would call the urgent-future – a state of affairs that is urgently desired in the immediate future. The urgent-future is similar to the *à-venir,* which, Caputo observes, is not 'the future-present', but remains 'the object of a faith, not a plan'; it opens up 'the adventure *(aventure)* of the future'.[75] For Jennings, optimism and pessimism seek to control and domesticate the future by projecting the past and

---

[70] For polite and bald imperatives, see Mey, p.68.
[71] Thiselton, p.296.
[72] Jennings, p.104.
[73] Recanati, pp.11-16, 159.
[74] Pratt, p.83.
[75] Caputo, pp.56, 72.

present into it. This is 'the future-present', or what I would call the predictive-future. Rather, for Jennings, the future 'is an advent that befalls me'. It ruptures both temporal structures and language because it may lead either to the annihilation of God's absence or to the future of encounter with God's presence. Both these possibilities are beyond our control. This is the *à-venir*, or urgent-future.[76]

Plea-poems often set up a powerful tension between the desired presence of a loving God and his seeming absence or anger:

> How long wilt thou forget me, O Lord? For ever? How long wilt thou hide thy face from me?
> How long shall I take counsel in my soul, having sorrow in my heart daily? How long shall mine enemy be exalted over me?
> Consider and hear me, O Lord my God: lighten mine eyes, lest I sleep the sleep of death.
> Lest mine enemy say, I have prevailed against him; and those that trouble me rejoice when I am moved.
> But I have trusted in thy mercy; my heart shall rejoice in thy salvation.
> I will sing unto the Lord, because he hath dealt bountifully with me.
>
> Psalm 13

The lexical content of this passage brings the desired actions of God (considering, hearing, lightening, having mercy, saving, and dealing bountifully) powerfully to the reader's mind. At the same time, the plea-imperatives ('Consider... hear... lighten) and interrogatives suggest that these actions remain in the future: they may never actually take place – the Lord may indeed forget the speaker 'for ever'. Although the psalm ends with an expression of trust, this does not fully overcome the agitated doubt of the five questions, the repeated cries of 'how long?' that start the poem.

This doubt allows plea-poems to operate in the gaps of language. Praise-poems tend to use the present or past tense to make statements about God in the indicative mood (any imperatives are usually addressed to the worshippers): they claim to relate facts about God. They thus attempt to capture the reality of God in language, suggesting that in some ways he is actually available to the speaker. Moreover, their lexis and syntax can even become distracted from God by the delight they take in describing his creation. Plea-poems, however, construct God as other, as available only in some tenuous future, as desired with all the anguish of uncertainty. They show little interest in creation, but focus mainly on the speaker's longing for God's presence and his fear that God may not come quickly. They express the positive (God's presence) through their lexis; they express the negative (his absence) through their syntax (interrogatives and plea-imperatives). They set up a tension between God's presence and absence that places God outside human language, in the gaps between the lexis and the syntax; they depict God, in Hart's term, as 'an absent presence'.[77] In this way, they avoid certainty and closure. Plea-prayer enables a poet to convey an encounter with the divine that goes beyond the

---

[76] Jennings, pp.106-7, 116, 131.

[77] Hart, pp.6-7. See also Jennings, p.188.

comforting certainty that takes religious truths for granted. It conveys the anguish with which the seeking soul encounters a God who is beyond human conceptions.

Perhaps the only ground on which Man can in any sense match God is the ground of his own need for God – the one thing in which Man himself touches infinity. In plea-poems it is notable that the poet speaks to God on almost equal terms. He pleads, promises, and even threatens, often taking up as much space in both the grammar and the lexis as God does. This grammatical equality between God and Man is achieved largely through the demand (plea) function of dialogue, as in Psalm 6. Verses 1-4 express an anguished plea to God for God's help:

> O Lord, *rebuke* me not in thine anger, neither *chasten* me in thy hot displeasure.
> *Have mercy* upon me O Lord; for I *am* weak: O Lord, *heal* me; for my bones *are vexed*.
> My soul *is also sore vexed*: but thou, O Lord, how long?
> *Return*, O Lord, *deliver* my soul: O *save* me for thy mercies' sake.

Here the dialogue is tightly focused: the only participants are God and the speaker. The passage is rich in verbs (ten verbs in 59 words – 17 per cent) God is powerful, the agent/subject of all the active, material processes: rebuke, chasten, have mercy, heal, return, deliver, save. The speaker is weak, the subject of one relational process and two passive verbs: 'I am weak... my bones are vexed. My soul is also sore vexed.' The main message is a simple plea, 'God have mercy on me', repeated, with variations, in simple words: 'O Lord' is repeated five times; 'mercy' and 'vexed' twice each. The grammar reinforces the speaker's weakness and uncertainty with a question that may never be answered ('O Lord, how long?') and seven plea-imperatives. The two opening plea imperatives are even more urgent because they are negative pleas, imploring God to stop rebuking and chastening the speaker. The positive pleas ('Have mercy... heal... Return... deliver... save') are given added urgency by the continued interjections of 'O Lord' and 'O'. Yet in this uncertainty, the speaker is in intimate grammatical relationship with God.

In verses 5-7, the dialogue changes from demand function to giving function, from a plea for help to a reproach:

> For in death there *is* no remembrance of thee: in the grave who *shall give* thee thanks?
> I *am* weary with my groaning; all the night *make I my bed to swim*; I *water* my couch with tears.
> Mine eye *is consumed* because of grief; it *waxeth* old because of all mine enemies.

Here the poet, rather than pleading for (or demanding) God's help, gives God information about his suffering. There are fewer verbs (7 in 53 words: 13 per cent), and God is not the agent of any of them. The poet begins to dwell on things other than God: death, the grave, his bed, his couch, his eye. These things shift attention away from God to other things, and the focus moves to the poet's enemies, a third major participant in the action.

In verses 8-9, it is the enemies who are directly addressed:

Depart from me, all ye workers of iniquity; for the Lord *hath heard* the voice of my weeping.
The Lord *hath heard* my supplication; the Lord *will receive* my prayer.
Let all mine enemies be ashamed and *sore vexed*: *let them return* and *be shamed* suddenly.

The passage is more verbal (7 verbs in 46 words: 16 per cent), but the participant roles have changed. The speaker fails to maintain the tight focus of a plea-dialogue in which God and the speaker are held, as it were, in balance, by being given equal weight in the poem's lexis and syntax. Here he addresses his enemies rather than God.

Whereas in the first section the speaker expressed his abject need for God, here he seems full of confidence. The only imperative is a confident command-imperative that he addresses to his enemies, 'Depart from me'. He reinforces this command and attempts closure with his indicative statements that God has heard his supplication and will receive his prayer. Yet in allowing his enemies into grammatical relationship with himself, the speaker loses grammatical intimacy with God. He also becomes less active himself. In the last verse, he is no longer a direct participant in the action, no longer the subject of any verbs. He is reduced, grammatically, to the single possessive 'mine'. Nor is God as grammatically active as he was in the first section: in the passives 'be ashamed and sore vexed... be shamed', the agent is unexpressed, and thus God is grammatically removed from the verse. It is as if the poet is subconsciously ashamed of asking God to enact the vengeance he desires. Thus the psalm, starting in tightly focused demand or plea mode, moves away from encounter with God as it moves to the information-giving function of dialogue.

The linguistic characteristics of plea-poems allow them to operate in the gaps of language. In their use of direct address they are tightly focused on the Other. They use the demand function of dialogue, expressed in interrogatives and imperatives, to project their desire for God into the urgent-future. Theirs is the language of 'not yet'. Their frequent use of imperatives gives many plea-poems their intense urgency as the speaker realizes that he lacks the authority to force God to respond to his pleas, and the 'not yet' expands into a 'perhaps never'. Their focus on the desired actions of God allows them to avoid explaining God or describing his essence: by not objectifying God they escape the idolatry of language. They hesitantly suggest the nature of encounter rather than depicting it as a concrete, present reality.

Yet, at the same time, that concrete 'present' reality is an important feature of much Christian poetry. Christianity is a historical religion: it asserts that the Son of God became incarnate at a particular time, in a particular place, among particular people, and thus gave meaning to history.[78] Indeed, Jennings argues that

---

[78] Ricoeur says of the Incarnation, 'At that moment history acquired meaning': 'Christianity and History', in *History and Truth,* pp.84-5.

encounter itself is historical, that humans find meaning largely through 'the sphere of our encounter with one another, and thus with time... the region of ethical and historical existence'. He says that this encounter is expressed in the interpersonal linguistic acts of naming, commanding, and promising.[79] These, together with questioning, are the features of plea-poems.

All the poets in this study – the medieval lyricists, Langland, Donne and Milton – construct personae who experience an interpersonal encounter with the God or Christ of salvation history. In their use of biblical language and story, together with personae who enter into and respond to that story, these poets assert their own participation in the meaning of Christian history. Yet at the same time they avoid the idolatry of language by depicting this moment of encounter as incomplete, as fleeting, or as merely a potentiality. Rather than expressing the certainties of praise, these poets, to a large extent, as I shall argue, rely on the gaps and uncertainties of plea, challenging, questioning, commanding, and doubting both themselves and the God whom they dare to name.

---

[79] Jennings, pp.103-4.

Chapter 2

Redemption and Response in the Anonymous Middle Ages

Ihesu, my love, thou were so fre,
Al that thou didest for love of me.
What schal I for that yelde thee?
Thou axist nought but love of me...

Brown, XIV.89. 25-8

1. Why God became Man: two theories of atonement

The dominant theme of medieval English religious lyrics of the thirteenth to fifteenth centuries is the Crucifixion. These Crucifixion lyrics provide a useful point of departure for this study, because, as short lyrics, their whole focus is on the encounter between Christ and the individual Meditator. They were composed mostly by friars in order to help the laity to meditate on matters of faith, and therefore the reader is persuaded to imagine him or herself as actually taking part in the scenes that they describe.[1]

As poems intended to encourage meditation on matters of faith, the lyrics do not question that faith. Critics have remarked that in these poems 'Christianity is taken for granted',[2] that the Meditator is admonished not so much to believe, as to live by his beliefs,[3] and that he is expected not merely to grasp the theology of Redemption intellectually, but to gain access to its grace through a 'heart-felt response to God's offering of love'.[4] These views assume that the lyrics follow a homogeneous theology in which the nature of the Redemption and other matters of faith were undisputed. In this period, however, there were three major theories of Redemption, and this chapter will examine which of these predominated in the Crucifixion lyrics, and how this affected their depiction of encounter.

Gustaf Aulén, followed by later scholars, has identified three major theories of Atonement.[5] First, in the heroic (or classic) theory, 'God-in-Christ'[6]

---

[1] Rosemary Woolf, *The English Religious Lyric in the Middle Ages* (London, 1968), pp.19-20, 337.

[2] Douglas Gray, *Themes and Images in the Medieval English Religious Lyric* (London and Boston, 1972), p.59.

[3] Woolf, *The English Religious Lyric*, p.14.

[4] Susanna Greer Fein, *Moral Love Songs and Laments* (Kalamazoo, 1998), pp.1, 5.

[5] Gustaf Aulén, *Christus Victor*, tr. A.G. Herbert (New edn, New York, 1969), pp.1-2.

conquers the Devil and rescues Man from evil. Secondly, in 1098, St Anselm's *Cur Deus Homo?* developed the satisfaction theory in which the Son, the sinless God-Man, pays satisfaction to God on behalf of sinful Man. Thirdly, Peter Abelard's exemplarist theory argues that the Redemption depends solely on Christ's example of love, which wins man's love in return.[7]

The exemplarist view is concerned with human response to the Atonement, and thus it can often be found in conjunction with either of the other two theories.[8] This is seen in a number of the lyrics examined in this chapter. The main question, then, is whether the poet relies on the heroic theory or the satisfaction theory to account for God's motivation for the Atonement.

Although both these views sometimes appear in a single work,[9] there is a fundamental tension between them. The heroic theory stresses God-in-Christ's divinity, his victory over evil, and God's self-giving love and mercy.[10] The satisfaction theory, on the other hand, stresses Christ's manhood, his payment to God, and God's justice and dignity.

One of the most influential accounts of the heroic theory is St Augustine's *De Trinitate*. Augustine stresses the *continuity* of the divine action: it is God-in-Christ who overcomes the Devil.[11] Augustine sees Christ's death, not as a payment made by the Son to the Father, but as the work of the Trinity acting together:

> Is it really the case that when God the Father was angry with us he saw the death of his Son on our behalf, and was reconciled to us? Does this mean then that his Son was already so reconciled to us that he was even prepared to die for us, while the Father was still so angry with us that unless the Son died for us he would not be reconciled to us?... Would the Father have... handed [the Son] over for us, if he had not already been reconciled... the Father loved us not merely before the Son died for us, but before he founded the world... Nor does the Father's not sparing him mean that the Son was handed over for us against his will... the Father and the Son and the Spirit... work all things together equally. (XIII.1v.15)[12]

For Augustine, God's mercy is eternal: there was no need to placate his justice before his mercy could take effect. Although God imposes 'a wholly just death on the sinner', he also chooses to become 'a just man to intercede with God for sinful man' (IV.i.4-iii.15). Rather than exerting his power over the Devil, God relies on

---

[6] See James McClendon, *Doctrine Systematic Theology. Vol.II* (Nashville, 1994), p.206.

[7] Peter Abelard, *Commentariorum super S. Pauli Epsitolam ad Romanos,* Lib II, *Patralogia Latina,* 178.836. St Thomas Aquinas gave this as the first reason for God's chosen method of Redemption: *ST*.III.xlvi.3, ed. Petri Marietti (Taurini, 1915), IV.687.

[8] For Macquarrie, the heroic model unites the other two, including Abelard's subjective view by giving an example of perfect obedience for Man to follow, and Anselm's objective view by stressing that Man is powerless to save himself: *Principles,* pp.287-9.

[9] McClendon notes that Calvin combines the two views (p.20).

[10] Macquarrie, *Principles,* pp.287-9.

[11] Macquarrie, *Principles,* pp.287-9.

[12] *St* Augustine, *De Trinitate,* tr. Edmund Hill, in *The Works of Saint Augustine,* ed. John E. Rotelle, Part 1, vol 5 (Brooklyn, 1991).

justice: the Devil justly has power over sinful Man, but when he also kills the innocent Son, he justly loses his power over Mankind as a whole (XIII.iv.16-18).

God chose this means of Atonement because his gratuitous display of love enabled humanity 'to believe how much God loved us and to hope at last for what we had despaired of' (XIII.iv.13). Augustine does not overstress the sinfulness and helplessness of Man; rather, he believes that Man can contribute to his salvation through a *response* of faith and obedience (IV.iii.13).

In *De Trinitate* there are three points to Augustine's triangle of Redemption – God-in-Christ, Man, and the Devil. The 'Devil', as Maquarrie notes, should not be taken literally, but rather as standing for the demonic and enslaving effect of sin.[13]

The satisfaction theory, as found in Anselm's *Cur Deus Homo*, is very different. The three points of Anselm's triangle of Redemption are the Father, Man, and the Son. He sees God's mercy as restricted by the claims of justice: it would not be 'fitting' for God to forgive the debt of sin without punishment (I.12);[14] as Supreme Justice, God cannot violate justice's claim to satisfaction (I.23). Because Man owes everything to God already, and has nothing left to offer in reparation for his sin (I.20), it is necessary for the Son to become the perfect Man, so that he can repay God for Man's sin (II.6-9).

Since Anselm's God voluntarily provides the means for overcoming the dilemma caused by human sin, this model of the Atonement can still be seen as the work of a loving God.[15] Indeed, Anselm's prayers and meditations stress the sinner's trust that Christ will act through mercy rather than justice to save him.[16] Nevertheless, as Aulén observes, in Anselm's account, the Atonement may 'be called a *discontinuous* Divine work'.[17] Anselm's view, no doubt unintentionally, sets up a sense of two-way division in the Godhead. Unlike Augustine, when he discusses whether or not the Father compelled the Son to die, Anselm makes no mention of the Spirit (I.8-10). Unlike Augustine, who said that God was reconciled to Man 'before he made the world',[18] Anselm's division between justice and mercy undermines the view of God as eternally unchanging. The satisfaction theory stresses the need to placate God's justice *before* his mercy can operate. It thus makes God's mercy *consequent* upon satisfaction and God's eternal will becomes subject to time and history.[19]

---

[13] Macquarrie, *Principles*, pp.287-9. Augustine does not believe that evil is a substance, but rather a perversion of the will that turns asside from God : *Confessions*, VII.16.

[14] St Anselm, *Why God Became Man* in *Anselm of Canterbury:The Major Works*, ed. Brian Davies and G.R. Evans (Oxford, 1998), p.284. This translation uses the term 'righteousness' rather than the *justicia* of the Latin text; *Opera Omnia*, ed. F.S. Schmitt, 6 vols. (Stuttgart: Fromman, 1946), II.69-70.

[15] Ellen M. Ross, *The Grief of God* (New York, 1997), p.85.

[16] Fulton, pp.176-7.

[17] Aulén, p.5n.

[18] See also Macquarrie, *Principles*, p.283.

[19] Charles Mazouer, 'Dieu, justice et miséricorde dans le *Mistére du Viel Testament*', *Moyen Age*, 91 (1985), 53-73 (p.60).

In brief, the heroic theory represents the Atonement as a continuous act in which the eternal mercy of God-in-Christ redeems Man. The satisfaction theory represents it as a discontinuous act in which Christ-as-Man must make a repayment to satisfy God's justice before his mercy can take effect. The exemplarist stress on *human response* to God's mercy and love can appear in conjunction with either the heroic or the satisfaction theory.[20] What concerns me is whether the medieval Crucifixion lyrics account for *God's motivation* for the Incarnation using the heroic theory or (as critics have assumed) the satisfaction theory.

R.W. Southern relates these two theories to the two main divisions of the medieval era – the epic or heroic Dark Ages, and the 'romance' period of the Middle Ages.[21] In the heroic period, dominant until the eleventh century, a strong Christ was needed to appeal to pagans and recent converts. Artists minimized Christ's humanity and suffering, and tended to avoid representing the Crucifixion until around 800 AD.[22] In early Crucifixion scenes, Christ appears as a king or hero – upright, alive, eyes open, sometimes wearing a crown.[23] However, by the time of Anselm, he is shown as human – dying or dead, his body sagging and disfigured by suffering.[24]

Southern argues that the heroic model presents Man as a 'helpless spectator in the cosmic struggle' between God and the Devil, and overlooks Christ's humanity, with 'little or no place for tender compassion for the sufferings of Jesus'. On the other hand, in the satisfaction theory, with its 'intense commiseration' for Christ's suffering, 'The Devil slipped out of the drama and left God and man face to face.'[25] Rosemary Woolf argues for a similar pattern in the medieval religious lyrics: she sees the heroic theory in terms of God's defeat of the Devil, with Man playing a subordinate role, while the satisfaction and exemplarist theories demand a loving human response to Christ's humanity.[26]

However, the two periods cannot be treated as completely distinct from each other: an emphasis on Christ's sufferings developed as early as the late tenth-century Gero Crucifix;[27] features of the satisfaction theory were apparent earlier than Anselm;[28] and the heroic theory remained popular in late medieval depictions

---

[20] Ross, pp.15-17.

[21] R.W. Southern, *The Making of the Middle Ages* (London, 1967), pp.209-44. See also Woolf, *The English Religious Lyric*, pp.21-22; J.A.W. Bennett, *Poetry of the Passion* (Oxford, 1982), pp.7-26, 32-61; Barbara C. Raw, *Anglo-Saxon Crucifixion Iconography* (Cambridge, 1990), pp.168-76.

[22] Mitchell B. Merback, *The Thief, the Cross and the Wheel* (Chicago, 1999), p.49.

[23] For example, Merback, fig. 16 and Southern, plate 2.

[24] Southern, pp. 226-7; frontispiece, plates II and III.

[25] Southern, pp.224-5. See also Woolf, *The English Religious Lyric*, p.21; Ross, p.84.

[26] Woolf, *The English Religious Lyric*, pp.21-3.

[27] Bennett notes that the suffering Christ appeared in Anglo-Saxon art before 1066: pp.32-3. See also Merback, pp.55-8, fig.18. Fulton argues that in these turn-of-the-millennium crucifixes the suffering Christ was 'an image not of pathos but of justice... the terrible, weeping, bloody Christ of Judgement... whom they could do naught but dread': p.87.

[28] Woolf, 'Doctrinal Influences on *The Dream of the Rood*', *MÆ*, 27 (1958), 137-53 (pp.142-3).

of the Harrowing of Hell. Literature is able to use a mixture of theories, presenting different aspects of the Redemption in a creative tension.

In the rest of this chapter I will argue: first, that, pace Woolf, the medieval English Crucifixion lyrics do not use the satisfaction theory to account for God's motivation in the Atonement. Rather, they combine the heroic and exemplarist theories, using the heroic theory to account for God's motivation in the Atonement, and the exemplarist theory to stress the need for human response. Moreover, their use of the heroic theory coexists with a stress on Christ's suffering and an anguish at the human sinfulness that has caused it. The satisfaction theory's stress on the need to placate God's justice is not apparent in the lyrics. It occurs later in the period than Woolf suggests, and in *narrative* rather than lyric texts – in the mystery plays and in treatments of the Debate between the Four Daughters of God. Its appearance coincides with a development of encounter that goes beyond the simple anguish of sin displayed in the lyrics to include the beginnings of a new focus on the anguish of doubt.

2. The importance of human response: the exemplarist theory in the Crucifixion lyrics

Critics have generally accepted Southern's idea that the satisfaction theory was dominant in the 'romance' period.[29] However, due to critical neglect of the lyrics,[30] there has been very little close discussion of their treatment of the Redemption,[31] and almost none of their *differences* from the art of the period.[32]

Early medieval English art depicts the Crucifixion using the simplest, traditional arrangements: Christ is either alone, or in the centre of the picture with the Virgin Mary on his right and St John on his left.[33] An excellent example is the *Crucifixion* in the Gospels of the Countess Judith (Fig.2.1), which Southern uses to illustrate the romance period's stress on Christ's suffering humanity.[34] The painting is tightly focused on Christ's drooping body (his eyes closed in death). A small female figure, probably Mary Magdalen, embraces the foot of the Cross, eyes raised to Christ's feet. Mary and John look up at his face, Mary's hand reaching to wipe his side, John writing what he sees in his Gospel. Above Christ's head, the Sun and Moon weep while God's hand, appearing from the clouds, points to

---

[29] Woolf, *The English Religious Lyric*, pp.21-7; Bennett, pp.95-8; James Simpson, *Piers Plowman: An Introduction to the B-text* (London and New York, 1990), p.215; C.W. Marx, *The Devil's Rights and the Redemption in the Literature of Medieval England* (Cambridge, 1995) pp.111-12; Lawrence Warner, 'Jesus the Jouster: The Christ-Knight and Medieval Theories of Atonement', *YLS,* 10 (1996) 129-43.

[30] O.S. Pickering (ed.) *Individuality and Achievement in Middle English Poetry* (Cambridge, 1997), p.vii.

[31] See Woolf, *The English Religious Lyric*, pp.21-2. Gray does not discuss the topic.

[32] Ross, for example, discusses sermons, art, and drama, but not lyrics.

[33] See Margaret Rickert, *Painting in Britain: The Middle Ages* (2nd edn) (Harmondsworth, Penguin, 1965), plates 24, 30, 37b, 43, 52, 53, 60, 106, 107, 144.

[34] Southern, frontispiece and p.226.

Figure. 2.1. Crucifixion, *The Gospels of the Countess Judith*, The Pierpont Morgan Library, New York, MS M.709, f.1v.

Christ's head. But although the painting strongly suggests both the emotional and intellectual responses desired in the viewer, it cannot place the viewer in the actual painting.

The Crucifixion lyrics are different from the art in three major aspects. First, the reader *can* enter the text in a deeply personal way by accepting the role of the 'I' who speaks them. Secondly, although the *art* of the period depicts Christ as dead, in the *lyrics* he is usually alive and speaking to the Meditator.[35] Thirdly, unlike the paintings and sculptures of the period, the lyrics fall into two groups offering two distinct perspectives – that of the Meditator and that of Christ.

One short poem displays several features of the Meditator's point of view:

> Whanne hic se on rode
> Ihesu, mi lemman,
> An be-siden him stonden
> Marie and Iohan,
> And his rig i-suongen,
> And his side i-stungen,
> For the luve of man,
> Well ou hic to wepen,
> And sinnes for-leten,
> Yif hic of luve kan,
> Yif hic of luve kan,
> Yif hic of luve kan.
>
> Brown, XIII. 35B [36]

The use of the first person allows the writer to avoid preaching by conveying the desired response as his own, while at the same time inviting each reader to embrace it as his or her own.[37] The poet shares with his readers, not what makes him unique and different from them, but what makes him the same. The lack of personal or contemporary details in the poem give the sense that it was written, not by a particular person for a particular audience in a particular time, but for all believers in universal time.[38]

---

[35] Woolf notes that the third-person lyrics, with a preacher as intermediary, are less effective: *The English Religious Lyric*, p.20. A number of lyrics also depict a dialogue between Christ and the Virgin.

[36] See also 34, 35 (A), 36, 37. Unless otherwise specified, I have cited Carleton Brown's editions: *English Lyrics of the XIIIth Century* (Oxford, 1932); *Religious Lyrics of the XIVth Century*, 2nd edn, rev. G.V. Smithers (Oxford, 1957); and *Religious Lyrics of the XVth Century* (Oxford, 1939). I have modernized the orthography (*thorn, yogh*, and 'u' or 'w' for 'v') of all Middle English texts to make them more accessible to the non-specialist reader.

[37] Gray, p.60; Bennett, p.35. Woolf sees the lyrics as displaying an 'abnegation of individuality': *The English Religious Lyric*, p.6.

[38] Gray, p.141. Woolf, *The English Religious Lyric*, p.19; Marta Gebinska 'Some Observations on the Themes and Techniques of the Medieval English Religious Love Lyrics', *ES*, 57(1976), 103-14 (p.111).

These poems were written to encourage meditation on matters of faith. Their sense of a common, unquestioned belief gives them a certain security:[39] the sinner is expected not merely to understand what he or she is supposed to believe, but to respond with love, and to live according to these beliefs.[40] It is this emphasis on response that indicates the lyrics' reliance on the exemplarist theory.

Thus, the first half of 'Whanne hic se on rode' uses the present tense[41] and indicative mood (lines 1-7) to suggest certainty that Christ's redemptive actions are already an actuality, happening before the Meditator's eyes: Jesus is the 'lemman' or 'beloved' who dies 'for the luve of man'. However, the 'when' of the first line, as a subordinating conjunction, throws the emphasis onto the main clauses in the second part of the poem (8-12). Here the poet uses repeated conditional clauses to convey the speaker's frustration at not being able to respond as he should to Christ's love:[42] in this poem, the Redemption is a present reality, human response only a future possibility.

In 'Whanne hic se on rode', the sole motivation for the Atonement is love: there is no mention of placating God's justice. Christ's love is perhaps the strongest feature of the lyrics as a whole, with a corresponding emphasis on the Meditator's obligation to respond with love, a response which is sometimes forthcoming, as in this short poem:

> Ihesu cryst, myn leman swete,
> That for me deye-des on rode tre,
> Wiht al myn herte i the bi-seke
> For thi wndes to and thre,
> That al so faste in myn herte
> Thi love roted mute be,
> As was the spere in-to thi side,
> When thow suffredis ded for me.

Brown, XIV.52

The poet expresses a passionate physical attachment to his *lemman*, Christ,[43] with the image of love transfixing the heart like a spear. Other lyrics speak of the Meditator's 'love-longing', ask that Christ be buried in the speaker's breast, or even long to be clad in Christ's skin.[44] In one lyric, all sixteen stanzas begin with the words 'Sweet Jesus', addressing Christ as 'myn herte light... myn herte gleem... my soule fode,' and asking him to plant a root of love in the Meditator's

---

[39] Gray says that in them 'Christianity is taken for granted', p.59.

[40] Woolf, *The English Religious Lyric*, p.14; Fein, pp.1, 5.

[41] Edmund Reiss, *The Art of the Middle English Lyric* (Athens, Georgia, 1972), p.31. See also Gray, pp.40-56. Peter Dronke notes the liveliness, the vigorous language, and the sense of things happening '*now*' that distinguish the English lyrics from their Latin models: *The Medieval Lyric* (London, 1968), pp.63-9.

[42] Reiss, pp.31-6.

[43] See also Sarah Beckwith, *Christ's Body* (London and New York, 1993), pp.45-77.

[44] Brown, XIV.83, 79 and 71 respectively.

heart. Trusting in Christ's response, the speaker is confident of his own, declaring his repentance, and promising to sin no more:

> Suete ihesu, me reoweth sore
> Gultes that y ha wroht yore
> Thar-fore y bidde thin mylse & ore.
> Merci, lord! y nul na more.

Brown, XIV.7.33-6

Other poems have less confidence in the Meditator's response. In one, the Meditator laments his dilatory behaviour:

> Loverd, thu clepedest me
> An ich nagt ne ansuarede the
> Bute wordes scloe and sclepie:
> 'Thole yet! Thole a litel!'
> Bute 'yiet' and 'yiet' was endelis,
>   And 'Thole a litel' a long wey is.

Brown, XIV.5

Another poem pleads for over 150 lines that Christ should engrave his love upon the Meditator's hard heart:

> Ihesu, yit write in my hert
> How bloode out of thy woundes stert;
> And with that blode write thou so ofte,
> Myn hard hert til hit be softe.

Brown, XIV.91.49-52

The Meditator implores assistance so that he may not flee Christ (75-8) and so that he may forsake worldly joy (91-104) and suffer hardship 'for love of thee' (105-24). Yet for all his anxiety about himself, the Meditator has confidence in Christ:

> Ihesu that art so corteysly,
> Make me bold on the to cry;
> For wel I wot with-out drede
> Thy mercy is more than my mysdede...
>
> At my deynge I hop I-wis,
> Of thy presens I shal noght mysshe.

ll.137-40, 149-50

Sometimes, when the Meditator raises doubts as to his own response, he answers himself positively:

> Ihesu, my love, thou were so fre,
> Al that thou didest for love of me.
> What schal I for that yelde thee?
> Thou axist nought but love of me...

> Ihesu my love, ihesu my lyght,
> I wole thee love & that is right;
> Do me love thee with all my might,
> & for thee moorne bothe day & nyght.
>
>   Brown, XIV.89. 25-8, 33-6

The pleas of the Psalmist or Donne call on the help of a distant God who may answer them in the urgent-future. Here the Meditator's are far less anguished: he sees Christ with his mind's eye, and it is human response that remains only a future possibility. Moreover, the speaker has power over this possibility: by definition, someone who is meditating sincerely is at least trying to respond to Christ.

The fear that Man may not respond appropriately is much stronger in poems where Christ appeals to the Meditator:

> Men rent me on rode
> Wiht wndes woliche wode,
> Al blet mi blode –
> Thenk, man, al it is the to gode.
>
> Thenk who the first wroghte
> For what werk helle thow sowhte;
> Thenk who the ageyn bowhte –
> Werk warli, fayle me nowhte.
>
>   Brown, XIV.51. 1-8

The tone of the imperatives here suggests not the authority of command-imperatives, but the uncertainty of plea-imperatives. Here, Christ's repeated pleas (eleven plea-imperatives in the twenty-four lines of the whole poem) suggest fear that the Meditator is not listening.

Christ's repeated appeals and complaints about his suffering can give these poems a plaintive tone:

> Com home againe!
> Com home againe!
> Mine owene swet hart, com home againe!
> Ye are gone astray
> Out of youer way,
> Therefore, com home againe...
>
> My blod so red
> For thee was shed,
> The prise it was not smale.
> Remembre welle
> What I thee telle,
> And com whan I thee cale.
>
>   Davies, 150.1-6, 13-18[45]

---

[45] R.T. Davies, *Medieval English Lyrics* (London, 1963).

Weakness in the rhyme and rhythm cause this poem to slip into querulousness,[46] but another poem, 'Wofully araide', expresses Christ's anguish more successfully:

> Thus nakid am I nailid, O man, for thi sake.
> I love the, thenne love me. Why slepist thu? awake!
> Remember my tender hert-rote for the brake,
> With paynes my vaines constrayned to crake.
>
> Brown, XV.103.10-13

Here the variation of statement, command, question, and exclamation, together with the alliteration, antithesis, and the hard doubled rhyme, give power to Christ's appeal. In many of the Psalms and Donne's Divine Poems it is Man who pleads with God; here Christ places himself in a position of weakness before Man, using the interrogatives and imperatives characteristic of plea-prayer. These poems suggest that God has given Man free will, and that the one thing he does not have power over is Man's response to his love. This is where the lyrics avoid idolatry by creating a gap in the language as Christ invites the Meditator with questions that he may choose not to answer and plea-imperatives that he may choose not to obey.

In these poems the anguish of sin is the dominant anguish. Both the Meditator and Christ lament that the Meditator's sin has placed Christ upon the Cross, and both fear that he will not respond to Christ's suffering with love and repentance, but will keep on sinning. Sin is described in general terms:[47] the poet may say that one must leave sin, or may mention a traditional sin such as pride,[48] but there is nothing as specific and concrete as Langland's wrestling with his unproductive life throughout *Piers Plowman*. The poet cannot afford to confess to sins with which the reader might not identify: for him the important thing is not the particularity and variety of sin, but the fact that all sin is a failure of response to Christ, and risks alienating the Meditator from him.

3. God's motivation for Atonement: the heroic theory in the Crucifixion lyrics

The lyrics discussed so far follow the exemplarist theory, stressing the importance of human response to the Atonement. However, they do not use the satisfaction theory to explain God's motivation for the Atonement. Although the lyrics stress Christ's manhood, two key features of Anselm's view are absent – the sense of division in the Godhead, and the idea that Christ had to satisfy God's justice before his mercy could operate. These lyrics are love poems addressed to Christ, and they focus on his love and mercy; God's justice is barely, if ever, mentioned.

There is little, if any, evidence in the lyrics of Anselm's idea that God's justice must be satisfied before his mercy can take effect. Nor is there any sense of

---

[46] Gray, p.140.

[47] Siegfried Wenzel, *Preachers, Poets, and the Early English Lyric* (Princeton, 1986), p.54; Woolf, p.6.

[48] For example, Brown, XIV.127; XV.96, 107.

division within the Godhead. Rather, these poems present the Atonement as simply the work of God's mercy and love:

> Love me brouthte,
> & love me wrothte,
> Man, to be thi fere.
> Love me fedde,
> & love me ledde,
> & love me lettet here.
>
> Love me slou,
> & love me drou,
> & love me leyde on bere.
> Love is my pes,
> For love i ches,
> Man to byghen dere.
>
> Brown, XIV.66.1-12

Another poem uses two refrains to alternate Man's cries for mercy with God's refrain that 'I lost my myght and toke mercy' and his promise to the penitent:

> Yyt leve thi synnus, & turne to me,
> & for thi gylte be thu sory,
> And now as welcum schalte thu be
> As he that nedud nevur any mercy.
>
> Brown, XV.107.93-6

Poems like this do not overstress the sinfulness of Mankind, making it a barrier to Atonement: rather they present the Atonement as a matter of course. One simply declares that when God *liked* 'he made purviance,/Mankynd for to bryng unto salvacioun'.[49] In another, Christ states that 'To save mane yt was devyned/ That I shulde dye upone a tre', without any comment on how this was 'divined'.[50] A third says that *God* (not the Son) was 'agreeable' to save Man simply because Man could not save himself:

> Whether these shulde be savyd, it was examyned,
> Man or angell; then gode was greabyll
> To answer for man (for man was not abyll)
> And seid, 'man hade mocyon & angell hade none;
> Wherefore god and man shulde be sett at one.'
>
> Brown, XV.118.12-16

The lyrics convey a sense that the Atonement took place without delay. One stresses that Christ, with humility and 'paternal' pity, acted 'anon' and 'soon':

---

[49] Brown, XV.14.32-3.
[50] Brown, XV.105.61-2.

> Cryst thene, beholdynge thy grete and grevous fall,
> Perseyvynge the spoyled off thy gyftis naturall,
> Was Anone meked with pyte paternall,
> The to make fre that by synne was thrall...
>
> The to redeme He founde sone remedye,
> Usinge humylite to thi pride clene contrarye...
>
> Brown, XV.106. 13-20

Another stresses the speed of his action:

> And, of grett love a-noone, I dyd devise
> The to delyver out of this wrechidnese.
> And by and by, with-out long procese,
> I lefte my trone and regall mageste
> And hither I came, a maydyns childe to be...
>
> Brown, XV.109.24-8

Here there is no division in the Godhead, no debate, no mention of justice or satisfaction, no stress even on Man's sinfulness.

Nor do the lyrics insist only on Christ's manhood. Woolf argues that the lyrics avoid the intellectual and paradoxical language that would 'compel the reader to... understand imaginatively, that the man who is suffering is God'. She claims that in most lyrics 'a reader who did not know of the divinity of Christ would not learn of it from them'.[51] To the contrary, the lyrics can and do express both the humanity and the divinity of Christ.[52] As one lyric puts it:

> A wonder it es to se, wha sa understude,
> How God of mageste was dyand on te rude.[53]

Likewise, William Dunbar's 'Of the Passion of Christ' recalls the Passion of 'the michtie king of glorie'.[54] In another lyric, using the lament 'My people what have I done to thee', Christ alternates images of his divine power with images of the human suffering inflicted by his creatures. He describes how he led his people from Egypt, parted the Red Sea, fed and watered them in the desert, and defeated their enemies, while they have buffeted and scourged him, crowned him with thorns, and crucified him.[55] Many lyrics describe Christ fighting and defeating the Devil in order to ransom humanity from his power, a feature of the heroic theory.[56]

---

[51] Woolf, *Religious Lyrics*, pp.9-10; 'The Theme of Christ the Lover-Knight in Medieval English Literature', *RES*, ns. 13, No. 49 (1962), pp.1-16 (p.1). See also Southern, p.225. Peter Moore notes that art tends 'to play down Christ's real divinity': 'Cross and Crucifixion in Christian Iconography', *Religion*, IV (Autumn 1974), 104-13 (p.112).

[52] Ross also notes this in the drama, pp.77-81.

[53] Hope Emily Allen, *English Writings of Richard Rolle* (Oxford, 1931), p.68, lines 235-6.

[54] *The Poems of William Dunbar*, ed. W. Mackay Mackenzie (London, 1970) no. 80.

[55] Brown, XIV.15.

[56] Brown, XIV.13, 20, 21, 22, 24, 48, 59, 63, 66; XV. 95, 97; Davies, 150.

The lyrics can suggest simultaneously Christ's suffering and his triumph:

Luveli ter of loveli eyghe, whi dostu me so wo?
Sorful ter of sorful eyghe, thu brekst myn herte a-to.

Thu sikest sore,
Thy sorwe is more
Than mannis muth may telle;
Thus singest of sorwe
Manken to borwe
Out of the pit of helle.   Luveli etc.

I prud & kene,
Thu meke an clene,
With-outen wo or wile.
Thu art ded for me,
& I live thoru thee,
So blissed be that wile....   Luveli etc.

Thin herte is rent,
Thy bodi is bent
Up-on the rode tree.
The weder is went,
The devel is schent,
Christ, thoru the might of the.   Luveli etc.
                                                            Brown, XIV.69

This poem juxtaposes Christ's tears and sighs with the heroic image of his 'borrowing' or ransoming mankind from hell. Woolf argues that medieval literature stresses Christ's suffering at the expense of his triumph,[57] but although here Christ is weak in relation to Man, he remains powerful in relation to the Devil. Indeed it is by his weakness that he triumphs: while Christ's death conquers the Devil and gives life to the Meditator, his tear 'woes' the Meditator and breaks his heart, ensuring his response. The final stanza neatly balances Christ's suffering manhood with his triumphant divinity.

These lyrics stress Christ's willing mercy, balance his humanity with his divinity, and refer to his victory over the Devil. In accounting for God's motivation for Atonement, they follow the heroic theory rather than the satisfaction theory.

4. The Crucifixion lyrics and the anguish of sin

Unlike Anselm's *Cur Deus Homo*, which stressed human sinfulness as a barrier *before* the Atonement, the lyrics stress sinfulness as a barrier *after* the Atonement – the possible failure to respond to Christ's love and thus to benefit, as an individual, from Christ's Redemption. According to Rachel Fulton, Anselm's meditative

---

[57] 'Doctrinal Influences', p.143.

writing stresses 'the infinite weight of even the tiniest sin', and suggests that since Christ's death is a debt that cannot be repaid, the only necessary response is love and praise.[58] However, some lyrics in fact suggest that more is needed. Perhaps because of their use in preaching, they require that the sinner should perform 'works' in order to merit redemption.[59]

In one poem, Christ goes on to suggest that if the Meditator responds with love he can not only receive mercy, but can actually *earn* a heavenly reward:

> Off tendure love, all this I dyd endure;
> Love dyde me lede, love dyde me thus constrayne;
> And for my dede & grevouse adventure,
> More aske I nott but love for love a-gayne.
> Brother, be kynde, & for a good certayne,
> By-side al this, rewardede shalt thou be
> In the blysse of hevyne, where ther ys no poverte.
>
> Brown, XV.109, 190-6

The lyrics suggest that human virtue is possible with God's help. Thus two short poems to the Trinity appeal for help to serve God 'with all my might' and 'with such werkes my lif to lede' that the Meditator may face Doomsday fearlessly.[60] Another says that because God wills 'every mannes savacioun' he will assist souls to earn salvation by 'reason' as well as mercy:

> Then wilt thu, goodly, graunt us grace
> So to do her to yeve the enchesoun
> For to save us by mercy and resoun.
>
> Brown, XV.57.26-28

Another lyric declares:

> That ever was thralle, now is he free;
> That ever was smalle, now grete is she;
> Now shall God deme both thee and me
> Unto his blisse, if we do well.
>
> Davies, 100.18-21

Douglas Gray remarks that in this poem, the Incarnation is seen 'almost as much as the triumph of man as the triumph of Christ... There is nothing here of that denigration of man which is sometimes supposed to be characteristic of medieval religious poetry.'[61] Thus the lyrics stress that Redemption demonstrates God's love for Man, that it has already occurred, and that each individual has the power to partake in it, if only he or she will respond to Christ's love.

---

[58] Fulton, p.176.

[59] Bennett notes that devotional writers like Richard Rolle and Walter Hilton urge Christians to put devotion into action by helping the poor (pp.59-61).

[60] Brown, XV.49 and 50; see also Brown, XV.52.49.

[61] Gray, p.97.

With their simple emotional appeal and sustained focus on two main ideas – Christ's suffering and the speaker's response – the lyrics do not confront most of Ricoeur's anguishes. Although many other lyrics confront the anguish of death,[62] the Crucifixion lyrics do not: the death they contemplate is Christ's, not the Meditator's. Nor can they confront the anguish of psychic disintegration: they are too certain of what they believe and how they should respond. As Everyman, the Meditator can feel a simple sorrow, but not the mental wrestling that usually marks this anguish: there is no sense here of an individual searching for the truth. With their anonymity and lack of contemporary detail, the lyrics cannot confront the anguish of history. They concentrate almost entirely on the anguish of sin.

Even this anguish is treated in a limited way: the poets do not seem at all concerned with the effect sin has on fellow creatures, that is, with sin's temporal aspect. Rather they represent the Redemption in its eternal aspect. The Meditator is 'present' at Christ's redeeming death, and laments his own sinfulness, not because it may lead to damnation, nor because it harms others, but because it has crucified Christ and demonstrates a rejection of his love.

These poems do not display the anguish of doubt. They emphasize God's love and availability, and the possibility of his wickedness or absence is not an issue. Even when, towards the end of the period, a poem asks whether God could have created Man only to damn him, it answers immediately and with confidence:

> Whi woldest thu, lord, mankynd make
> The worthiest Creature of all this werkes?
> Nought to dampn hym ne to forsake,
> But for tu lovist hym, as witness clerkis...
>
> Then, good lord, wilt thu Constren
> My wykked wil fro wrong governance.
> I am bridelid, thu holdist the reyne –
> Then rule me, lord, at thi ordenance...
>
> For thu wilt every mannes savacioun;
> For no thing in this worldis space
> Is half so dere in reputacioun
> As mannes soule, before thi face.
>
> Brown, XV.57.8-11, 15-18, 22-25

The lyrics are certain of God's goodness, mercy and love. Their only doubt concerns human response. As I have argued, Christ appears to feel more anguish over this doubt than the Meditator does. Ultimately the Meditator is confident, both in Christ's mercy and love and in his own urge to meditate: while his poem lasts, he is in connection with Christ.

The Crucifixion lyrics represent Redemption as a present reality, valid for the meditating Everyman who represents humanity. As love lyrics addressed to

---

[62] For example, Brown, XIII. 10, 11, 12, 13, 14, 15(X), 16(M), 17(M), 19, 20; XIV. 53, 81, 97, 106, 135; XV.149-64.

Christ, they seem more certain of Redemption than do any other poems discussed in this book. [63] Their very certainty, however, limits their representation of encounter, for several reasons. First, the poems meditate on a Christ who is already present, rather than narrating the soul's search for a distant God. There is thus little story in these poems,[64] no sudden, unpredictable inbreaking of God or Christ, such as is found in *Piers Plowman* or the Book of Job. In order for a full sense of *encounter* to be conveyed, God must be absent initially, and the persona's meeting with him must have elements of conflict as well as love.

Secondly, a true sense of encounter can only occur between two individuals: God speaks to Job alone, and Job responds. I cannot think of any poem that depicts encounter as occurring between God and a group of people. But in the lyrics, the sense of individuality is muted: there is no sense of the Meditator's personality, no sense of his individual sins, doubts or struggles. These lyrics do not confront the individual anguish of psychic disintegration or the anguish of a particular historical period, but present traditional images for Everyman to contemplate. However, Everyman cannot encounter God in the way that an individual might, because he has no real self to surrender to God.

Thirdly, the lyrics' limited view of anguish and their focus on Christ's suffering love limits their view of God. His powerful, awesome, or frightening aspects are left out, or directed towards Satan rather than Man. The poems suggest a trusting intimacy, a certainty of Redemption, rather than the disconcerting, unpredictable and challenging irruptions that mark encounter.

This confident but limited view of God is possible because the lyrics are short meditative pieces, written largely in the present tense. Rather than attempting to construct a temporal narrative, they seek to convey eternal truths. As a group, they do not suggest any division in the Godhead, any sense that Christ's death placates the Father. There is, however, one curious poem in which Christ himself implores his Father to notice his sufferings, and gaze on his white breast, his long, stiff arms and his darkened eyes:[65]

> Thou that madist alle thinc,
> mi suete fadir, hevene kinc,
> Bi-sue to me thad am thi sone,
> Thad for monkine habe fles ynomin.

> Mi wite breste, suene & brit,
> Blodi is min side rist
> & mi licam on rode i-stist.

---

[63] Fulton (throughout) and Ross (pp.17-22) argue that the sense of Christ's presence is related to the doctrine of the real presence of Christ's historical, human body in the Eucharist.

[64] In some lyrics, the narrative structure is so weak that they could be expanded indefinitely; see Gray, pp.138-40.

[65] Woolf notes that this is the only extant adaptation of the popular Latin texts *Respice in faciem Christi tui*, and *Candet nudatum pectus* to do this: *The English Religious Lyric*, pp.28-39.

Figure. 2.2. Lamentation, *Grandes Heures de Rohan*, Bibliothèque nationale de France, Latin 9471, Folio 135.

Mine lonke armes, stive & sterke,
Min heyin arrin dim & derke,
Min theyis honket so marbre-ston in werke;

Tho flod of min rede blod
Al over-weint min thurled fod.
Fadir, thau monkine ab idon folie,
Mid mine wondis for them mercy ic the crie.

Brown, XIII.33

In the last two lines Christ appeals to the Father for mercy that might otherwise be unavailable, suggesting that the writer was thinking of the satisfaction theory. This is the only lyric I have found that seems to have any connection with the satisfaction theory, and that suggests any kind of division in the Godhead.

However, this sense of division does appear in an unusual *Lamentation* by the Master of the Hours of Roan (Fig.2.2). God the Father looks down from heaven at Christ's dead body lying at the foot of the Cross. The Father's divinity is stressed by the gold orb in his left hand, by the gold trim of his garment, and by the host of angels surrounding him. Christ's humanity is stressed by the rigidity of his body, by his wounds, his complete nakedness, and the earth on which he lies. But the most unusual thing is the relationship between the Father and St John. John is not looking at Christ, nor at the fainting Virgin in his arms; instead, his head turns upwards over his shoulder, as if challenging the Father. The Father does not meet his gaze, but looks sorrowfully down at his Son, right hand touching his head in dismay. Despite his symbols of power, he appears weak.

In the later Middle Ages this sense of division and this suggestion of weakness in the Father appear in narrative representations of the conflict between divine justice and mercy. This narrative approach to the theme of justice and mercy opens up possibilities for the anguish of doubt.

5. Justice versus mercy: dramatic narratives and the anguish of doubt

A common medieval motif is the Parliament of Heaven in which the Four Daughters of God – Truth, Mercy, Justice, and Peace (Psalm 85:10-11) – debate whether God's justice or mercy is paramount.[66] For reasons of space, three examples will have to suffice. In one the narrative avoids creating a sense of division in the Godhead; in the other two it does not.[67]

In 'The Parliament of Heaven' in the *N-Town Play*,[68] Contemplacio pleads for Man's Redemption. The Father then announces the time of reconciliation, and each of the Daughters simply states her case. There is a short debate between

---

[66] See Hope Traver, *The Four Daughters of God* (Bryn Mawr, 1907); Ross, pp.15-17.
[67] Langland's treatment of the theme in *Piers Plowman* will be discussed in Chapter 3, Milton's in Chapter 5.
[68] *The N-town Play*, ed. Stephen Spector (Oxford, New York, 1991).

Truth, Mercy, and Justice, but when Peace reminds them that 'It is not onest in vertuys to ben dyscencion' (l.114), and suggests that 'oure lorde' in his wisdom should resolve the issue, the Debate instantly ceases. The Son solves the problem, eagerly offering to become man in order to save Mankind, and urging Gabriel to hurry:

> Hie thee, be there apace
> Else we shall be there thee before,
> I have so great haste to be man there...

ll.199-201

This approach avoids depicting either an angry God who demands satisfaction, or a weak and indecisive God. There is no suggestion of debate between the Father and Son.

The *Gesta Romanorum*, however, sets the Debate at the court of an Emperor,[69] later identified as 'the fadir of hevin' (p.135). The Emperor has cast an unfaithful servant into prison to be tormented and slain. When Mercy discovers this,

> ...she rente of the clothinges of hir body, and of hir hede, and pullid of hir heer, and yellid and cride; and ranne with alle hir myght to hir fadir, the Emperour, and knelid to him, and seide, 'Alas! my dere fadir, am I not thi dowter, and art thow not mercyfulle? Have mercy of suche a sarvaunt; for yf thow have no mercy of him, thou art not mercyfulle, and yf thow be not mercyfulle, withe oute dowte thow shalt not have me thy dowter.' (p.133)

After this somewhat threatening beginning to the Debate, Sothfastness (Truth) and Rightwiseness (Justice) add counter claims and threats until Peace forsakes the Emperor:

> And when the Emperoure hard telle how that she was gon ther-fore out of his londe, and saw swich a distance amonge the systeres, he wist not what was beste to be done; for yf he turne to Mercye, he shulde offende Truth and Rightwysnesse, and yf he folow the wille of Truth and of Ryghtwisness, he shulde not have Mercy and Pes to his dowteres. He clepid to him his wise sone, and upon this matter askid his counscill. (p.134)

Thus the Father is ineffectual, threatened by his daughters, and uncertain how to act. The Son, however, is confident and resourceful: he offers to solve the problem, sets out with Mercy, takes pity on the prisoner, and releases him. The story does not explain how this satisfies the claims of Truth and Rightwiseness, but all ends well.

An extreme form of the Debate is found in the *Procès de Justice et de Miséricorde* by Arnoul Gréban.[70] Here God pleads with Justice, imploring her to

---

[69] S.J.H. Herrtage, *The Early English Versions of the Gesta Romanorum*, EETS e.s. 33 (London, repr. 1962), pp.132-5.
[70] *Le Mystére de la passion*, ed. Gaston Paris and Gaston Raynaud (Geneva, 1970).

set a lower price than the death of his Son (ll.3250-6). She insists that she will never be content until Christ suffers all the pain prophesied by Scripture (ll.3257-66). During the Agony in the Garden, she concedes that a drop of Christ's blood would suffice for Atonement, but she insists that he must render full payment, demonstrating his love for humanity by suffering crucifixion (which she describes with almost ghoulish glee), and God consents (ll.18842-62). Gréban presumably intends to show how much the Incarnation cost God, and thus to emphasize his love for man. However the effect of allowing lesser characters to dictate to God on stage is extremely unfortunate: God appears weak and vacillating. Rather than being eternal, he becomes subject to time.[71]

The tendency to subject God to time seems to be a tendency in narrative texts. The English medieval mystery cycles narrate the whole of salvation history, from the Creation to the Day of Judgement. Thus they place the Redemption within time, rather than treating its eternal aspects as the lyrics do. This leads to some interesting developments in their treatment of anguish and encounter with God.

The earlier parts of these plays continue to stress features of the heroic theory such as God's eternal mercy and Christ's victory over Satan. In the Towneley 'Annunciation', God announces the time of mercy; because Adam was deceived by the Devil and has 'boght his syn full sore' for five thousand years in hell', God can free him:

> All wyth reson and with right,
> Both thrugh mercy and thrugh myght...
> My son shall in a madyn light,
> Agans the feynd of hell to fight.[72]

Similarly the York 'Annunciation' describes how God sent his Son in order to deceive the fiend.[73] In the Towneley 'Crucifixion', Christ laments at length the unkindness of his people whose sins have brought him to such pain, and begs his Father to forgive them (ll.233-96). However, he does not mention any need for God's justice to be placated; rather, he says that the Father wishes his Son to die to free those who are in the Devil's power (ll.509-13). In stressing God's mercy and Christ's victory over the Devil, the cycles take a heroic view of the Redemption. The heroic view is also apparent in their accounts of Christ's Harrowing of Hell.[74]

As Ellen M. Ross has observed, the plays also follow the exemplarist theory of Redemption, stressing the importance of the good works that show a human response to Christ's love.[75] This is especially so in the Doomsday plays which draw on Christ's account of Doomsday in Matt. 25: Christ's judgement is based on the souls' performance or non-performance of the works of mercy. Robert Potter notes that Doomsday is:

[71] Mazouer, p.60.

[72] *The Towneley Plays*, ed. Martin Stevens and A.C. Cawley (New York, 1994), ll. 19-20, 35-6.

[73] *The York Plays*, ed. Richard Beadle (London, 1982), ll.19-30.

[74] Marx, pp.114-25.

[75] See also Ross, pp.85-8.

...not so much a 'Day of Wrath' as a day of equal justice before the heavenly law – a time at the end of time when earthly privilege will be laid aside and due reward given for actions performed... actions... turn out to be the ultimate evidence, the final grounds for divine justice.[76]

Potter, however, does not explore the full implications of the idea that justice triumphs at the end of time.

The Doomsday plays depict the ending of the time of mercy and Christ's final insistence on justice. Thus they end by focusing, not on the eternal truth of the Redemption, but on the question of whether individual souls can make this Redemption valid for themselves, achieving salvation through the works of mercy that mirror Christ's mercy and must be practised in this life rather than the next.[77] In the York 'Judgement', God catalogues his mercies and Man's ingratitude, concluding:

> Therefore now is it time to me
> To make ending of man's folly.
>
> I have tholed mankind many a year
> In lust and liking for to lend;
> And uneaths find I far or near
> A man that will his miss amend.
> On earth I see but sins sere;
> Therefor my angels will I send
> To blow their bemes, that all may hear
>   The time is come I will make end.

                                                                    ll.55-64

This temporal narrative of salvation history, as opposed to the lyrics' meditation on the eternal truth of Redemption, demands a more complex treatment of God: God's anger as well as his love must be dealt with.

As Potter suggests, the concept of due reward for good works has its attractive side, representing an end of the injustices of earthly privilege. However this view is less attractive in that it also represents the termination of divine mercy. Two of the plays go beyond Matt. 25 and allow the damned to appeal for mercy, an appeal that Christ disconcertingly rejects.[78]

In the *N-Town* 'Doomsday', the damned repeatedly appeal for mercy:

> A mercy lorde for oure mysdede
> And lett thi mercy sprynge and sprede
> But alas we byden in drede
> It is to late to aske mercye...

---

[76] 'Divine and Human Justice', in *Aspects of Early English Drama*, ed. Paula Neuss (Cambridge, 1983), pp.139-40.

[77] Ross, p.94.

[78] In *The English Mystery Plays* (London, 1972), p.296, Woolf finds Christ's severity in the Continental plays 'disconcerting'; she does not remark on his severity in the English cycles.

> Ha ha mercy mercy we crye and crave
> A mercy lorde for oure mysdede
> A mercy mercy we rubbe we rave
> A helpe us good lord in this nede.
>
> 11.36-9, 66-9

Christ rejects them on the grounds that they have not followed his example of mercy:

> *Deus*: How wolde ye wrecchis any mercy have
> Why aske ye mercy now in this nede
> What have ye wrought your sowle to save
> To whom have ye done any merciful dede
>   Mercy for to wynne.
>
> 11.70-74

The last words of the play as it now stands (the end is missing) are a piteous cry from the damned:

> A mercy lord, mekyl of myght
> We aske thi mercy and not thi right
> Not after oure dede so us quyth
>   We have synnyd we be to blame.
>
> 11.127-30

In the Chester 'Judgement', Christ insists that his judgement is righteous (11.366, 434-6).[79] The demons appeal to him to cease acting through mercy and to act through justice (11.509-72); one declares that, unless Christ hands over the sinners to the devils, 'thou art as false as wee' (1.571). At the end of the demons' speeches, Christ says:

> Loe, you men that wycked have benne,
> What Sathan sayth you heren and seene.
> Rightuouse doome may you not fleene,
> For grace ys put awaye.
> When tyme of grace was endurynge,
> To seeke yt you had no lykinge.
> Therefore must I, for anythinge,
> Doe rightuousenes todaye.
>
> And though my sweete mother deare
> And all the sayntes that ever were
> Prayed for you right nowe here,
> All yt were to late.
> Noe grace may growe through theire prayere.
> Then rightuousenes had no powere.

---

[79] R.M. Lumiansky, and David Mills, *The Chester Mystery Cycle*, EETS (London, New York, 1974).

Therefore, goe to the fyre in feere.
There gaynes noe other grace.

ll.605-20

The play ends with the Evangelists' affirmations of these words.

Such depictions of the Judgement were no doubt intended to involve the audience, to warn them of the dangers of continuing in sin, and to ensure their conversion and ultimate salvation.[80] V.A. Kolve says of the ending of the Chester 'Judgement' that:

> ...in terms of drama time the Evangelists are justifying Christ's judgement by saying that they gave warning to all through their teachings and writings; but in terms of audience time they are issuing a call to alertness and repentance. The spectators still live in the time of mercy; grace is not yet put away, and they may avail themselves of it if they will.[81]

Kolve does not, however, comment on the desperate pleas of the damned.[82]

The Chester passage is disconcerting for several reasons. First, it concedes a certain power and right to the devils. Secondly, it suggests that Christ himself lacks freedom, and 'must' do justice. Thirdly, it suggests that mercy is a temporal attribute of God, while justice is the eternal one. In taking a narrative approach to Redemption, the plays begin to convey the anguish of history – anguish at the thought that Christ's eternal Redemption may not result, historically, in the Redemption of all individuals.

The plays and the Debates of the Four Daughters of God also make possible the beginnings of the anguish of doubt. The conflict between divine justice and mercy suggests the possibility of division within the Godhead. Ross argues that the ending of the plays 'does not undercut or minimize the privileged place of divine love'.[83] However, in placing the termination of God's mercy at the end of the drama, and suggesting that justice is the final truth about God, the plays do in fact question the primacy of God's love. In the Doomsday plays, Christ is no longer the eternally loving, merciful, and suffering Saviour. Instead, he becomes the awesome Judge, announcing that mercy is finite, that justice is God's final attribute, and that sinners will be punished eternally at the end of time. This opens up the awesome possibility that, from the perspective of some individuals, God may appear malign.

This more complex, narrative and historical approach to Redemption makes possible a fuller sense of encounter with the awesome as well as the loving aspects of God. However, like the lyrics, the plays do not confront the full range of human anguish. Lacking any sense of a particular individual who is narrating them, they do not confront the anguish of psychic disintegration, of the individual's

---

[80] Christine Richardson and Jackie Johnstone, *Medieval Drama* (Houndmills and London, 1991), pp.83-85.
[81] V.A. Kolve, *The Play Called Corpus Christi* (Stanford, 1966), p.103.
[82] Nor do Richardson and Johnstone, who take a view similar to Kolve's (p.88).
[83] Ross, p.93.

struggle to find God. Written to convey the eternal truth of the Redemption, they do not engage with the historical anguishes of the particular times in which they were written.

Like the lyrics, the cycles, taken as a whole, stress God's mercy, Christ's victory over the Devil, and the importance of human response. They are thus both heroic and exemplarist in approach. Neither the plays nor the lyrics embrace the satisfaction theory in the way that critics have assumed. Anselm saw *divine justice* as a force that had to be placated *before* divine mercy could operate. The plays, however, do not stress the need for divine justice to be placated: even in the N-Town cycle, the issue is swiftly dealt with by the willingness of the Trinity to restore Man. Rather, they stress the need for *human justice* to be practised *after* Christ's Atonement: the just response to Christ's merciful love is to avoid sin and perform the works of mercy. If this is not done, the dramatists fear that God too will reject mercy and turn to justice. As with the lyrics, the cycles locate the gap between God and Man in the human failure to respond, not in the absence or unavailability of God.

A similar stress on the heroic-exemplarist theory of Redemption, a similar stress on good works, and a similar fear that failure to live well will result in damnation, are central to William Langland's poem, *Piers Plowman*. However, Langland goes beyond the plays and lyrics in using an individual persona who can confront all the anguishes. His poem deals not only with salvation history, but also with the social and religious dilemmas of fourteenth-century England.

Chapter 3

Finding the Balance in the C-revision of *Piers Plowman*: Faith-Grace-Mercy versus Hope-Works-Justice

Ac grace ne groweth nat til gode-wil gyve reyne
And woky thorw gode werkes wikkede hertes.
Ac ar such a wil wexe, worcheth God sulve
And sent forth the Seynt Espirit to do love sprynge:
     Spiritus ubi vult spirat.
So grace withouten grace of God, and also gode werkes
May nat be, be thou syker, though we bidde evere.

C.XIV.23-9

1. The C-Text: Langland's final narrative of anguish and encounter

The medieval Crucifixion lyrics are simple poems in which the message is more important than the artistry or individuality of the author. William Langland's poem, *Piers Plowman*, is different in many respects. First, its protagonist, Will, is a powerfully individual figure – a recalcitrant, backsliding, argumentative, but above all, a thinking and questioning man. He lacks self-knowledge, but is ardently committed to his struggle to understand both personal and social salvation. Will bears at least some resemblance to the poem's author,[1] and the urgency of his quest suggests a similar urgency in Langland's own mind. Whereas the Meditator in the lyrics spoke predominantly in the indicative, Will speaks habitually in the interrogative: the whole poem is driven by a series of cranky, satirical, anxious, or

---

[1] Simpson, *Piers Plowman*, pp.1-5. Kathryn Kerby-Fulton points out that the medieval persona and author cannot be clearly distinguished from each other: 'Langland and the Bibliographic Ego', in Steven Justice and Kerby-Fulton, *Written Work: Langland, Labor, and Authorship* (Philadelphia, 1997), p.67. Anne Middleton observes that Langland is unusual in presenting himself as a participant in the poem rather than as its author: 'The Audience and Public of Piers Plowman', in Middle English Alliterative Poetry and its Literary Background, ed. David Lawton (Cambridge, 1982), pp.101-23 (pp.111-13). Some critics, however, warn against reading Will as 'a single personality': Malcolm Godden, *The Making of Piers Plowman* (London and New York, 1990), p.23; David Lawton, 'The Subject of Piers Plowman', *YLS*, 1 (1987), 1-30; John Burrow, *Langland's Fictions* (Oxford, 1993), pp.90-1.

downright anguished questions that he directs to a variety of guides, [2] and, ultimately, to God.

Secondly, *Piers Plowman* is a long narrative rather than a lyric poem. It is thus concerned more with the progress of human time than it is with the state of eternity. The main thread of the narrative traces Will's arduous and circuitous journey towards encounter and finally the loss of that encounter. However, in narrating that journey, Langland does incorporate lyrical moments that convey a sense of present encounter: while he depicts God as entering time in the Incarnation, he does not depict him as being subject to time.

Thirdly, as I suggested in the previous chapter, this narrative mode also opens up the need to confront the awesome, frightening aspects of God, including his justice and the possibility of damnation. Langland's extensive narrative exploration allows him to interrogate his faith in a way that is not possible in the simpler lyric mode. Whereas the Crucifixion lyrics almost exclusively depict encounter with the crucified, merciful Christ, Langland depicts encounter with God as Truth, as Kynde the Creator, as Christ the Redeemer and Judge, and as Grace or the Holy Spirit.

Fourthly, Langland counterbalances this confrontation with God's awesome aspects with the idea, particularly marked in the C-Text, that it is not only Christ, but God who suffers for the sake of his creation. This provides a further dimension to anguish in the poem – Langland's anguish that God's generous, loving, and creative suffering is not met with a loving human response in the historical world.

Finally, Langland's poem is more concerned with the anguish of history – with the struggle to find meaning in the history of the fourteenth century – than any other poem in this book. Beyond the likelihood that he was an educated man with a circle of readers and probably a patron,[3] almost nothing is known of Langland's personal history, but his England was a time of religious and social ferment. It was the period of the Great Schism, marked by tension between the friars and the secular clergy, between the church hierarchy and would-be reformers. John Wyclif rejected the doctrine of transubstantiation and attacked the abuses of the institutional church, denying the ability of corrupt clergy to administer the sacraments.[4] The role of the very church itself had become controversial.[5] On the social front, work was an urgent problem: the Black Death had led to labour

---

[2] A.V.C. Schmidt, 'Langland and the Mystical Tradition', in *The Medieval Mystical Tradition in England: Papers Read at the Exeter Symposium, July 1980*, ed. Marion Glasscoe (University of Exeter, 1980), pp.17-38 (p.30).

[3] Kerby-Fulton, 'Langland and the Bibliographic Ego', pp.97-122.

[4] Anne Hudson suggests that Langland influenced Wycliffite texts rather than the other way around and as a result *Piers Plowman* came to be seen as more and more radical: *The Premature Reformation* (Oxford, 1988), pp.398-408.

[5] David Aers, *Chaucer, Langland and the Creative Imagination* (London, 1980), p.38. See also R.B. Dobson, *The Peasant's Revolt of 1381* (London and Basingstoke, 1983), pp.59-71; 83-144. Anna P. Baldwin, 'The Historical Context', in *A Companion to Piers Plowman*, ed. John A. Alford (Berkeley, Los Angeles and London, 1988), pp.67-86; Aers, pp.9-10; Wendy Scase, *Piers Plowman and the New Anti-clericalism* (Cambridge, 1989) throughout.

shortages and a new class of urban poor; labourers were agitating for higher wages, culminating in the Peasant's Revolt of 1381; and mendicant friars were espousing voluntary poverty as a virtue.[6] In response, some thinkers redefined work, which had been seen as a curse on fallen humanity, as a virtue and a duty.[7]

Work is a key issue, if not *the* key issue in the C-revision and my main concern is to explore the anguish with which C discusses the spiritual and moral significance of work. This is the anguish of history, for, as Ricoeur says,

> To create leisure is very often to hand man over to... a sort of civilized idleness, and in the end, to his own vacuity, his lack of purpose... Man cannot convert the anguish of Narcissus if he does not associate himself to a work at once communal and personal, universal and subjective... We may call the new level of anguish which we have attained *historical*, for man appears herein as the protagonist – the craftsman and the sufferer – of the history of mankind on its collective level.[8]

Langland's heartfelt concern at the failure of individuals to join in this essential and healing work is one of the structural principles of the C-Text.

Langland seems to have spent his whole poetic life struggling to express his agonized concern for the social and moral evils that threatened to destroy his society, evils that he saw as threatening damnation for the individuals responsible. He made four attempts to complete *Piers Plowman*,[9] starting with the brief Z-Text of c.1362,[10] abandoning the A-Text (1367-70) midway, completing the narrative in the B-Text (1377-9), and refining and expanding it in the C-Text (1385-6).[11]

For many years, critics focused on the B-Text. C had an unfortunate reputation, even amongst its adherents,[12] for a loss of poetic power. But although C removes some famous passages such as Piers's tearing of the Pardon and Hawkin's Confession, it adds equally fine passages such as the Dreamer's Confession and the

---

[6] Godden, pp.102, 180-1.

[7] Kathleen Hewett-Smith, 'Allegory on the Half-Acre: The Demands of History', *YLS*, 10 (1996), 1-22 (p.6); Derek Pearsall, 'Poverty and Poor People in *Piers Plowman*', in Edward Kennedy et al. (eds.) *Medieval English Studies Presented to George Kane* (Woodbridge, U.K., 1988) pp.170-4.

[8] Ricoeur, *History and Truth*, p.293.

[9] Unless otherwise stated, all references are to *Piers Plowman: A Parallel-Text Edition of the A, B, C, and Z Versions*, ed. A.V.C. Scmidt, Vol.1 (London and New York, 1995). I also refer to *Piers Plowman: The C Version*, ed. George Russell and George Kane (London, 1997), and *Piers Plowman by William Langland: An Edition of the C-Text*, ed. Derek Pearsall (London, 1978). I have modernized the orthography throughout.

[10] Godden, pp.3, 171.

[11] Schmidt, *The Vision of Piers Plowman: A Complete Edition of the B-Text* (London, 1978), p.xvi. See also the debate between Jill Mann, John M. Bowers, Charlotte Brewer and Traugott Lawler in *YLS*, 8 (1994), 21-50 and *YLS*, 9 (1995), 65-98. Middleton argues that the C V apologia was the last addition, written after the 1388 Statute of Laborers: 'Acts of Vagrancy', in Justice and Kerby-Fulton, pp.208-317.

[12] E. Talbot Donaldson, *The C-Text and Its Poet* (New Haven, 1949), p.17; G.H. Russell, 'Some Aspects of the Process of Revision in *Piers Plowman*', in *Piers Plowman: Critical Approaches*, ed. S.S. Hussey (London, 1969) pp.27-49 (p.44).

lament for poor cottagers. More recently, various critics have recognized that, taken as a single poem rather than as a series of striking moments, C may in fact be stronger than B: it 'makes better sense';[13] it is more concerned with 'theological accuracy' and avoiding heresy;[14] its thematic development 'strengthens and enriches the dramatic fabric of the poem';[15] in it, 'Langland's spiritual concerns receive their fullest expression'.[16]

Yet the C-text has still received insufficient attention. Apart from Malcolm Godden's brief thematic analysis (which I disagree with in many respects)[17] there has been very little discussion of Langland's overall motivation for the C-revisions and how they affect our understanding of Langland's deepest religious concerns and the structure of the C-Text as a whole. Even the recent collection edited by Steven Justice and Kathryn Kerby-Fulton is mainly concerned with a single passage, the *apologia* (C.V1-108).[18] C is Langland's last word on issues that he explored, with a heartfelt anguish, throughout his poetic life.[19] It is extraordinary that so many of his admirers have continued to privilege his penultimate draft rather than paying Langland the respect of giving their greatest attention to the text as he finally left it.

2. The anguish of death and the poem's central dilemma

The anguish of death runs throughout Langland's poem, from the opening vision of the Tower of Truth and the Dale of Death to the moment when Age and Death attack Will at the close of the poem. However, this anguish is not a merely personal anguish over Will's own mortality. Rather it links with an urgent distress at the sufferings of the poor in this world and an equally passionate fear for the possible fate of sinners after death.

---

[13] Pearsall, *C-Text*, p.11.

[14] Bruce Harbert, 'A Will with a Reason: Theological Development in the C-Revision of *Piers Plowman*', in *Religion in the Poetry and Drama of the Late Middle Ages in England*, ed. by Piero Boitani and Anna Torti (Cambridge, 1990), pp.149-61 (p.150). Kerby-Fulton, 'Langland and the Biblio-graphic Ego', pp.75-6; Simpson, 'The Constraints of Satire', in *Langland, the Mystics and the Medieval English Religious Tradition*, ed. Helen Phillips (Cambridge, 1990), pp.11-30; Hudson, p.408.

[15] John Ruffing, 'The Crucifixion Drink in *Piers Plowman* B.18 and C.20', *YLS* (1991), 99-109 (p.108). See also A.C. Spearing, 'The Development of a Theme in *Piers Plowman*', *RES*, n.s. 11 (1960), 241-53; Lorraine Kochanske Stock, 'Will, Actyf, Pacience, and *Liberum Arbitrium*, Passus V, XV, XVI', *Texas Studies in Literature & Language*, 30 (1988), 461-77; Martyn J. Miller, 'Meed, Mercede, and Mercy: Langland's Grammatical Metaphor', *Medieval Perspectives*, 9 (1994), 73-84.

[16] Kerby-Fulton, *Reformist Apocalypticism and Piers Plowman* (Cambridge, 1990), p.204, n2; however, she concentrates on the single issue of apocalypticism.

[17] Godden, pp.176-201. I will discuss points of disagreement as they occur.

[18] See note 1.

[19] Alan J. Fletcher thinks that the ongoing revision process was part of his poem's ethical essence': see 'The Essential (Ephemeral) William Langland: Textual Revision as Ethical Process in *Piers Plowman*', *YLS*, 15 (2001), 61-84 (p.63.)

From the start of the poem, the C-reviser offers a more focused and bleaker vision than B. He replaces B's romantic details of the stream whose waters lulled the Dreamer to sleep in a wilderness, 'wiste Y nevere where' (B.Pro.1-22), with details more suited to a spiritual autobiography, announcing that this dream concerns truth, treachery, treason, and guile (C.Pro.12).[20] Unlike B, C names the inhabitants of Tower and Dale, adding poignancy to the image of the 'fair feld ful of folk' who, unaware of their tenuous position between Truth and Death, are

> Worchyng and wandryng as the world ascuth.
> Somme potte hem to the plogh, and playde ful selde,
> In settynge and in sowynge swonken ful harde
> And wonne that this wastors with glotony destrueth.
>
> C.Pro.21-4.

Langland makes a crucial, structurally significant contrast between the 'winners' who work and the wandering 'wasters' who prefer idleness and irresponsibility.[21] In the Prologue, the ploughmen are the only workers. The rest of the folk are wanderers: the beggars who cram their bags and bellies; itinerant friars who preach 'for profit of the wombe; gluttonous pardoners who cheat *lewed*[22]men; parsons who abandon their parishes for better livings in London; bishops who fail to 'till' [23] charity and belief in the *lewed* (C.Pro.57-102). A King attempts to establish 'crafts', or occupations, in order to feed the *comune* (C.Pro.139-50),[24] but he is replaced by a vision of legal corruption and inadequate kingship (C.Pro.151-218). The Prologue depicts a world of avarice, idleness, and gluttony, ending with the cries of street sellers offering wine and hot pies (C.Pro.227-31).

In both B and C the poem's action arises from two interrelated questions that Will asks Holy Church in the next passus. Holy Church descends from the Tower of Truth and awakens the Dreamer from his spiritual torpor with the words 'Wille, slepestou?' By using Will's name, as B does not, C underlines the need for the human will to embrace the offer of salvation and articulates the poem's central problem: although God's mercy is always available, and Redemption has already taken place, most people *will* nothing beyond this world and have no care for 'other hevene then here' (C.I.5-9).[25] In response, Will asks his first question, 'what may this be to mene?' (B.I.11; C.I.11). I take 'this' to refer to the graceless state of

---

[20] Kerby-Fulton, 'Langland and the Bibliographic Ego', p.72. See also Godden, p.177; Middleton, 'The Audience and Public', p.116.

[21] Schmidt, 'Langland's Structural Imagery', *Essays in Criticism*, 30 (1986) 311-25 (p.312). Middleton argues that vagrancy was a particular concern of the 1388 Statute of Laborers: 'Acts of Vagrancy', pp.217-46.

[22] Unlearned.

[23] The agricultural imagery is added in C.

[24] *Comune* can mean the common people or the common good of the community.

[25] R.E. Kaske, 'Holy Church's Speech and the Structure of *Piers Plowman*', in *Chaucer and Middle English Studies in Honour of Rossell Hope Robbins*, ed. Beryl Rowland (London, 1974), pp.320-7.

the Field of Folk. Shortly afterwards, Will falls on his knees and asks Holy Church for grace to amend,

> And also kenne me kyndly on Crist to bileve:
> 'Teche me to no tresor, but telle me this ilke –
> How Y may save my soule, that saynt art yholde.'

C.I.78-80

Will's two questions provide the initial impetus for the urgent search that drives the poem's linear narrative – the search for Truth that transmutes first into the search for Dowel, then the search for Charity, and finally the search for Christ.

Yet this linear drive coexists with a circular structure.[26] When Will asks Holy Church who she is, she rebukes him: he ought to know her, for she made him a free man at his baptism, and he has forgotten his promises to believe, obey, and love her (C.I.72-7). The Dreamer is embarking on a search that he has already completed: he has lost the freedom that he once had, and must now regain it. The search requires recovery of *kynde knowyng* – a 'natural' knowledge from experience, knowledge of the heart rather than of the head, a knowledge that must be attained through suffering.[27] Such knowledge remains elusive, forgotten under stress, always to be rediscovered by painful effort, effort which the fallen human will can make only sporadically. As Will discovers, the search for social and individual salvation can never be complete, but must be continually renewed.

There are two threads to Holy Church's instruction of Will. On the one hand she stresses the generous and gratuitous love of God. Truth is 'fader of faith and formor of alle' who 'of his cortesye' has ordained food, clothing and drink to assist humans 'to worschipe hym' (C.I.12-22). She goes on to explain that God's love, as shown in the Incarnation, is the remedy for sin:

> For Treuthe telleth that love ys triacle fo synne,
> And most soverayne salve for soule and for body.
> Love is the plonte of pees, most precious of vertues,
> For hevene holde hit ne myghte, so hevy hit semede,
> Till hit hadde of earth ygotten hitsilve.

C.I.145-9

This is the first of several passages that demonstrate Langland's dynamic concept of a God whose love is immediate and active, without interruption or division: [28]

---

[26] Schmidt, *The B-Text*, pp.xx-xxiv; Bennett, p.85. Robert Adams argues that while individual progress is possible, social achievements circle from promise to decay: 'Langland's Theology', in Alford, *A Companion*, pp.87-114 (p.88).

[27] Mary Clemente Davlin, '*Kynde Knowyng* as a Middle English Equivalent for "Wisdom" in *Piers Plowman* B', *MÆ*, 50 (1981), 5-17 (p.12) and '*Kynde Knowyng* as a Major Theme in *Piers Plowman* B', *RES*, n.s. 22 (1971) 1-19; John Lawlor, *Piers Plowman: An Essay in Criticism* (London, 1962), pp.88, 228-33; Hugh White, *Nature and Salvation in Piers Plowman* (Cambridge, 1988), pp.41-59.

[28] Bennett remarks that the third-person singular pronouns suggest unity of purpose, and that Langland's names for God – Truth, Love, Kynde, and Grace – are qualities that can only

> ... the Fader that formede us alle,
> Lokede on us with love and let his sone deye
> Mekeliche for oure mysdedes, to amende us alle.

C.I.161-3

There is no sense of God's justice having to be placated before his mercy can take effect: Redemption is mentioned *before* sin, as if the Incarnation were the purpose of Creation, not merely a result of the Fall.

On the other hand, Holy Church insists on the need for a virtuous human response that follows God's example of love and goodness in the social world. This is ultimately a spiritual goal: Holy Church warns that failure to use God's material gifts with 'mesure' is spiritually destructive (C.I.12-67); conversely, she stresses that spiritual needs are met through practical, socially based actions, rather than by specifically religious or mystical actions. Truth, she says, is the best treasure:

> For who is trewe of his tonge and of his two handes,
> And doth the werkes therwith and wilneth no man ylle,
> He is a god by the Gospel...

C.I.84-6

Stressing the need for work with the hands (added in C), she insists that salvation is won, not by withdrawal from the world, but by working in it.

Holy Church warns that:

> ... alle that worchen that wikked is, wenden thei sholle,
> Aftur here deth day and dwelle ther Wrong is,
> And alle that han wel ywroughte, wende they sholle,
> Estward til hevene, evere to abyde
> There Treuthe is, the trone that Trinite ynne sitteth.

C.I.129-33

The active verb *wend* suggests that damnation is not so much something that God does to humans as something that humans do to themselves[29] – a feature that recurs throughout the poem. Conversely, humans can achieve salvation through *doing* well.

Holy Church explains that 'Kynde knowing in herte' is demonstrated by God's gift of his Son in the Incarnation and by Christ's mercy towards his executioners. Following the exemplarist theory, she stresses that God's love gives 'ensaumples', requiring a loving response from his creatures (C.I.160-9). Her conclusion is somewhat surprising in its particularity: *therefore*, the rich should show mercy to the poor, for after death they will be weighed with the same

---

exist in action: pp.87-89. See also Traugott Lawler, 'The Gracious Imagining of Redemption in *Piers Plowman* ', *English*, 28 (1979) 203-16 (p.203).

[29] See also Davlin, *The Place of God*, p.28.

measure that they have given (C.I.170-3). She sees giving to the poor as *the* essential virtuous action:

> But yf ye love leeliche and lene the pore,
> Of such good as God you sent goodliche parte,
> Ye na haveth na more meryte in masse ne in oures
> Than Malkyn of her maydenheed wham no man desireth.
> For James the gentele jugeth in his bokes
> That fayth withouten feet is feblore then nauhth.
>
> C.I.176-81

That is, religious observance is worthless without practical good works. Holy Church, the foundational guide of the poem,[30] offers a view of poverty that is diametrically opposed to the later formulations of Recklessness, Patience, and Need. She aligns Christ with the rich rather than with the poor: as Christ behaved to his enemies, so the rich should behave to the poor. Poverty is here the *recipient* rather than the *agent* of virtuous acts (a point to which I shall return).[31] For Holy Church, salvation depends upon works rather than upon faith alone: following Christ truly involves the development of *kyndeness*,[32] construed here as a willingness to give to others.

Holy Church's advice expresses the poem's central dilemma – the struggle to find a balance between faith and works, mercy and justice. On the one hand Christ was merciful even to those who killed him; on the other, justice threatens damnation for the rich who fail to help the poor. It seems that Langland's God can forgive anything except the failure to follow his example of mercy by performing good works for the benefit of fellow Christians.

Several critics have discussed the B-Text's position in the debate between Augustinianism (which believes that grace is paramount) and Pelagianism (which believes that human good works are possible).[33] Conceding that there are some Augustinian passages, John Adams demonstrates that it is nevertheless impossible to explain away the many passages that emphasize 'the primacy of good works and taking the semi-Pelagian view – while God does not *owe* anything to anyone, he has freely and mercifully 'agreed to honor good deeds'.[34]

---

[30] Aers is sceptical of her 'abstractions' and simplifications (*Chaucer, Langland*, pp.6-7), but she is stressing timeless moral precepts rather than providing a blueprint for a particular society.

[31] Anne M. Scott notes that giving to the poor is 'a *sine qua non* for salvation': '"Nevere noon so nedy ne poverer deide": *Piers Plowman* and the Value of Poverty', *YLS*, 15 (2001), 141-53 (p.143).

[32] Aers, 'Christ's Humanity and *Piers Plowman*', *YLS*, 8 (1994), 107-25 (pp.118-19).

[33] Daniel Murtaugh, *Piers Plowman and the Image of God* (Gainesville, 1978), pp.76-84; Adams, 'Piers' Pardon and Langland's Semi-Pelagianism', *Traditio*, 39 (1983), 367-418 (p.389), and 'Mede and Mercede in *Piers Plowman*', in Kennedy et al., pp.217-32; Denise Baker, 'From Ploughing to Penitence', *Speculum*, 55 (1980), 715-25. Simpson suggests a peculiar combination of Wycliffism and the opposing doctrine of semi-Pelagianism: 'The Constraints of Satire', p.18.

[34] John Adams, 'Langland's Theology', pp.96-7

Myra Stokes gives the most extensive account of the tension in B between justice and mercy, arguing that, for Langland, justice is God's predominant attribute, and it is 'unthinkable that a just God could countenance the non-punishment of transgression'.[35] Anna P. Baldwin also argues that the poem 'consistently upholds justice'.[36] James Simpson argues that God 'is represented as essentially a judgemental figure in His aspect of Truthe', although he concedes the paradox that God is also Love and that 'Love's predisposition will be to ignore the demands of justice'.[37]

However, Holy Church's teaching clearly privileges mercy. Her vision of Truth is not 'judgemental', but shows God as acting only in loving ways: providing the necessities of life; generating the love that is shown in the Incarnation; and, in the person of Christ, showing mercy to his executioners. She does not depict God as actively dispensing reward and punishment. It is, as I have already observed, sinners who decide whether they will 'wend' to the Tower of Truth or the Dungeon of Death. She warns the rich that 'the same mesure that ye meteth... ye shal be weye therwith' (C.I.171-3). By using the active voice for human activities, and the agentless passive 'shal be weye' for the consequences, she again suggests that eternal rewards spring from human decisions rather than divine. She does not say that rich men will be 'cheyned in helle', but that the abstract quality 'Chastite withouten charite' will be (C.I.183). This is the stance that Langland takes throughout the poem: his God is primarily a God of mercy. This mercy is always available for the asking, even, as Christ suggests in the Harrowing of Hell, at the moment of final judgement. However, at the same time, Langland fears that sinners may render themselves incapable of asking for, and thus of benefiting from, this mercy.

Critics have paid little attention to the effect of this dilemma on the C-revisions and the structure of Langland's final narrative.[38] In both texts, Will's questions to Holy Church, 'what does this world mean?' and 'how may I save my soul?' are the mainsprings of the poem's action, but C's answers are substantially different from the answers given in B. This, I believe, is because the way that the B-Text ended – in near despair at the failure of humanity to respond properly to the Redemption – drove Langland to revise the whole poem.

Towards the end of B, there are four significant developments in relation to these themes. First, Will asks the Good Samaritan whether, if he had sinned against the Holy Spirit through *unkyndeness* towards his fellow Christians, he could be saved by repenting. *Yes,* says the Samaritan, *if you are able to repent*

---

[35] Myra Stokes, *Justice and Mercy in Piers Plowman: A Reading of the B Text Visio* (London and Canberra, 1984), p.20.

[36] Anna P. Baldwin, 'The Double Duel in *Piers Plowman* B XVIII and C XXI', *MÆ*, 50 (1981), 64-78 (p.64).

[37] James Simpson, *Piers Plowman*, pp.29-30. Simpson tends to overstress the judgemental aspects of God (pp.71, 88, 161-5, 220).

[38] Godden touches on this, but his views are almost diametrically opposed to mine, since he argues that many of the revisions privilege poverty and challenge the idealization of labour (pp.176-201).

(B.XVII.299). He goes on to warn that if people persist in their sins until the time of death, then:

> Drede of desperacion thanne dryueth awey grace,
> That mercy in hir mynde may noght thanne falle;
> Good hope, that helpe sholde, to wanhope turneth –
> Noght of the nounpower of God, that he ne is myghtful
> To amende al that amys is, and his mercy gretter
> Than alle oure wikkede werkes, as Holy Writ telleth –
> Ac er his rightwisnesse to ruthe torne, som restitucion bihoveth:
> His sorwe is satisfaccion for [swich] that may noght paye.
>
> B.XVII. 309-16

That is, God's mercy *is* always available, but it does depend upon the human being willing and able to ask for it. Persistent sin may render the sinner unable to feel and express the sorrow that will win grace.

Secondly, following a brief but powerful vision of the suffering involved in Christ's death, Will sees the Four Daughters of God debating whether Mankind can be saved by Christ. In marked contrast to the earlier speech where Repentance insisted that neither Father nor Son 'no sorwe in deeth feledest' (B.V.478), Peace insists that God became incarnate and 'suffrede to be solde to se the sorwe of deying' (B.XVIII.213).

Thirdly, in the Harrowing of Hell, Christ says that his *kynde* will require that he is 'merciable to man' and promises that 'alle that beth myne hole bretheren in blood and in baptisme' will be spared final damnation (B.XVIII.376-9). He privileges grace over works when he says that 'it lith in my grace/ Wheither thei deye or deye noght for that thei diden ille' (387-8), and he resolves the debate between justice and mercy by declaring:

> Ac my rightwisnesse and right shal rulen al helle,
> And mercy al mankynde bifore me in hevene.
>
> B.XVIII.397-8

This passage hints at the possibility of universal salvation[39] (a message which is strengthened in C).

Fourthly, despite the Dreamer's enthusiastic embracing of the cross, the Christian world is unable to profit from Christ's Redemption. In the next vision, Christ appears as Judge rather than as Redeemer. Conscience warns that Christ will punish those who do not pay Piers's pardon *redde quod debes*:

> And demen hem at domesday, bothe quyke and dede –
> The goode to the Godhede and to grete joye,
> The wikkede to wonye in wo withouten ende.
>
> B.XIX.197-9

---

[39] W.O. Evans, 'Charity in *Piers Plowman*', in Hussey, pp.245-78; Thomas Hill, 'Universal Salvation and its Literary Context in *Piers Plowman* B.18', *YLS*, 5 (1991), 65-76; Davlin, *The Place of God*, p.135.

These lines are the only ones depicting God or Christ as *actively* meting out damnation that Langland allows to stand in his final version as a bitter warning.

Grace attempts to fulfil Christ's work by instituting a just Christian society. He directs Piers and Conscience to summon the *commune*, and gives each man 'a grace' to ward off the sins of Idleness, Envy and Pride by labouring at his 'craft', and thus loving 'as bretheren' (B.XIX.226-56). Christian society fails to perform these good works and to bring the crop of truth into the barn of Unity which is mortared with Christ's mercy (B.XIX.324-31). Instead, it almost immediately disintegrates into sinful anarchy, and the Dreamer becomes as lost as he was at the outset.

The later part of the B-Text thus develops a complex understanding of the interconnectedness of faith and hope, grace and works, justice and mercy: first, Langland's God is a god of mercy, willing to suffer for his creatures and desiring to save all of them if only they will ask for his mercy; secondly, the Christian should respond by doing socially useful good works that will demonstrate a love of fellow Christians and in some sense earn God's grace and mercy; and finally, Langland fears, persistence in sin after all that God has done may destroy the *kynde* relationship, rendering the soul incapable of asking for and receiving God's mercy.

Justice is crucially important in the poem, but Langland is less concerned with divine justice than with the failure of human justice to perform the good works that can reform society. Aers argues that this 'displays a terrifying rejection of the final good' offered by the Good Samaritan and Christ.[40] It, is, I believe, anguish at this 'terrifying rejection' that drove Langland to revise the poem, focusing on the moral and spiritual significance of work. For Langland, the key social problem, the key test of good works, is how to provide the necessities of both physical and spiritual life for all. Working and wasting, begging and patient poverty, the duty of the rich to the poor, and of the clergy to the *lewed*, anger at the covetousness and gluttony which grasp more than a fair share of worldly goods, a deep concern for the plight of the poor – these themes dominate the C-revision of *Piers Plowman* with an anguished intensity. Images of food, clothing, and agriculture have both social and spiritual significance in the poem: the quests for individual and social salvation, for spiritual and literal bread, are united in its hero, Piers Plowman, the honest worker who also represents Christ's human nature (C.XX.21-2).[41] When he disappears, the poem ends in confusion and near despair.

Key terms in this quest for social and spiritual salvation are '*leute*' or '*leel* labour', the quality that Holy Church insists on when she emphasizes that faith is useless unless 'ye lovye *leeliche* and lene the pore' (C.I.175). *Leute* can mean 'virtue' or 'justice',[42] but, as I have argued elsewhere, it can also stand for the hope of salvation that arises from good works, while a lack of good works, caused by the

---

[40] Aers, *Faith, Ethics and Church: Writing in England, 1360-1409* (Cambridge, 2000), pp.56-75, especially p.74. Aers, however, does not draw a distinction between human justice and divine.

[41] R.W. Frank, *Piers Plowman and the Scheme of Salvation* (New Haven, 1957), p.81.

[42] P.M. Kean, 'Love, Law and *Lewte* in *Piers Plowman*', *RES*, n.s. 15 (1964), 241-61 (pp.255-6).

sin of sloth, leads to *wanhope* or despair.[43] For Langland, this quality *may* ensure that individual salvation is to some extent earned, and it *does* ensure social salvation.

Langland's bleak and anguished vision at the close of B demonstrated the absolute necessity of good works if society is not to collapse into misery and chaos. Yet, at the same time, Langland is driven by another anguish – the fear of damnation, not so much for himself, as for others. As John Burrow argues, although a poet of passionate convictions, Langland suffered from a 'divided mind' on this and other dilemmas, a division reflected in his use of 'the strong adversative conjunction *ac* – "but", or "on the other hand".'[44] Thus Langland stresses God's love, insists that mercy is always available to the penitent, and is unable to conceive of a God who could damn a sinner for all eternity. *Ac*, seeing all around him the famine and social havoc caused by sin, he urges again and again the importance of good works. *Ac*, he knows that insistence on works may drive sinners to despair. *Ac*, he reiterates, good works foster hope. This is Langland's key dilemma, and it informs all the anguishes: the fear of death and the afterlife; the psychic anguish of a mind struggling with irreconcilable opposites; the anguish of searching for meaning in a chaotic historical period; the anguish of guilt for Will's own sinful contribution to that chaos; the anguish of doubt as to God's ultimate mercy.

Several critics have briefly noticed an increased concern for works in C,[45] but none of them discuss the significance of this for the structure and argument of the revision as a whole. It is the aim of this chapter to show in detail that the tension between faith and works, between mercy and justice, between the needs of the individual and the needs of society, drives most of the C-revisions, large and small. In the C-Text the claims of both justice and mercy are strengthened, and with them, the thematic unity of the poem. The C-reviser's view of Redemption does not follow the Anselmian insistence on *God's* justice, but the heroic-exemplarist view that stresses both God's loving mercy and the need for humans to respond with a love that issues in good works. Salvation, for Langland, requires both mercy *and* justice, faith *and* hope, grace *and* works. On the one hand the individual Christian must have faith in salvation as a free gift of God's grace and mercy; on the other, if there is to be any hope of a harmonious society, its members must embrace the *leel* works that will both make a fitting response to God's loving suffering on their behalf, and allow them to hope that God's justice will ultimately reward them. Thus the key theme in the C-revision is the balance between faith-grace-mercy and hope-works-justice.

---

[43] Charlotte Clutterbuck, 'Hope and Good Works: *Leaute* in the C-Text of *Piers Plowman*', *RES*, n.s. 28 (1977), 129-40. According to Aquinas, hope fosters good works (S.T. I-II.xl.8); despair allows people to fall into unrestrained vice (II-II.xx.3).

[44] John Burrow, *Langland's Fictions*, pp.28-9.

[45] John Bowers, *The Crisis of Will in Piers Plowman* (Washington, 1986), pp.197ff; Pearsall, 'Poverty', pp.167, 180; Harbert, 'A Will with a Reason', pp.151, 159; Theodore L. Steinberg, *Piers Plowman and Prophecy: An Approach to the C-Text* (New York and London, 1991), p.127.

3. The suffering or sorrow of God in the C-revisions

There are two primary meanings of the word *suffer*: to endure some kind of painful experience (*OED* I); and to tolerate or allow (*OED* II). The idea of God's suffering (in both senses) gains an increasing importance throughout the B and C revisions.

Its first appearance is B's addition to Repentance's speech (B.V.478-509). This explicitly denies that either God or his Son felt any suffering in death: rather, our human flesh felt 'that sorwe, and Thy sone it ladde' (490-91). This makes Christ a heroic figure who is in control of sorrow and pain. B's Reason uses the word in its second sense, telling Will that, if God suffers (tolerates) the wrongs of the world, he too should hold his tongue rather than criticizing others (XI.379-91). B-Peace extends the idea, contradicting B-Repentance by saying that God became Man in order to know what Adam had suffered (XVIII.202-24). C develops the issue still further, flatly contradicting B-Repentance, strengthening the other two passages, and adding two more.

It seems that the impetus for the C-revisions comes from B-Reason's speech, the first time that B concedes that God does suffer. B-Reason tells Will that God suffers 'for som mannes goode' (B.XI.378-81). C's alterations make God's motivation clearer and increase the value of suffering:

> 'Ho soffreth more then God?' quod he; 'no gome, as Y leve.
> He myhte amende in a mynte-while al that amys standeth,
> Ac he soffreth, in ensaumple that we sholde soffren alle.
> Is no vertue so fair, ne of valewe ne of profit,
> So is soffrance sovereynliche, so hit be for Godes love.'
>
> C.XIII.198-202

C's addition of the word 'ensaumple' suggests that Langland is here following the exemplarist theory. The intransitive use of *suffer* suggests 'enduring' rather than 'allowing': God might like to 'amende... al that amys standeth', but he does not or cannot force his creatures to love him. Rather, he endures the suffering caused by evil in the hope that they will follow his example and suffer for love of him. In the remaining four passages, C develops the theme so as to underline the necessity for the soul to respond to the example of a God who suffers in both senses of the word.

In C, Peace uses the word in both senses, but primarily in the sense of *endure*, stressing that suffering has value: no one can really know 'wele' who has not known 'wo' (C.XX.209-15). Most unusual is her insistence (added in C) that God too *needs* this knowledge by experience and becomes man in order to get it:

> Ne hadde God ysoffred of some other then hymsulve,
> He hadde nat wist witterly where deth were sour or swete.
>
> C.XX.216-17

Peace suggests that God takes responsibility for all the experiences of his creatures: his purpose in the Incarnation was not merely to save Mankind from sin, but also to experience their suffering for himself:

> *So* [my italics] God that bigan al of his gode wille
> Bycam man of a mayde mankyne to save,
> And soffred to be sold, to se the sorwe of dying.
>
> C.XX.220-2

God also allowed Adam to learn through suffering: he set him 'in solace',

> And sethe he soffrede hym to synne, sorwe to fele –
> To wyte what wele was ther-thorw, kyndeliche to knowe.
> And aftur, God auntred hymsulve and toek Adames kynde
> To wyte what he hath soffred in thre sundry places,
> Bothe in hevene and in erthe – and now to helle he thenketh,
> To wyte what al wo is, that woet of alle ioye.
>
> C.XX.228-33

God and Man both need to suffer because it gives them *kynde*, experiential knowledge of good and evil.[46] God needs this because of his loving desire to share all his creature's experiences. Man needs it because it teaches him to follow God's example and reject evil.

Like Peace, Repentance speaks of God's suffering in the context of the drama of the Redemption:

> God, that of Thi goodnesse gonne the world make,
> And of nauhte madest auhte and man liche Thysulve,
> And sethe soffredest hym to synege, a syknesse to us alle –
> And for our beste, as Y beleve, whatever the Boek telle;
> *O felix culpa! O necessarium peccatum Ade!*
> For thorw that synne Thy sone ysent was til erthe
> And bicam man of a mayde, mankynde to amende –
> And madest Thysulve with Thy sone oure soule and body ilyche:
> *Ego in Patre, et Pater in me; et qui me videt, videt Patrrem meum...*
> And sethe in oure secte, as hit semed, deyedest,
> On a Friday, in fourme of man, feledest oure sorwe.
>
> C.VII.122-30

Repentance focuses on the positive results of God's suffering love: God 'soffredeste' (allowed) Adam to sin 'for oure beste'. This was the 'happy sin' that brought God's Son to earth. Whereas B denied that either Father or Son felt sorrow in death, C insists on the Father's full involvement with the suffering involved; B's Son *led* sorrow, but C's Son *feels* it. Langland's view of Redemption here is heroic/exemplarist rather than Anselmian:[47] God made Man like himself and allowed Man to sin, not so that he could be punished, but so that he could be redeemed when God made himself like us. There is no anger here, no mention of

---

[46] Davlin shows that this insistence on the need for *kynde* knowledge of suffering recalls Will's experience in the Inner Dream: '*Kynde Knowyng* as a Major Theme', p.13.

[47] Bennett notes the stress on love, but still considers that the passage fulfils Anselmian notions of justice (pp.92-8). He does not mention the C-revisions.

God's justice. Nor is there any division in the Godhead: God made 'Thysulve with Thy sone' like us – a unity that C emphasizes by changing the Latin tag to '*Ego in Patre*'.[48]

Repentance moves beyond his account of the Redemption of Mankind to encourage a mass of individual sinners to seek access to the *grace* it provides. C extends Repentance's brief prayer for mercy (B.V.504-6) into an assurance that God has promised salvation to all who ask it:

> That what tyme we synnefole men wolden be sory
> For dedes that we han done ylle, dampned sholde we ben nevere,
> Yf we knowlechede and cryde Crist therfore mercy.
>
> C.VII.145-7

The passage underlines the need for sinners to respond to God's willingness to feel 'oure sorwe' with sorrow of their own, repenting their sins and turning to God for his ever-available mercy and grace.

C adds two new passages which explore what happens when sinners fail to respond to God's offer of grace. In the first, Conscience makes a disconcerting analogy between God and earthly rulers who give gifts 'To here lele and to lege', but withdraw them if their liegemen subsequently become wicked (C.III.314-22):

> For God gaf Salomon grace upon erthe,
> Richesse and resoun, the while he ryhte lyuede;
> And as sone as God seyh a sewed nat his wille,
> A refte hym of his richesse and of his ryhte mynde
> And soffrede hym lyve in misbileve – Y leve he be in helle.
> So God gyveth nothyng that *si* ne is the glose,
> And ryhte so, sothly, may [cesar] and pope
> Bothe gyve and graunte there his grace lyketh,
> And efte have it ageyne of hem that don ylle.
>
> C.III.323-31

Conscience is here unusually fierce (probably influenced by the severity of Conscience's warning in B.XIX.197-9, mentioned above). He depicts God as actively depriving Solomon of 'richesse and of his ryhte mynde' and *allowing* him to continue in 'misbileve'. He suggests, again disconcertingly, that God's grace is provisional, and will be withdrawn from those who persist in evil. The revision suggests Langland's growing concern with the possibility that if the soul *chooses*, despite the gift of Redemption, to follow self-will rather than God's will, God will respect the creature's right to *free will*, even if that means the creature putting himself beyond the pale of God's *grace*.

Similarly, C's Wit describes Kynde as the Creator who made Man 'semblable in soule to God'. However, the sunshine of God's grace can be obscured by the clouds of sin (C.X.152-61), with the result:

---

[48] 'I am in the Father and the Father in me; and who sees me sees My Father' (John 14:9-10).

That God sheweth nat suche synnefole men, and soffreth hem mysfare,
And somme hangeth hemsulve and otherwhile adrencheth.
God wol nat of hem wyte bute [yworthe lat hem],
As the Sauter sayth by synnefole shrewes:
Et dimis eos secundum desideria eorum.
Such lyther-lyvyng men lome been ryche
Of gold and of other goed, ac Goddes grace hem fayleth,
For they louyeth and bylyveth al here lyf-tyme
On catel more then on Kynde, that all kyne thynges wrouhte,
The which is love and lyf that last withouten ende.

C.X.162-71

This stark message may well have been influenced by the Good Samaritan's warning at the end of B, mentioned above: sinners who destroy their relationship with God risk killing themselves in despair. By desiring 'catel' rather than Kynde 'al here lyf-tyme', they render themselves unable to access God's grace and the love that means eternal life. Wit, however, depicts God as *allowing* sin rather than as actively punishing sinners. The sun of God's grace is always shining, and it is the 'shrewes' who create a barrier to that grace through sin.

C's treatment of God's suffering suggests that Langland sees grace and free will as equally important. Peace and Repentance stress the validity of the Redemption that has been achieved by God's willingness to *endure* sorrow with his creatures, offering them *grace*. Wit and Reason, as befits intellectual faculties who are concerned to instruct Will in the nature of vice and virtue, focus on the idea that God does not control his creatures, but *allows* humans to sin: Man has *free will*, and thus responsibility for the sinful actions that may cut him off from the grace that God offers him.

In all five passages, the issue of the *kynde* or natural relationship between God and Man is essential: Conscience's discussion immediately precedes his discussion of the *kynde* grammatical relationship between Man and God (see below); Repentance stresses the kinship between Man and a God who is 'furste oure fadur, and of flesch oure brother' (C.VII.143); Wit relates how *Kynde* the creator made Man 'semblable in soule to God but if synne hit make' (C.X.158); Reason's discussion of God's 'soffrance' follows Will's vision of a world created by Kynde; Peace insists on the need for God and Man to know death and suffering *kyndely* in order to understand 'wele'. This *kynde* (natural) relationship between the creature and a loving God is crucial to the poem. It demands, as the Good Samaritan and Holy Church both suggest, a *kynde* (kind) response from all Christians to the *emcristene* (fellow Christians) who share their nature. This *kynde* response requires useful work for the benefit of the *comune*. This need, as I will attempt to show, is the driving force behind most of C's revisions. Whatever the case in B, in C there is none of what Aers has called 'an imaginative *withdrawal*' from the spiritual and social significance of productive labour.[49] Quite the reverse.

---

[49] Aers, *Community, Gender, and Individual Identity: English Writing, 1360-1430* (London and New York, 1988), p.67.

4. The first and second visions: the anguish of sin and the affirmation of work

For Langland, sin is a social as well as a spiritual problem: unlike the Crucifixion lyricists he is deeply concerned with the way that a sinner affects other people. The first and second visions are dominated by the anguish of sin – sins involving the corruption of social institutions in the first vision, and sins of the individual in the second vision. The action of the first vision is driven by Will's request that Holy Church 'Kenne me by sum craft to knowe the false'. (C.II.4) and by the subsequent exploration of the role of Meed in society. This episode is mainly a social satire on the corruption of the legal and clerical systems.

However, a major C-revision strengthens the idea that humans can and should 'earn' a heavenly reward.[50] Following his discussion of how Solomon, by rejecting God's gifts, was himself rejected, Conscience moves on to the right or 'direct' relationship between the adjective (Man) and the noun or substantive (God).[51] He says that this 'right' relationship merits 'retribution':

> And that the gyft that God gyveth to alle lele lyuynge –
> Grace of good ende, and gret joye aftur.
>
> C. III.338-9

Both these additions strengthen the Pelagian notion that heavenly rewards are in some sense dependent upon human merit.[52]

Conscience extends the grammatical metaphor by drawing a parallel between this relationship and that between labourer and master:

> 'Relacioun rect,' quod Conscience, 'is a record of treuthe...
> Folowynge and fyndynge out the fundement of a strenghe,
> And styfliche stande forth to strenghe the fundement
> In kynde and in case and in the cours of nombre;
> As a leel laborer, byleveth with his maister
> In his pay and in his pite and in his puyr treuthe –
> To pay hym yf he parforme and have pite yf he faileth
> And take him for his travaile al that treuthe wolde.
> So of hol herte cometh hope and hardy relacioun
> Seketh and seweth his "sustantif" savacioun –
> That is God, the ground of al, a graciouse "antecedent".
> And man is "relatif rect" yf he be rihte trewe...'
>
> C.III.347-54

---

[50] C also adds St Lawrence's claim to have deserved 'mede' from God (II.132-3).

[51] For more discussion of the grammar, see: Paula Carlson, 'Lady Meed and God's Meed', *Traditio*, 46 (1961), 291-311 (pp.297, 306); Adams, 'Mede', pp.221-30; D. Vance Smith 'The Labors of Reward', *YLS*, 8 (1995), 5, 127-54 (p.134); Martyn J. Miller, pp.73-84.

[52] Adams argues that while some revisions are intended to 'defuse' criticisms of B's Pelagian leanings, the image of the labourer suggests Langland's semi-Pelagian view that 'salvation itself... can also be regarded as a kind of wage earned by the righteous' ('Mede', pp.219, 232). Vance Smith notices Langland's nostalgia for a time of 'direct' or healthy labour relations (p.150).

Conscience suggests that the rich and intellectually gifted Solomon destroyed his relationship with God, while the humble labourer maintains his. This foreshadows Recklessness's later claim that while clerks are soon 'yraveschid fro the rihte bileue', 'Lewed lele laboreres and land-tulyng peple... passen purgatorie penaunceles for here parfit bileue' (C.XI.294-300). However, unlike Recklessness, Conscience stresses the effort involved with vigorous verbs, 'Folowynge and fyndynge out... styfliche stande... to strenghe... seketh and seweth'. God may take pity on those who fail in their attempts at virtue, but it is essential for them to make that attempt. The relationship of labourer and master is the best analogy for the relationship Man should have with God because it stresses the importance of human effort and reinforces the spiritual significance of physical labour.

Conscience goes on to say that in the indirect relationship, people want benefits without the effort of 'coest and care and alle kyn travayle' (C.III.371) and that most people are now 'indirect':

> Ac the moste partie of peple now puyr indirect semth
> For thei wilnen and wolden as beste were for hemsulve,
> Thow the Kynge and the comune al the coest hadde.

C.III.382-4

This is a dominant theme of C – the destructiveness of an idle, reckless greed that takes more than a fair share of society's resources without working to produce those resources. Conscience contrasts the Lord 'that for oure love deyede,/ And coveytede oure kynde' (C.III.400-1) with the 'coveytise of mede' that destroyed Saul (C.III.430). The C-additions link strongly to Conscience's vision of a just society in which Meed will 'mishap' when 'kynde love' and Conscience make law into a labourer, priests pray for the sinful, and knights and kings avoid exploiting the *comune* (C.III.451-81). However, Conscience warns that reform will be difficult 'without the comune helpe' (C.IV.176). C's increased stress on the moral and spiritual significance of labour prepares for the second vision in which the *comune*, the mass of individuals, will attempt to assist in the reform of society by taking part in the Ploughing.

Before the second vision, Langland inserts one of the major C-additions, often called the Dreamer's apologia. At the beginning of this episode, Langland briefly identifies Will as a satirical 'maker', whose literary efforts are despised by the 'lollares of London and lewede ermytes' because 'Y made of tho men as resoun me tauhte' (C.V.1-5). Kerby-Fulton argues persuasively that Langland is here 'working with his *own* authorial experience' and that Will is here not just a fictional character, but an external authority figure whom Langland uses to reassert control over his poem after its 'misappropriation... by the rebels in 1381'.[53] However, she does not discuss why Langland places his 'apologia' at this particular point in the poem, and how that affects its larger meaning for the poem as a whole.

---

[53] Kerby-Fulton, 'Langland and the Bibliographic Ego', pp.70-4.

The mention of the Dreamer's 'making' is very short, and other moral issues quickly dominate the episode. I believe that the 'apologia' is not so much a defence of Langland's way of life or his poem[54] as a confession: the Dreamer examines his life and social responsibilities, finds himself guilty of the idle, selfish greed that Conscience saw as 'indirect', and is rebuked by Reason for his failure to contribute to the welfare of the *comune*. As Middleton comments, Langland is 'never outside the ethical reach of his own writings'.[55] Just as Dante depicts himself as joining in the cleansing punishments of Purgatory, here Langland interrogates his own life and finds it wanting.

The name of Will's wife, 'Kitte', may suggest lechery, or at least uxoriousness, since it is a 'Kitte' who shortly afterwards prevents Active from following the Pilgrimage to Truth (C.VII.304). However, Will's predominant sin is sloth.[56] He leads a lazy and gluttonous life:

> In an hot hervest whenne Y hadde myn hele
> And lymes to labory with, and lovede wel fare
> And no dede to do but to drynke and to slepe.
>
> C.V.7-9

However, when Reason rebukes him, asking him what work he does 'that to the comune needeth,' Will makes a feeble excuse:

> 'Sertes,' Y sayde, 'and so me God helpe,
> Y am to wayke to worche with sykel or with sythe,
> And to long, lef me, lowe to stoupe, .
> To wurche as a werkeman, eny while to duyren.'
>
> C.V.22-5

Will's language here foreshadows the Wasters who undermine the Ploughing episode, complaining that they have 'none lymes to labory with, Lord God we thonketh' (C.VIII.135). Reason presses Will further, asking him if he has rich relations to support him, for he seems prodigal, 'A spendour that spene mot' (C.V.28).[57] Reason then demands to know whether Will is a fraudulent beggar who 'faytest uppon Frydayes', living a 'lollarne lyf' that will be little valued when

---

[54] For this view, see *Ibid.*, p.86; Godden, pp.183-4; Lawler, pp.214-16; Geoffrey Shepherd, 'Poverty in *Piers Plowman*', in *Social Relations and Ideas*, ed. T.H. Aston et al. (Cambridge, 1983), pp.169-89 (p.180).

[55] Middleton, 'Acts of Vagrancy', p.261. Middleton argues that the passage depicts the Dreamer's prosecution under the Statute of labourers. Wittig is unconvinced, saying that 'in remembraunce' suggests an inward encounter rather than a 'trial': '"Culture Wars" and the Persona in *Piers Plowman*', *YLS*, 15 (2001), 167-95 (pp.168-71).

[56] Bower, *The Crisis of Will*, pp.167-76. Sloth's lament, 'Heu michi quod sterilem duxi vitam iuvenilem' (C.VII.54a) is the same as Holy Church uses to rebuke Will for the first time in the poem (C.I.139a).

[57] Dante sees prodigality as punishable in the same way as avarice (*Inferno* VII: *Purgatorio* XXII).

'ryhtfulnesse rewardeth ryht as men deserveth'; the only acceptable excuse would be if Will is crippled 'thorw som myshap' (C.V.29-34).[58]

Faced with the question of whether he lives in such a way as to *deserve* a reward from 'rightulnesse', Will replies to Reason with a shrill passage of self-justification[59] that shows evidence of the three spiritual sins – anger, envy and pride. Will uses the words 'I', 'me', or 'mine' 25 times in 17 lines (C.V.36-52). He claims that his clerical education has allowed him to know 'witterly' or truly 'what Holy Writ menede'. This is a large claim for one in minor orders, and one that foreshadows Pride's confession, added in C, that 'Y trowed me wysor/ To carpe and to consayle then eny clerk or lewed' (VI.28-9). The Dreamer's argument that, since his friends died, he has found no other 'Lyf that me lykede' seems both feeble and self-centred, and hardly meets his obligations to engage in useful work. Will claims that he 'deserves' his livelihood because the 'limbs' that he labours with are his prayers, *Placebo* and *Dirige*: unlike the professional beggars he despises, he prays for his wealthy benefactors and begs 'Withoute bagge or botel but my wombe one' (C.V.45-52).

Will thus tries to construct himself, not as an agricultural labourer, but as a spiritual labourer. However, he lacks the full clerical education that would allow him to provide the spiritual bread of the sacraments or to instruct the *lewed*. He does not follow Conscience's prophetic vision in which the clergy will say the *Placebo* and *Dirige* 'for alle synful' (C.III.464 – added in C). Will prays only for his rich patrons: even his prayers are not intended to benefit the *comune* as a whole. Since he has just described himself as liking to do nothing but drink and sleep, it is clear that he contributes nothing beyond what he has to in order to secure his own food supply.

Will next claims that 'Hit bycometh for clerkes Crist for to serve'. He shows contempt (reinforced by the harsh consonants) for the suggestion that one with his clerical education should do work fitting for 'Bondemen and bastardus and beggares children'. This sits uneasily with all the passages where Langland expresses sympathetic concern for the poor.[60] Will's tone becomes increasingly angry and envious as he accuses the clergy (including the Pope) of simony in offering preferment to 'bondemen barnes' and 'barnes bastardus' while overlooking 'pore gentel blood' and 'Lyf-holynesse and love' – qualities that Will himself hardly displays at this point (C.V.53-81). Finally, Will begs Reason not to rebuke him:

---

[58] Pearsall notes that Reason thinks of agricultural labour rather than 'London work' as 'the only true work': 'Langland's London', in Justice and Kerby-Fulton, pp.185-207 (p.190). See also Middleton, 'Acts of Vagrancy', p.248.

[59] Wendy Scase argues that Langland's use of the anticlerical satirical figure of the gyrovague shows that the Dreamer's excuses are quite unjustified: *Piers Plowman and the New Anticlericalism* (Cambridge, 1989), pp.125-40. Middleton argues that his tirade suggests suspect motives ('Acts of Vagrancy', pp.259-60).

[60] Kerby-Fulton reads it as a reactionary, orthodox passage intended to mitigate Langland's dangerous political situation after the Peasants' Revolt, establishing his social and educational status and his 'authority to speak': 'Langland and the Bibliographic Ego', pp.87-9.

> For in my conscience Y knowe what Crist wolde Y wrouhte.
> Preyers of a parfit man and penaunce discrete
> Is the levest labour that Oure Lord pleseth.
>
> C.V.83-5

Will here offers a specious rationalization of his behaviour to Reason,[61] just as Will-Recklessness later reasons, first with Clergy (C.XIII.129), and then with Reason himself (C.XIII.194-245).

Langland depicts Will as an ardent man, but not as a wise or a virtuous one: he never speaks at any length without being rebuked. His claim to perfection is dubious, and again foreshadows the Wasters who offer to pray for Piers. Piers responds tartly, 'Your preyeres... and ye parfyt weren,/Myhte helpe' (C.VIII.136-7), and here Conscience rebukes Will with similar acidity:

> Quod Conscience, 'By Crist, Y can nat see this lyeth;
> Ac it semeth no sad parfitnesse in citees to begge
> But he be obediencer to prior or to mynstre.'
>
> C.V.89-91

It is also important to note that none of the major guides in C endorses begging of any kind (see below).

The Dreamer capitulates with a passionate hope that despite his idleness, God's mercy will extend to him as well:

> 'That is soth,' Y saide, 'and so Y beknowe –
> That Y have ytynt tyme, and tyme myspened;
> Ac yut, Y hope – as he that ofte hath ychaffared
> And ay loste and loste, and at the laste hym happed
> A bouhte suche a bargayn he was the bet evere,
> And sette al his lost at a leef at the laste ende,
> Suche a wynnyng hym warth thorw wordes of grace...
> So hope Y to have of Hym that is almyghty
> A gobet of his grace, and bigynne a tyme
> That alle tymes of my tyme to profit shal turne.'
>
> C.V.92-101

Although this passage is not necessarily a literal account of Langland's own life,[62] it may be *spiritual* autobiography.[63] Its shifts in tone suggest searing self-criticism,[64] anguish at his shared responsibility for the sinful state of the world, and a passionate hope that he can yet be redeemed despite his idleness. His repentant speech suggests that he can be, that he is not one whose sin is so great that he falls into *wanhope* and loses access to God's mercy. Furthermore, it is significant that

---

[61] Aers, *Faith, Ethics*, pp.60-1, 71.
[62] Donaldson accepts its literal truth (pp.218-19).
[63] Bowers, *The Crisis of Will*, p.171.
[64] Burrow, *Langland's Fictions*, p.106; Wittig, '"Culture Wars"', p.186.

he must reform 'a tyme' – he must attempt to act virtuously in the temporal world instead of relying solely on God's mercy.

Will here imagines turning, with God's grace, from the life of a waster to the life of a winner. These lines, stressing the need not to misspend time, prepare for the C-revisions to the teachings of Wit and Imaginative: C adds Wit's injunction that friends and the Church should help 'so sholde no man begge' (C.X.184-8); C's Imaginative instructs Will to position himself in the lay life of Dowel, separating him from the 'Clerkes that conne al' and may be able to 'do bettere' (C.XIV.1-11), and thus scotching his pretensions to clerical status.

Middleton reads this passage as releasing 'Will into a form of penitential rectification that is quickly transformed into the dreaming and "making" of *the rest of Langland's poem*.'[65] However, the 'making' that Langland was concerned with in the first vision was satirical writing, directed 'as resoun me tauhte' against the evils committed by 'tho men', that is, against evils committed *by others*. At this point, however, the emphasis of the poem shifts. Although the poem never completely loses its satirical, social concerns, it becomes more concerned with the spiritual development of the Dreamer as he directs his criticism against himself. Here, and in the third and fourth visions, he writes about what Reason has taught him *about himself*. The modes of allegory, confessional literature, and apocalyptic vision predominate over the satirical mode for the rest of the poem. That is, the poem that Langland continues to 'make' is different from the one he was 'making' before Reason and Conscience accosted him, and his *penance* is the self-examination that he undergoes in the rest of the poem.

Will then goes to church and kneels before the Cross, beating his breast, weeping and wailing for his sins (C.V.107-8). The Dreamer here shows his willingness to attempt to rectify his sinfulness, to *act well*. However, as Middleton notes, his penance cannot be perfect, for that would stop the poem.[66] He, like the other sinners he depicts, will be unable to bring this willingness to fruition until he aligns his will with the grace available through Christ's redemption – a fulfilment that takes place after the Harrowing of Hell and Resurrection, when Will once again kneels before the Cross, finally taking responsibility for his wife and daughter (C.XX.470-8).

The episode opens the way for the Confession of the Seven Deadly Sins by making the Dreamer not merely an observer, as he was in B, but himself a sinner who must confess and commit himself to reform. Will's confession of time wasting provides an excellent introduction to the second vision, which starts with Reason's sermon on good living:

---

[65] Middleton, 'Acts of Vagrancy', p.260.
[66] Middleton, 'Audience', pp.15-16. See also Judith Dale, 'The Author, the Dreamer, his Wife and their Poet: Thoughts on an Essential-Ephemeral "Langland"', *YLS*, 15 (2001) 89-94. Fletcher argues that since *sola contrition delet peccatum* the Dreamer's penance is perfect: p.69. Kerby-Fulton notes that the Blackfriars Council of 1382 banned this opinion as heretical: 'Langland and the Bibliographic Ego', p.75. C revises Patience's endorsement of contrition alone (B.XIV.182-92) insisting on satisfaction of *works* (C.XVI.28-32).

He bad wastoures go worche and wynne here sustinaunce
Thorw some trewe travail, and no tyme spille.

C.V.126-7

Reason's sermon precipitates the Confession of the Seven Deadly Sins.[67] In the first vision, the Folk were presented socially, according to their crafts or professions. Now they are presented morally, as Sins who must repent and confess in order to find God. Because the sins are in fact repenting at this point, Langland's writing here is lively and humorous, and the tone is almost optimistic: many sins are confessed, enough for all readers to find that they are guilty of some, but on the whole, they are not mortal sins.[68] The two most serious sins, the ones which are *unkynde*, are Covetise (VI.294), which cheats others out of the necessities of life, and Sloth (VII.43), which fails to contribute to these necessities.[69] Yet even here the tone is optimistic. When Repentance warns that Covetise must make restitution before he can be absolved (VI.294-307), and Robert the Robber weeps because he lacks means for restitution, Repentance urges him to trust in God's mercy:

For al the wrecchednesse of this world and wikkede dedes
Fareth as a fonk of fuyr that ful amydde Temese
And deyede with a drop water; so doth alle synnes
Of alle manere men that [myd] goode wille
Confessen hem and cryen Hym mercy, shal nevere come in helle.

C.VI.333-7

C strengthens Repentance's speech (cf. B.V.281-5), adding the promise that those who seek mercy will never go to hell.

Sloth, the sin that fails to contribute to social needs, is the most dangerous: he is the last one to repent,[70] the one who sleeps during his confession and fails to perform his penance; he is wasteful, ignorant, careless about God, and 'unkynde' to his fellow Christians, recognizing no obligations; he has been a beggar because of his 'foule sleuthe'. Because of his lack of good works, he is prone to *wanhope*, but again, Repentance encourages him to beg God for grace, 'For is no gult so greet that His goodnesse is more' (.VII.1-61).

Repentance goes on to warn Sloth, and rich men generally, against feeding flatterers and liars rather than God's minstrels – beggars, the poor, the learned, the blind and the bedridden (C.VII.69-118). This passage reinforces Holy Church's message that the key duty of the rich is to help the poor freely. At the same time, C tempers B's warning that loving corrupt minstrelsy will lead to 'Luciferis feste' with the additional line, 'To perpetual payne or purgatorie as wikke' (C.VII.117): although unkind behaviour deserves punishment, this punishment may not be eternal. Similarly, as I noted above, C strengthens

---

[67] For reasons that I will discuss later, C has moved many details from B's account of Hawkin-*Activa Vita* (B.XIII.275-457) to this spot.
[68] Morton W. Bloomfield, *The Seven Deadly Sins* (East Lansing, 1952), p.43.
[69] Stokes (pp.165-72).
[70] See also C.II.83-104, and Bowers, *Crisis of Will*, pp.79-96.

Repentance's promise that, if sinners repent, 'dampned sholde we ben nevere' (CVII.145-7). If C stresses the need for good works more than B does, it also stresses God's mercy more.

Hearing Repentance's account of God's willingness to suffer to redeem them, the Folk set out on a Pilgrimage to Truth (C.VII.152-7). Piers Plowman suddenly appears, claiming to know Truth *kyndely*, since for forty years he has served Truth 'in alle kyne craftes.../ Profitable as for the plouh' (C.VII.182-97). Piers fulfils Conscience's grammatical metaphor and his prophecy of the society of love that will arise when each man will 'pley with a plogh' (C.IV.460): his response to God's suffering sacrifice has been to do essential work for the benefit of all – he is Conscience's ideal labourer who is in the grammatically right relationship with God and deserves his payment.

Piers tells the Folk that following the path of virtue (or good works) will enable each of them to 'se Treuthe sitte in thy sulve herte' (C.VII.254). C adds the lines that describe Charity making a church

> 'In thyne hole herte to herborwe alle trewe
> And fynde alle mannere folke fode to here soules.'
>
>   C.VII.257-8

These lines foreshadow Piers's leadership of the Christian society in the Barn of Unity in Passus C.XXI, and develop the spiritual symbolism of food.

Like all of Langland's visions of union with God, this vision is only momentary. Several disreputable characters withdraw from the Pilgrimage, using the excuses of the guests who failed to come to the Wedding Feast (Luke 14:16-24). One of them is Active, who has just married, and who says that 'I may nat come for a Kitte, so a cleveth on me.' Contemplation, however, undertakes the Pilgrimage (C.VII.291-308). This episode is puzzling, for the Pilgrimage itself represents the virtuous active life [71] that is a necessary preparation for the contemplative life.[72] Unlike Godden, I do not think that C intends to dismiss the active life as one that is *unable* to pursue Truth: later, C replaces B's rascally Hawkin-*Activa Vita* with the more virtuous Active (C.XV.195ff).[73] Rather, he recognizes the possibility that working to fulfil the material needs of the world may lead to becoming fixated on the responsibilities and relationships of that world – the farms, oxen, and wives. He warns of the danger of confining oneself to that active, material world without proceeding to contemplation.[74] It is surely no accident that Active's wife is called 'Kitte', for his sin is the same as the Dreamer's: those who refuse the Pilgrimage are slothful, spiritually careless, lacking in the hope that inspires good works.

---

[71] Donaldson notes this, but still thinks that Active's refusal shows the inadequacy of the active life (pp.167-8). Derek Pearsall thinks the episode is out of place, and rejects a too spiritual reading of the Ploughing (*C-Text*, VII.199n).

[72] Stock, p.465.

[73] Godden, p.185.

[74] Cf. Gillian Rudd, *Managing Language in Piers Plowman* (Cambridge, 1994) p.129.

Piers offers to guide the remaining pilgrims when he has finished ploughing and sowing his half-acre. In fact, the Ploughing replaces the Pilgrimage as Piers becomes 'a pilgrim at the plough for profyt to pore and ryche' (C.VIII.111). Most of the folk help Piers to work, but gluttony and sloth disrupt their efforts as the wasters sing, drink ale, and pretend to be crippled when Piers accosts them.[75] Piers calls on Hunger, who beats the wasters so severely that a thousand cripples are cured and willing to work for horse-bread (C.VIII.171-96).[76] Piers is 'proud' of their new attitude (C.VIII.197, 203), but it does not last long.

Hewett-Smith believes that the point of this episode is to show 'the moral inadequacy' of the pride that Piers, as 'manager of the economy', feels at the 'return to the ideal, estate-based labor relations'.[77] However, Piers is surely proud of the wasters because their work will ensure enough food for the 'pore peple' on whom he immediately takes pity (C.VIII.205). It is Piers who asks Hunger how he can teach the wasters to labour out of love[78] rather than fear, and asks to what extent he is responsible for the beggars who are 'my blody bretherne, for god bouhte us alle' (C.VIII.209-22).[79] Hunger advises him to take a stern approach, citing various biblical texts commonly used against the sin of sloth.[80] Hunger stays with Piers until harvest, and the folk struggle to assuage him with herbs and beans. As soon as harvest arrives, the wasters stop working, and start eating gluttonously. The scene ends with an urgent prophecy of impending famine (C.VIII.343-54). The episode thus shows on a small scale the cyclical problem that Langland explores in the poem as a whole: people reform under the pressure of fear and/or enthusiasm, and relapse as soon as the pressure abates.

The Ploughing has an allegorical dimension, standing both for the provision of food for the soul, and for completion of the sacrament of Confession through works of penance.[81] However, its literal meaning is paramount, and based on the historical realities of fourteenth-century famines.[82] Unlike many other religious poets, Langland is urgently concerned with daily life, especially the life of the poor. The details of this passage show how familiar he must have been with the realities of physical work and hardship. The Ploughing scene insists that practical work for the common good is necessary for both the physical and spiritual health of a society.

---

[75] Bowers, *The Crisis of Will*, pp.125-6; Kaske, 'Holy Church's Speech', p.324, and 'The Character Hunger in *Piers Plowman*', in Kennedy, pp.187-97 (pp.192-3).

[76] Aers sees a tension between Langland's ideological disapproval of their quest for higher wages and his imaginative involvement with their lives (*Chaucer, Langland*, p.17)

[77] Hewett-Smith, p.13.

[78] Spearing notes that the C-revision here stresses the problem of love (pp.243-4).

[79] Hewett-Smith discusses the fourteenth-century controversies over the need to discriminate in charity between the deserving, involuntary poor, and the undeserving, whether lay or friars, who choose to live in idleness, pp.14-17.

[80] Wenzel, *The Sin of Sloth* (Chapel Hill, 1967), p.142.

[81] Burrow, 'The Action of Langland's Second Vision', *Essays in Criticism*, 15 (1965), 247-68 (p.248).

[82] Hewett-Smith, pp.11-12.

Several small C-revisions emphasize the conflict between the need for good works (in this case, physical labour) and the need for compassion for genuine poverty: C expands the Parable of the Talents so that it specifically warns against sloth (C.VIII.253); he replaces B's statement that Christ approves both the active and contemplative lives (B.VI.237-51) with an injunction to 'lele labour, as thorw lymes and handes' (C.VIII.247-63);[83] he adds the story of Dives and Lazarus as a warning against failure to share wealth with the poor. However, rather than making God the agent of punishment, C says that 'Dives for his delicat lyf to the devel wente' (C.VIII.278), representing damnation as a result of human actions. C also deletes the text *Mihi vindictam et ego retribuam* (B.VI.225a) which attributes vengeance to God. C's revisions are again designed to emphasize both God's mercy and the need for human response through socially useful work.

The conflict between the need for labour and the need for compassion grows more acute in the Pardon scene. The gloss on the Pardon explains that it applies to kings, knights, clergy, merchants and lawyers, but only if they perform their duties as they should, helping the poor. Labourers, however, are pardoned without further conditions (C.IX.9-60). But by far the greatest part of this episode, expanded by about 140 lines in C, involves an anguished discussion of whether beggars and mendicant religious are included in the Pardon (C.IX.61-281).

Here the C-additions, with their anger against the social disease of false begging[84] and their heartfelt compassion for the truly poor, show just how deeply this issue concerned Langland. He warns that false beggars are not included in the Pardon, because they defraud the needy and deceive 'hym that gyveth' (C.IX.64-5). He scorns those who live 'In idelnesse and in ese and by others travayle' (C.IX.152), and who deliberately break their children's bones, saying that God's law damns such beggars, 'til they ben amended' (C.IX.160). The rich should not care if such beggars starve (C.IX.98-101), but should heed the plight of their poorest neighbours, the 'prisones in puttes and pore folke in cotes', especially the women who struggle to feed their crying children, suffering much hunger, rising at night to rock the cradle, doing the most menial work, scraping flax and peeling rushes. Unlike the idle Will, these poor women work hard, but still 'turne the faire outward,/ And been abasched for to begge' (C.IX.72-87): true poverty does not beg, but rather endures and works as hard as possible. The homeliness of the details shows that Langland understood the misery of poverty.[85]

Langland suggests that the old, the crippled, women who cannot work because they have children, 'And all pore pacient.../ That taketh thise meschiefes mekeliche and myldeliche at herte' are granted the privilege of suffering Purgatory on earth (C.IX.178-86). This passage introduces the theme of patient poverty, crucial to the discussion of social issues throughout the rest of the poem. Langland,

---

[83] Rudd notes that C also replaces a later discussion of the contemplative life (B.IX.95-99) with 'an increased obligation to help and love our neighbours and enemies' (p.141).
[84] Shepherd, pp.170-1.
[85] Shepherd, p.127. Pearsall observes that whereas most medieval writers give a theoretical view of poverty, Langland probes the reality: 'Poverty', pp.168, 179. Scott points out that the plague had left many families 'without fathers and sons to farm the land' (p.146).

however, does not offer *voluntary* poverty as a desirable way of life: he criticizes those who had a trade, but, tired of 'long labour and little wynnynge', left their labour and became wandering, begging clerics (C.IX.203-54); his sympathies are with those who meekly suffer *involuntary* poverty.

Finally a Priest asks Piers to open the Pardon, and they find a text from the Athanasian Creed saying that those who do well will go into eternal life, and those who do evil into eternal fire (C.IX.288-9), which the Priest says is no pardon. In B, Piers tears the Pardon, vowing to abandon his agricultural labour for spiritual labour:

> 'I shal cessen of my sowyng,' quod Piers, 'and swynke noght so harde,
> Ne about my bely joye so bisy be na moore;
> Of preieres and of penaunce my plough shal ben herafter,
> And wepen when Y sholde slepe, though whete breed me faille.'
>
> B.VII.118-21

This scene has caused intense debate amongst critics of the B-Text, and has even led Baker and Woolf to suggest that Langland deliberately misleads the reader by representing the Ploughing as virtuous, only to reject it in this passage.[86] However, these critics make little of the fact that Langland deletes this passage from C.

The tearing of the Pardon does not suit C's purpose. For one thing, tearing the Pardon suggests a rejection of the authority of the Church (which issues pardons) and Truth (who sent this one). Instead of rejecting the structures of the Church, Langland wishes to renew them – with an ideal Pilgrimage and an ideal Pardon which are not as other pilgrimages and pardons. For another thing, the tearing of the Pardon suggests that Piers has been mistaken, is himself unable to fulfil the Pardon, and must throw himself on God's grace and mercy.[87] This may be true for B, but it makes Piers a limited (rather than a transcendental) figure who has been mistaken (and therefore prideful) in his assessment of his own virtue and his relationship with Truth. Such a figure would need major reform before he was worthy to represent Christ's human nature, or to become the partner of Grace in the founding of Christian society, or to be the only hope of destroying pride at the end of the poem. But in no version of the poem does Piers undergo this reform. Revising the poem in the light of B's ending, C reinforces Piers's stature by removing this passage with its suggestion of error, by having Piers rather than Patience give the final definition of Dowel, and by *Liberum Arbitrium*'s statement that Piers is the one who knows charity 'most parfitlyche' (C.XVI.338)

In B, Langland suggests that a life of prayers, poverty, and penance may be better than a life of active labour, but in C he is fully aware that if Piers stopped ploughing society would starve. C removes the tearing of the Pardon, moving straight to Will's waking assertion that on Doomsday a poke-full of pardons will

---

[86] Baker (p.724), and Woolf, 'The Tearing of the Pardon', in Hussey, pp.50-75.

[87] John Lawlor, '"Piers Plowman": The Pardon Reconsidered', *MLR*, 45 (1950), 459-68. Godden argues that the C-revision of the Pardon redefines Do-wel as patient poverty (I disagree), rendering the tearing of the Pardon unnecessary; he does not explain C's omission of Piers's rejection of work (p.190).

not be worth a pie-crust 'but Dowel us helpe' (C.IX.332-53). The reader can give credence to this speech, because it is only when Will is awake that he is able to take spiritual action, going to church to sigh for his sins before the Cross (C.V.105-8), bringing his family to reverence the Resurrection (C.XX.471-8), and going to Mass and the Eucharist (C.XIX.2-3).

Many of the minor C-revisions relate to the tension between social salvation (dependent on human effort) and personal salvation (dependent on God's grace): they stress the dangers of sloth; they reject begging as an acceptable way of life (the truly poor are ashamed to beg); they insist on the value of physical, agricultural labour with limbs and hands; and, on the other hand, they also stress the availability of God's mercy to all who repent. The major revisions all reinforce these themes. The grammatical metaphor insists on the need for man to act towards God like a *leel* labourer to his master, but also to trust in God's pity if he fails. The Dreamer confesses to leading a socially parasitic life and appeals to God's grace to help him to amend. The Pardon displays pity for genuine, involuntary poverty, and anger at the voluntary choice of begging as a way of life. The omission of the tearing of the Pardon and Piers's rejection of labour avoids suggesting that Piers's work is in any way morally defective. On the one hand, C stresses the need for *leel* labour in order to in some sense earn salvation and ensure that all are fed; on the other, he stresses the need to trust to the mercy of God when one has failed to live *leelly*. The *Visio* deals largely with the anguish of sin, particularly the sins of covetousness (that takes an unfair share of the common good) or sloth (that fails to work to produce that good). This anguish is particularly evident in the confessions of the Dreamer and Robert the Robber.

As well as having thematic significance, the major C-revisions tighten the poem's narrative structure. Conscience's grammatical metaphor stresses the 'rightness' of labour for the common good, strengthening his vision of a loving society in which all do useful work, and developing the theme of the whole first vision: that the realm can only be well run when all members of the *comune* are ready to work in accordance with Reason and Conscience rather than Meed. This prepares for the way in which Reason and Conscience interrogate the Dreamer and convince him that he too needs to reform. His confession that his idle life does not contribute to the *comune* links to the Confession of the Seven Deadly Sins and the Ploughing scene. The omission of the lines where Piers rejects ploughing prevents the weakening of Piers's stature as a guide and the possible undermining of the fundamental significance of useful work. Will's greater involvement in the general Confession paves the way for his increased importance in the second part of the poem, where he pursues an individual quest for Dowel, and the key anguishes are the anguish of psychic disintegration and the anguish of doubt.

5. The search for Dowel and the anguish of psychic disintegration

In the third vision, Will embarks on a quest to find Dowel with the help of the intellectual guides – Thought, Wit, Study, Clergy, Scripture, Reason, and Imaginative. Unfortunately he persists in thinking of Dowel as a noun rather than as an imperative verb and adverb, as a thing he can find rather than as an action he must do,[88] and keeps asking for 'a more kyndore knowynge' (C.X.55-6, 108; XI.92), when this experiential knowledge could only come from the actions he is unwilling to undertake.[89] As a result his search leads to a crisis of psychic disintegration.

C makes several changes to the intellectual guides' definitions of Dowel in order to stress the importance of work for the common good. Instead of saying that Dowel wins his livelihood through 'his labour *or thorugh his land*' (B.VIII.81), C's Thought insists that he 'thorw lele labour lyveth and loveth his emcristene' (C.X.79). C's Wit stresses the need to provide for those who cannot look after themselves, adding a condemnation of begging and idleness in terms that echo Will's confession, with its admission of misspent time:

> And Holy Church helpe to, so sholde no man begge
> Ne spille speche ne tyme, ne myspende noyther
> Meble ne unmeble, mete nother drynke.
> Ac thenne dede we alle wel...
>
> C. X.186-9

Whereas B's Clergy tells Will that Dowel is faith in the church's teaching (B.X.232-43), C's Clergy adds acidly, 'and loke thou *do* theraftur' (C.XI.142-8).

Although the intellectual faculties cannot directly enable Will to *act*, he should apply their instructions to his own particular situation, turning them over in his mind until the meaning of what he is told becomes real in his own heart. This can happen only if he looks closely at himself. Scripture puts her finger on Will's problem, scorning his lack of self-knowledge (C.XI.162-5). Her attack precipitates a crisis of psychic disintegration,[90] as Will falls into an Inner Dream and abandons the search for Dowel (C.XI.167-XIII.213).

C changes this episode radically. Will's angry argument with Scripture and Clergy (B.X.371-475) is now spoken by Recklessness, and becomes a part of the Inner Dream, rather than the prologue to it (C.XI.200-306). Godden and Pearsall both argue that C distances himself from the intellectual questionings of the episode by reassigning them from the Dreamer to Recklessness[91] But Recklessness *is* the Dreamer: Covetise of Eyes comforts Will, addressing him as 'Reckelesnesse' (C.XII.3-4), and when Kynde makes Recklessness look in the mirror of Middle Earth, it is Will who looks (C.XIII.129-34). Psychic disintegration is so strong that Will loses his sense of self and merges into the

---

[88] David Mills, 'The Role of the Dreamer', in Hussey, pp.180-212 (pp.194-5); Mary Carruthers, *The Search for St Truth* (Evanston, 1973), pp.81-2. Joseph Wittig, '"Piers Plowman", Passus IX-XII: Elements in the Design of the Inward Journey', *Traditio*, 28 (1972), 211-80.

[89] Davlin, '*Kynde Knowyng* as a Major Theme', p.3.

[90] Pearsall says that this 'crisis of intellect' caused Langland to abandon the A-text at this point (*C-text*, XI.163n); see also Godden, p.190. Mary Dove, *The Perfect Age of Man's Life* (Cambridge, 1986), p.113.

[91] Godden (p.191); Pearsall, XI.196n.

figure of Recklessness. By placing the diatribe against Scripture and Clergy inside the Inner Dream rather than outside it, C suggests that Will is having a kind of nightmare in which he acts out of character.

The structure of the inner dream is nicely balanced in C, documenting Will's slide to his lowest point in the poem. It starts with Will's meeting with Fortune, who shows him the Mirror of Middle-Earth so that he may 'knowe that thou coveytest, and come therto' (C.XI.166-72). Next comes his merging with Recklessness and the first diatribe against Clergy and Scripture, during which he argues that *faith* rather than works are the key to salvation. Then he follows the advice of Covetise of eyes to abandon the path to Dowel knowing that he can always 'confesse... to some frere' (C.XI.5). His nadir comes when he becomes old, Fortune abandons him, poverty 'potte me to be lowe', and the friar rejects him because he is no longer rich. When Scripture preaches on the text 'Many are called, but few chosen', Will-Recklessness becomes concerned for his own salvation, and, despite Trajan's insistence that it is *works* that matter, embarks upon a second diatribe, attempting to redefine the good life in terms of poverty. Kynde interrupts this diatribe, making Will-Recklessness look again in the mirror of Middle-Earth, so that creation can teach him 'Kynde to lovye' (C.XIII.129-33). Thus, in C, the Dreamer's lapse is neatly framed by the two mirrors and the two diatribes.

The Dreamer's lapse represents a disruption of the balance between faith-grace-mercy and hope-works-justice. Recklessness rebels against the intellectual, spiritual, and moral effort that is required in order to do well. He is the cousin of Wanhope, or despair, and he encourages Will to follow Fortune, declaring:

> 'Go Y to helle, go Y to hevene, Y shal not go myn one!'
>
> C.XI.200

So far, Will's response to his guides has been largely conciliatory, but Recklessness is aggressively argumentative. Whereas Will asks for guidance, Will-Recklessness's questions challenge his guides and seek to justify himself. The main thrust of his argument is that predestination makes all kinds of good works meaningless: *clergie* has little value; there is no point in doing the works taught by Solomon and Aristotle if they are in hell; the worst sinners – the Good Thief, Mary Magdalen, King David, and Paul – are now saints;[92] poor labourers 'passen purgatorie penaunceless for here parfit bileve' (C.XI.300). C adds two key points: Will-Recklessness states that he would rather have 'a lyppe of Goddes grace' than follow the teaching of Clergy and Scripture, and that 'At here moste meschef, mercy were the beste' (C.XI.225-33).

Will-Recklessness here relies on faith-grace-mercy rather than on hope-works-justice. He falls prey to all the sins against hope identified by Aquinas: the folly which, preferring worldly things to divine, leads to hatred of God and despair of heaven;[93] the sloth that makes the object of hope seem unattainable;[94] and the

---

[92] Wittig points out that these sinners led just lives after conversion, while Will uses the doctrine of predestination 'to justify an unreformed life': p.230. See also Murtaugh, p.73.
[93] *S.T.* II-II.xlvi.3.

despair that abandons good works and falls into unrestrained vice.[95] Recklessness's beliefs about predestination are particularly dangerous: Aquinas says that knowledge of predestination is concealed from man, lest it should cause despair in the non-elect and negligence in the elect.[96] Recklessness falls prey to both these sins, believing that if he is elect, no further effort is required, while if he is reprobate, no effort can save him.

This speech brings to a climax the tension between faith and works that has dominated Langland's thinking. Will's head (the intellectual faculties) tells him that good works are the proof of faith and the means of winning salvation.[97] However, his heart tells him that that sinners need only believe and ask for God's mercy and they will be saved. The intolerable tension between the two ideas brings him to a crisis of despair caused by self-will, and Elde and Holiness lament 'That wit shal turne to wrechednesse for Wil hath al his wille!' (C.XII.1-2).

Will-Recklessness follows Fortune until his old age, when, humbled by poverty, he tries to confess to a friar, who (unlike Repentance) refuses to absolve him because he cannot pay restitution. At this low point, Leaute appears as Will returns to the search for Dowel by asking for specific advice on his own moral problem – should he publicly condemn the friar. Leaute encourages Will to go on writing against fraternal corruption, because their 'dedly synne' is something 'that al the world woet' (C.XII.36-7).[98] However, he also warns Will against being the first to blame others, publishing private sins, and criticizing out of envy. He advises him 'Thouh thowe se, say nat sum tyme, that is treuthe' (C.XII.38-41) – advice that Will-Recklessness ignores in his subsequent diatribe against riches and clerical corruption.

Scripture preaches on the text, 'Many are called and few chosen', reopening the question of who will go to heaven. Will-Recklessness still relies on faith-mercy-grace, arguing that a Christian cannot renounce Christendom, but is saved by Baptism and Christ's Redemption; the worst he need fear is Purgatory, and not even that if he sincerely begs for mercy (C.XII.48-69). Scripture half-heartedly agrees with him that no sin can prevent mercy, which is above all God's works (C.XII.72), but the Emperor Trajan bursts out of hell, saying that he was saved, not by Christendom, but by 'love and leaute as in my lawes demynge' (81) – that is by *works*.[99]

In B, Trajan continues to praise the life of poverty. C replaces him with the disreputable Will-Recklessness who now tries to redefine the good life in terms

---

[94] *S.T.* II-II.xx.3.

[95] *S.T.* II-II.xx.4.

[96] *S.T.* I.xxiii.1. Willi Erzgräber notes that Langland is interested in the doctrine of predestination, not for what it reveals about God, but for its effects upon man: *William Langlands "Piers Plowman": Eine Interpretation des C-Textes* (Heidelberg, 1957), p.126.

[97] See B.J. Harwood, *Piers Plowman and the Problem of Belief* (Toronto, 1992), pp.152-6.

[98] Simpson reads this passage as endorsing satirical poetry, but argues that when Reason recommends 'suffrance', the Dreamer realizes that 'instead of satirising, he should "suffer"' ('The Constraints of Satire', pp.27-9). However, as I argued above, the main change from the satirical to the penitential mode occurs at the Dreamer's confession.

[99] Wittig, pp.258-9.

of poverty – a quality that has not been recommended by the intellectual guides, and a quality that he himself possesses in abundance. Recklessness praises *leute*, which he interprets as involving, first the duty of the rich to help the poor, and secondly the virtue of patient poverty.

The first part of his speech (C.XII.90-249), derived from B-Trajan, is a moving injunction to Christians to help the poor, because Christ's death has made us all 'blody bretherne... gentel men uchone,/ No beggare ne boy among us, but yf hit synne make' (C.XII.111-13). He argues that patient poverty makes a man remember God and crave his mercy, and that Christ recommended poverty to those seeking perfection (C.XII.146-73). In a beautiful agricultural image, added in C, he uses winter wheat as an image for the patient worldly suffering that will reap a heavenly harvest; he warns that the rich should fear the spiritual dangers of their wealth, which may cause others to rob or murder them, and both murderer and miser go to hell (C.XII.179-249).

So far, Will-Recklessness's speech is full of heartfelt concern for both poor and rich. He seems to represent carelessness about worldly wealth, and is set wholly on salvation. However, in the C-extension to his speech (C.XIII.1-128), his arguments become, as Pearsall notes, very presumptuous:[100] the poor need no virtue except patience; the rich must obey the commandments, but the poor do not need to bowe to the law; a beggar does not need to fast or do penance; the faith and will of a beggar is worth all the good works of a rich man (C.XIII.32-97). The last part of his speech degenerates into a diatribe against bishops who do not pay their clergy, and who ordain ignorant priests (C.XIII.98-127) – echoing the Dreamer's angry and envious diatribe preceding his confession. As Langland says, disapprovingly, 'Thus Rechelesnesse in a rage aresenede Clergie/ And Scripture scornede' (C.XIII.128-9). Lawrence Clopper points out that Recklessness is wrong to rely on poverty alone: patience (a virtue he hardly displays) is also necessary;[101] his 'sense that poverty has perfected him' is a symptom of pride.[102]

The C-reviser distances himself from Recklessness's doctrine of patient poverty:[103] first, he attributes this speech to Recklessness rather than to Trajan (B.X.170); secondly, he omits Scripture's endorsement of patient poverty (B.X.329-40) and Trajan's suggestion that Christ begs 'In a povere mannes apparaille' to test Christians' charity (B.XI.184-7). Recklessness' assertion that 'Oure prince Iesu poverte chees' (C.XIII.3) is in C supported only by Patience (C.XVI.113) and Need (C.XXII.49). Only three characters in the poem – Recklessness, Patience, and Need – see *poverty itself* (rather than the patient

---

[100] *C-text*, p.12. As Pearsall notes, Recklessness's praise of poverty must be read in the context of contemporary condemnation of the mendicant friars (C.XII.98.n).

[101] Lawwrence Clopper, 'Langland's Franciscanism', *Chaucer Review*, 25 (1990), 54-75.

[102] Clopper, 'The Life of the Dreamer, the Dreams of the Wanderer in *Piers Plowman*', *SP*, 86 (1989) 261-85 (p.277); 'Langland's Persona: An Anatomy of the Mendicant Orders', in Justice and Kerby-Fulton, pp.144-84.

[103] Shepherd, pp.179-82. Rudd thinks that Patience's support may indicate that Recklessness is trustworthy (p.187), but does not discuss the less trustworthy support of Need. Scase dismisses the view that C's attribution of the poverty polemic to Recklessness undermines it (pp.77-8).

acceptance of poverty) as a virtue. All of them are themselves poor: Recklessness has ragged clothes (C.XI.195); Patience is 'a pore thyng' (C.XV.33); and Need is the personification of poverty. All of them speak of beggary as if it were a respectable, even a virtuous way of life; none of them even mentions the need for work. Langland's frequent warnings against begging and injunctions to *leel* labour show that he would be very wary of this view. As I have already observed, Holy Church, the foundational guide of the poem, sees the poor, not as agents, but as recipients of virtuous acts (C.I.171-82).

Recklessness should not be taken in the same way as the other guides of this vision: his name hardly inspires confidence; he is identified with Will himself, and he appears at the point where Fortune offers Will the things that he covets. This suggests that Recklessness is a manifestation of self-will. Whereas C's Will may question his guides and even complain (C.X.107-10), he is usually polite, and he actually *listens* to them. Will-Recklessness, on the other hand, first embarks on an angry diatribe (C.XI.200-307), and then runs wild with Fortune and her retinue. When he repents, he embarks on another diatribe, passionate at first, and then merely angry C. (XII.90-248;XIII.1-128). He holds the stage for almost 400 lines, longer than any guide in the poem except *Liberum Arbitrium*. He appears at the heart of the poem, and both of his speeches discuss whether good works are rewarded in heaven, or whether the 'parfit bileve' of the poor is enough on its own. Since these are the key questions that dominate the C-revision, it seems possible that in Will-Recklessness Langland allows himself to vent his psychic anguish at the dilemma he finds so insoluble. All of Recklessness's questions and assertions are answered, soberly, by the next two guides, Reason and Imaginative.

6. Reason, Imaginative, and the return to psychic health

Kynde makes Will-Recklessness look in the mirror of Middle-Earth in order to teach him 'Kynde to love' (C.XIII.132). This second mirror suggests that Will is moving towards the works commanded by St James:

> For if any be a hearer of the word, and not a doer, he is like unto a man beholding his natural face in a glass: For he beholdeth himself, and goeth his way, and straightway forgetteth what manner of man he was. But whoso looketh into the perfect law of liberty, and continueth therein, he being not a forgetful hearer, but a doer of the work, this man shall be blessed in his deed. (Jas. 1:23-5)

In the Mirror, Will sees that animals are restrained and reasonable, while Man is unrestrained and unreasonable. With typical presumption, he reasons with Reason. When Reason rebukes him, saying that God 'soffreth, in ensaumple that we sholde soffren alle' (C.XIII.200, see above), Will is ashamed and wakes from the Inner Dream.

This time, however, he takes Reason's rebuke to heart, allowing it to lead him to self-knowledge, and lamenting that 'Slepynge had Y grace/ To wyte what Dowel is, ac wakynge nevere!' (C.XIII.217-18). In response to a question from

Imaginative,[104] who now appears, Will says that Dowel is to 'see moche and soffre al' (C.XIII.220-1): for the first time he has *kynde knowynge* of Dowel, based on his own experience, and applied to his own moral character.

Whereas B-Imaginative defines Dowel in general terms (B.XII.28-55), C-Imaginative uses second person pronouns to direct his instruction at Will himself:

> Y have folewed the, in fayth, mo then fourty wynter,
> And wissed the fol ofte what Dowel was to mene,
> And conseyled the for Cristes sake no creature to bygile,
> Nother to lye ne to lacke, ne lere that is defended,
> Ne to spille no speche, as for to speke an ydel,
> Ne no tyme to tyne ne trewe thyng tene.
> Lowe the and leue forth in the lawe of Holy Chirche,
> And then dost thow wel, without drede – ho can do bet, no force!
>
> C.XIV.3-10

These lines recapitulate the Dreamer's progress so far: Holy Church told him that he was to be 'trewe of his tonge and of his two handes' (C.I.84); he confessed to having 'ytynt tyme' (C.V.93); Thought, Wit, and Clergy advised him to avoid idleness and *do* as he is taught. The passage positions the Dreamer clearly in the lay life of Dowel, separating him from the 'Clerkes that conne al' and may be able to 'do bettere' (C.XIV.11), and showing that his claim to clerical status in the apologia was false.

Imaginative resolves Will-Recklessness's questions. His insistence on not wasting time does not support Recklessness's view that poverty and begging are the best way of life. On the contrary, Imaginative says that Charity involves both believing and living well (faith and works), and that Dobet is to help those who are poor and patient through no fault of their own, for, it is better to give than to receive (C.XIV.13-16). He omits the passage in which B-Imaginative rebuked Will for writing poetry when he could be praying 'for hem that gyveth thee breed' (B.XII.16-17). In C, Langland has changed his mind, and Reason and Conscience rebuke Will for following this advice, begging for food in return for praying for his benefactors when he should be working to help himself and others (C.V.1-104).

Conceding that riches and covetousness are dangerous, Imaginative says,

> Ac grace is a graes therfore to don hem [growe efte];
> Ac grace ne groweth nat til gode-wil gyve reyne
> And woky thorw gode werkes wikkede hertes.
> Ac ar such a wil wexe, worcheth God sulve
> And sent forth the Seynt Espirit to do love sprynge:
>   *Spiritus ubi vult spirat.*
> So grace withouten grace of God, and also gode werkes
> May nat be, be thou syker, though we bidde evere.
>
> C.XIV.23-9

---

[104] For Imaginative's role as memory and prudence, see Bloomfield, *Piers Plowman as a Fourteenth Century Apocalypse* (New Brunswick, 1961), p.171; Carruthers, p.103.

C omits B's assertion that grace grows especially among the patient poor (B.XII.60-1) and radically alters these beautiful lines to stress that grace and works nourish each other. C thus once again reinforces the view that salvation involves human effort as well as grace. On the other hand, C also omits B's warning that the Eucharist, taken in sin, causes damnation (B.XII.85-91), another example of C's reluctance to envisage God as inflicting eternal punishment.

Resolving Recklessness's questions, Imaginative insists on the value of the *clergie* that teaches sinners to trust that contrition by itself can wipe out their sins, and thus saves them from *wanhope* (C.XIV.99-130). He explains that the Good Thief is an example of mercy, but that works are still important: the Thief has a lowly spot, sitting on the floor of heaven (C.XIV.135-52). C-Imaginative strengthens B's claim that God's mercy is always available to those who ask for it and seek to amend (B.XII.193-5) by suggesting that mercy is always available (without qualification) and that damnation is a result of human will, not of divine will:

> And God is ay gracious to alle that gredeth to hym
> And wol no wikkede man be lost, bote yf he wol hymsulve.
>
> C.XIV.133-4

C also removes the passage in which B warns that the rich man who does not repent till his death-day will be damned, because his cries for mercy will sound to Christ like a magpie's chattering (B.XII.251-2). When Will brings up the question of the righteous heathen, Imaginative says, '*Vix salvabitur iustus in die iudicii; Ergo salvabitur!*' (C.XIV.203-4). This assertion that they are saved twists Peter's text, 'And if the righteous scarcely be saved, where shall the ungodly and the sinner appear?' (I Pet. 4:18).[105] Imaginative expresses a passionate belief that the virtuous heathen are saved, and that good works are rewarded:

> Ac treuth that trespassed nevere ne traversede agens his lawe,
> But lyved as his lawe tauhte and leveth ther be no bettere,
> And yf ther were, a wolde, and in such a wille deyeth –
> Ne woulde nevere trewe God but trewe treuthe were alloued...
> And hope hangeth ay theron to have that treuthe deserveth:
> *Quia super pauca fuisti fidelis...*
> And that is love and large huyre, yf the lord be trewe,
> And a cortesye more than covenant was, what so clerkes carpe!
>
> C.XIV.209-16

C adds the lovely images of God treating his creatures with 'cortesye more than covenant was' and 'loue and large huyre'. These additions recall the grammatical metaphor with its insistence that God would pay the labourer 'yf he parforme and have pite yf he faileth' (C.III.349) and reinforce Imaginative's insistence on God's mercy.

---

[105] Dove notes that the next passus reads the text more accurately and pessimistically (p.116).

In this episode, Langland confronts Ricoeur's fifth anguish – the possibility that God is not wholly good, and that his mercy and love may have limits. C omits B's references to damnation, and Langland here comes close to Origen's heretical belief in the ultimate salvation of all souls.[106] However, as Gillian Rudd notes, Imaginative is affirming faith rather than knowledge.[107] The same question will be debated – again with faith rather than knowledge – at the poem's climax.

In C, Langland gives different answers to the dilemmas that caused Will-Recklessness's crisis of psychic disintegration. C-Imaginative, while increasing his stress on the primacy of God's mercy, also increases his stress on works. He makes it clear that works of charity are more valuable than the mere acceptance of poverty. In the third vision, C continually emphasizes the value of works – by brief adjustments to the teachings of Thought, Wit, Clergy, and Imaginative, and by re-attributing Trajan's speech in praise of patient poverty to the disreputable figure of Recklessness. He thus undermines B's certainty of the virtuousness of patient poverty. The question is finally resolved in the fourth vision.

7. Patience versus good works: Will's dilemmas resolved through charity

In the fourth vision, many of the C-revisions stress the importance of good works and reduce the importance of patience and patient poverty. Will meets two characters, Patience and Active, who are both linked with Piers, but who seem to be diametrically opposed to each other. This dilemma is resolved by the appearance of *Liberum Arbitrium*.

Patience is introduced as being 'Ilyk Peres the ploghman, as he a palmere were' (C.XV.34). Given Langland's continuous criticism of palmers, the identification of Patience and Piers with one is disturbing.[108] C's Patience is a less impressive figure than B's: he no longer carries Dowel with him or gives the final definition of Dowel (B.XIII.136-52);[109] he begs, not only for 'mete' (B.XIII.30), but also for money (C.XV.33-6). C's Patience seems to have become a palmer in the disreputable sense of one who travels about begging for a living.

Piers, 'the palmer gent' (C.XV.132), is a true palmer/pilgrim in the sense that he was in the Ploughing Scene – 'a pilgrim at the plouh for profit to pore and ryche' (VIII.111). Piers sweeps away all the debates about Dowel with a final definition. He says that the patient will conquer because they are capable of the most arduous kind of love, love of enemies, which Piers defines in physical terms:

> Caste hote coles on his heved of alle kynde speche,
> Fond thorw wit and with word his love to wynne,

---

[106] Evans, p.269.
[107] Rudd, p.66.
[108] Godden p.196. Pearsall makes no comment (*C-Text*, XV.34n).
[109] Pace Donaldson (pp.176-7) and Erzgräber (pp.150-1) who both argue that C-Patience is Dowel.

Gef him eft and eft, evere at his nede,
Conforte hym with thy catel and with thy kynde speche,
And ley on hym thus with love til he lauhe on the;
And bote he bowe for this betynge, blynde mote he worthen!

C.XV.144-9

Whereas B-Patience recommended 'kynde speche' (B.XIII.136-48) Piers's definition is more vigorous and practical: he adds the commands to 'Give him eft and eft, evere at his nede' and to comfort the enemy with 'catel' as well as 'kynde speche'.

Patience is supposed to be like Piers, but when Piers vanishes as suddenly as he came, and Reason runs after him, Patience does not. Instead, he misapplies Piers's promise that the patient will conquer by suggesting that patience will bring material rather than spiritual benefits, enabling the person who has it

To have alle londes at thy likyng, and the here lord make
And maister of alle here mebles and of here moneye aftur,
The kyng and alle the comune and clergie to the loute
As for here lord and here leader, and live as thow techest.

C.XV.168-71

These seem curious (and naive) aspirations for Patience. Yet Conscience decides to set out 'with Pacience... parfitnesse to fynde' (C.XV.179-85). This is a dubious undertaking: Piers, not Patience, is the one who understands that Dowel is love; Patience is a beggar, and Conscience himself said earlier that begging is 'no sad parfitnesse' (C.V.89-91); and why is Conscience following Patience, rather than joining Reason, his usual companion, in pursuit of Piers?

Will follows Patience and Conscience 'with grete wille' (C.XV.186). This may be a sign that his will is beginning to operate,[110] but it could also suggest that he is relying on will (the moral faculties) without reason (the intellectual faculties) – a deficiency that is later rectified with the appearance of *Liberum Arbitrium*, whom C identifies as 'a wille with a resoun' (C.XVI.175).

The first person Patience, Conscience, and Will meet on their journey is *Activa Vita*. Pearsall dismisses Active as a scoundrelly, worldly minstrel who grudges all that he does for others, an erring pupil to be instructed by Patience.[111] This is hardly fair – C removes all the sinfulness that fouled Hawkin-*Activa Vita*'s coat in B, and adds it to the general confession in the second vision. C raises Active to the status of Piers's prentice, 'alle peple to conforte' (C.XV.196). Active makes men merry, providing communion wafers and bread, so that others laugh because of his labour; he pleases rich and poor by providing the necessities of life; he receives little reward for his labour, but contents himself with the fact that the priest and people pray for Piers 'And for me, Actyf, his man, that ydelnesse hate'; he wants to be 'bysy and buxum to helpe' all Christians; and he believes that peace among Christians can be achieved if pride is destroyed by lack of bread (XV.194-

---

[110] Spearing, pp.247-50; Shepherd, pp.184-5.
[111] Pearsall, *C-text*, XV.194n.

232). Active's hatred of idleness recalls Imaginative, who was never idle (C.XIV.1).[112]

In B, Patience was clearly virtuous and Hawkin sinful. In C, it is Active (if anyone) who represents Dowel: he performs the physical labour that Will's intellectual guides saw as essential to Dowel.[113] Alford thinks that B's Patience is a qualification of the Active Life rather than a repudiation.[114] In C, however, Active represents a qualification of Patience.[115] If Patience is like Piers in being a pilgrim or palmer, Active is like him in being a ploughman.

Patience and Active dramatize a clash between two possible ways of life, the life of labour (good works) and the life of patient poverty and prayer (faith). In hoping that lack of bread might destroy pride, Active naively echoes Piers's reliance on Hunger to control the disruptive wasters.[116] However, Patience's response is equally naive, saying 'Hit am Y that fynde alle folke and fram hunger save' (C.XV.237). As Priscilla Jenkins observes, Patience 'is almost comically idealistic... Man does not live by bread alone, but that does not make bread as dispensable as Patience implies.'[117] When Active asks what food he has with him, Patience offers a piece of the *pater-noster*, and says:

> 'Have, Actyf,' quod Pacience, 'and eet this when the hungreth,
> Or when thou claumsest for colde or clingest for drouthe;
> And shal neuere gyues the greue ne grete lordes wrathe,
> Prisoun ne other payne – for *pacientes vincunt...*
> Thar the not care for no corn ne for cloth ne for drynke,
> Ne deth drede, ne devel, deye as God liketh,
> Whether thorw hunger or thorw hete – at his will be hit.
> For if thow lyvest aftur his lore, the shorter lyf the betere.'
>
> C.XV.253-62

Given Langland's passionate concern for the truly poor, he is unlikely to have considered Patience's advice adequate. Indeed, it recalls the passage from St James cited by Holy Church (C.I.181-3):

> If a brother or sister be naked, and destitute of daily food, and one of you say unto them, Depart in peace, be ye warmed and filled; notwithstanding ye give them not those things which are needful to the body; what doth it profit? Even so faith, if it hath not works, is dead, being alone. (Jas. 2:15-17)

---

[112] Stock, p.468.

[113] Carruthers points out that the other allegorical figures *think*, but Active *does* (p.117).

[114] Alford, 'The Design of the Poem', p.51.

[115] Godden, however, argues that 'Langland seems to be suggesting the possibility of an enhancement of Actif's life through the virtues of Patience' (p.197).

[116] Spearing, pp.247-50.

[117] Priscilla Jenkins, 'Conscience: the Frustration of Allegory', in Hussey, pp.125-42 (pp.132-3).

Langland's continual concern with the poor and how they are to be fed means that Patience's words strike a bizarre, unfeeling note.[118]

When Active asks whether poverty and patience please God more than the reasonable and righteous use of riches (C.XV.281-2), Patience responds with lengthy praise of patient poverty. Like Recklessness, he shows much genuine compassion: he says that the poor who have lived their lives 'in langour and defaute' may beg extra consideration from God (C.XV.298); he is concerned that riches may 'robbe mannes soule/ Fro the love of oure lord at his laste ende,' (C.XVI.1-2) and prays that all may have *grace* to make a good confession. In B, Patience argued that confession alone was enough to save poor sinners, if they had the patent of poverty and 'parfit bileve' (B.XIV.182-92). C, however, stresses the need for satisfaction of *works*, 'the whiche folfilleth the Fader wille of hevene' (C.XVI.28-32).

However, like Recklessness, Patience presumes too much: he suggests that the poor are more capable of a true confession; that beggars are more virtuous than the rich; that the only virtue they need is patient poverty; that beggars are protected from the Seven Deadly Sins by their poverty and the penance they do; that they 'bereth the signe of poverte/ And in that secte Oure Saveour saved al mankynde'; and that the man who 'for Goddes love leveth al and lyveth as a beggare' can claim heaven by right (C.XVI.96-103).[119] Patience, like Recklessness, relies on faith-grace-mercy for salvation, while downplaying the necessity for hope-works-justice.

Active's view is vindicated when his leader, *Liberum Arbitrium* (replacing B's Anima) appears and resolves many of the dilemmas that have bothered Will (C.XVI.157). He represents the free will that, as Imaginative said, fosters grace through good works (C.XIV.19-29).[120] He is able 'To do wel or wykke – a wille with a resoun' (C.XVI.175), and in his company, Will is no longer separated from Reason. *Liberum Arbitrium* gives Patience some support by remarking laconically that a man who has land and lordship 'Shal be porest of power at his partynge hennes!' and saying that it is *sometimes* his role to suffer trouble and sorrows (C.XVI.159-76). However, C also adds to Anima's names the name *Liberum Arbitrium*, the faculty that is able to 'do or do nat gode dedes or ille' (191) – that is, able to do well.

Liberum Arbitrium does not agree with Patience that poverty is sufficient, or that begging is acceptable. Rather, he stresses the importance of practical works of charity. He warns that Will's lust for knowledge is a form of pride, a liability to its owner 'but if he wel worche' (C.XVI.209-21). He says that Charity is 'a childische thyng', careless of riches, 'As proud of a peny as of a pounde of golde'; he shares in the joys and sorrows of others (C.XVI.296-312). When Will asks who

---

[118] Aers, '*Chaucer, Langland*', pp.25-6.

[119] Clopper thinks that Langland sympathizes with Patience's view, but he ignores the corrective supplied by *Liberum Arbitrium*: 'Langland's Franciscanism', pp.61-3.

[120] As St Bernard of Clairvaux says, *Liberum Arbitrium* is the capacity to be saved: *De Gratia et Libero Arbitrio* i.2, in *Opera Omnia*. ed. J. Leclerq and H.M. Rochais (Rome, 1957), 7 vols., iii.166.

supports Charity's needs, *Liberum Arbitrium* replies that he lives on spiritual sustenance, such as '*fiat voluntas tua*' – appropriate food for a virtue. But whereas B's Charity was purely spiritual, helping men, not with bread, but with the 'swetter liflode' of love and concern (B.XV.184-5), C's Charity is practical: he pays for food for the poor, 'Clotheth hem and conforteth hem and of Christ precheth hem', telling them that patient poverty can help a man to face suffering (C.XVI.322-6). Unlike Patience, Charity sees the importance of real bread and clothing: patient poverty is a way of coping with the lack of these things rather than an end in itself.

In another C addition, Will declares that if he found Charity he would never leave him, 'Thogh Y my bylive sholde begge aboute at mennes hacches!' (C.XVI.336). *Liberum Arbitrium* replies that Piers (who works to provide food) knows Charity most perfectly. Whereas *Anima* said that charity is found not in words or works, 'but thorugh wil oone' (B.XV.210) *Liberum Arbitrium* says that it cannot be recognized 'By clothyng ne by carping... Ac thorw werkes' (C.XVI.339-40). He says that Charity has often been found in rich clothes, and once, in St Francis' time, even in the robes of a friar. However, he says firmly that 'biddyng als a beggare byhelde I hym nevere' (C.XVI.350):

> For nother he ne beggeth, ne biddeth, nor borweth to yelde,
> He halt hit for a vyce and a foule shame
> To begge or to borwe, but of God one.

> C.XVI.370-2

When Will protests that everyone borrows or begs at some time, *Liberum Arbitrium* reiterates that saintly hermits lived 'withoute borowynge or beggynge but of god one' (C.XVII.6-8).[121] This finally answers the question of whether it is virtuous to abandon active work in favour of a life of prayer and dependence on others for support: those who choose not to work must trust to God alone for food. *Liberum Arbitrium* shows that while patience may be the best way of enduring poverty, it is not the supreme virtue: it is not charity, which *gives* to the poor.

Liberum Arbitrium then discusses at length how clerical corruption undermines the charity that should bind the Church together (C.XVII.33-322). He defines the Church as the loving cooperation between all Christians:

> 'What is Holy Churche, chere frende?' quod I. 'Charite,' he saide;
> Lief and love and leutee, in o byleve a lawe
> A love-knotte of leutee and of lele byleve,
> Alle kyne Cristene clevynge on o wille,
> Withoute gyle and gabbyng gyve and sulle and lene.
> Love-lawe without leutee, allouable was hit nevere;
> God lereth no lyf to lovye withouten leel cause!'

> C.XVII.125-31

---

[121] Stock notes that *Liberum Arbitrium* condemns begging, but she does not say how this reflects on Patience's endorsement of it (pp.473-4).

Thus *Liberum Arbitrium* stresses both the need for *works* of charity and the need for the clergy, the keepers of *faith*, to enable charity by their teaching. He integrates Patience's reliance on faith and Active's reliance on works into one higher claim, the need for Charity. *Liberum Arbitrium* finally resolves the psychic anguish that Will has felt over this issue, at least for long enough for him to have a vision of Christ's redeeming love. The next vision dramatizes the insufficiency of both faith and works without the divine Charity that is at the core of salvation history.

8. The anguish of doubt resolved: the triumph of mercy

The high point of Will's personal search for salvation comes when *Liberum Arbitrium* leads him to the Tree of Charity. C describes how the Trinity has planted the Tree of *Imago-dei*, or 'Trewe-love' in the country of *Cor-hominis* (C.XVIII.1-9). This recalls Holy Church's teaching that True-love was the plant of peace, and C-Piers's directions for finding Truth 'in thy selve herte' and building there a church of Charity (C.VII.254-8). C's account of the Tree of Charity is more direct and confident than B's: in B, Will is still perplexed about the meaning of charity and sees the Tree only in an inner dream; in C, Will expresses a confident *belief* and *hope* that *Liberum Arbitrium* can lead him to Charity, and he sees the Tree directly. In B, the Tree is called 'Pacience... and pore symple of herte'; its leaves and blossoms are 'lele wordes, the lawe of Holy Chirche... buxom speche and benigne lokynge' (B.XVI.6-8). In C, its fruits are *works*

> Of holynesse, of hendenesse, of helpe-hym-that-nedeth,
> The whiche is *Caritas* y-cald, Cristes oune food.
>
> C.XVIII.12-14

Thus C again reduces the significance of patience, and suggests far more strongly the importance of practical works of charity. In making *Liberum Arbitrium* (one of Will's faculties), rather than Piers, the guardian of the Tree, C also brings Will himself closer to the practice of these works.

When Will begs *Liberum Arbitrium* to ask someone to shake down some fruit, Elde does so, but as soon as it falls, the Devil gathers it up and takes it to Limbo. Replacing *Liberum Arbitrium*, *Libera-Voluntas-Dei* snatches up a plank to rescue Mankind:

> Thenne moved him moed *in magestate Dei*,
> That *Libera Voluntas Dei* lauhte the myddel shoriare
> And hit aftur the fende, happe how hit myhte,
> *Filius*, by the Fadres wille, fley with *Spiritus Sanctus*
> To go ransake that ragman and reve hym of his apples...
>
> C.XVIII.118-22

Will's quest for salvation thus intersects with the life of Christ. In C, *Libera Voluntas Dei* rather than Piers (B.XVI.86-9) initiates the Incarnation. Schmidt believes that the change clarifies the theology but *loses* mystery and poetic urgency.[122] However, the change seems to me to *gain* poetic power: the sudden shift from *Liberum Arbitrium* to *Libera Voluntas Dei* demonstrates both how helpless the human will is without God, and how eager God is to help Mankind. In making Redemption seem so immediate, Langland uses the heroic theory rather than the satisfaction theory: there is no idea of division within the Godhead, no idea of God's anger. Langland speaks of Jesus as 'a justices sone' who will defeat the Devil 'by judgement of armes' (C.XVIII.126-30): God's justice is expressed in redeeming Man, not in demanding satisfaction.

Up to this point of the poem, Langland has set his narrative against the backdrop of the social and religious issues of fourteenth-century England. With the fall of the apples and the intervention of *Libera Voluntas Dei*, the poem suddenly moves from the moral to the historical dimension,[123] relating a vision of the key moments of salvation history that lasts until the arrival of Grace, the Holy Spirit (XXI.200-213).

Will has a brief vision of Christ's life up to his capture in Gethsemane, when Will awakes, 'nere frentyk' (C.XVIII.124-79):[124] Will, as an individual, is still not able to respond properly to the historical reality of the Redemption. Unable to find *Liberum Arbitrium*, he is unable to act, becoming once again a recalcitrant questioner who refuses to accept either Faith-Abraham's explanation of the Trinity or Hope-Moses insistence on *working* according to the law of love (C.XVIII.182-98; XIX.1-47). Even Faith and Hope, however, are unable to help a man who has been set upon by thieves, until a Samaritan (representing Christ and Charity) rescues him.

Once again faith and hope (works) are integrated in charity. The Samaritan explains the Trinity (a matter of faith) in terms of a hand and a taper. He also insists on Hope's works of love, or *kyndeness:* the only sin which extinguishes the fire of the Holy Ghost is *unkyndeness;* Dives is damned for being too *unkynde* to help 'the nedfol pore'; murder undoes the work of *Kynde*, and a man who shows no mercy to others cannot ask for mercy; at the last end, Christ will not love the sinner who destroys 'charity' by killing the innocent (C.XIX.151-275).[125]

This is C's harshest condemnation of a specific sin: to be *unkynde* is to go against the very nature of God's mercy,[126] and thus to shut oneself off from it. Will asks, pleadingly, whether, if he had committed this sin and repented at the hour of death, he could be saved. The Samaritan says 'yes', *if* he is able to repent (C.XIX.276-82), but warns that persistence in sin makes it more likely that the

---

[122] Schmidt, 'The Inner Dreams in *Piers Plowman*,' *MÆ*, 55 (1986), 24-40 (pp.27-9). Godden regrets the 'numinous' Piers (p.199), but Burrow thinks that C had to 'clear up the mess' caused by suggesting that Piers initiated the Incarnation: *Langland's Fictions*, p.75.

[123] Harwood, '*Liberum-Arbitrium* in the C-Text', *Philological Quarterly*, 52 (1973), 680-95 (pp.691-5).

[124] C retains the end of B's inner Dream, but forgets to start it.

[125] Frederic M. Biggs, '"For God is After an Hand": *Piers Plowman* B.17.138-205', *YLS* 5 (1991), 17-30 (pp.24-5).

[126] White, p.101.

sinner will despair instead of seeking grace and trusting God's ever-available mercy (C.XIX.293-8). The Samaritan concludes by saying that *unkyndeness* 'quencheth Godes mercy' because it is so unreasonable: no one is too poor to love his fellow men with good will and good words (C.XIX.325-33). He offers a partial solution to the poem's central dilemma: God's mercy is always available, but the persistent sinner, lacking the good works that foster hope, may despair, destroying the faith that relies on God's mercy.

The ultimate power of God's mercy is triumphantly revealed in the next vision when Will sees a knight who resembles the Samaritan and Piers riding an ass towards Jerusalem. Faith explains that Jesus has come to joust for 'Pers fruyt', wearing Piers's armour of human nature so 'That Crist be nat yknowe for *consummatus deus*' (C.XX.23). The image allows Langland to stress Christ's divinity. He uses both the heroic motif of tricking the devil, and the romance theme of Christ the Lover-Knight.[127] Both of these, however, construct Christ as an active, martial figure who fights against evil. C adds the line which says that Liberum-Dei-arbitrium is acting 'for love' (C.XX.20), reinforcing the heroic idea of God-in-Christ, motivated by love to rescue Mankind from the Devil. There is no suggestion of Christ-as-Man making satisfaction to God.

However, Langland then depicts Christ's human suffering in his death. Whereas the medieval lyrics use an intimate present-tense dialogue between Christ and the Meditator, Langland uses the more detached third person and past tense to suggest that his vision of Redemption is valid, not just for Will, but for all people in all times:

> '*Crucifige!*' quod a cachepole, 'he can of wycchecrafte.'
> '*Tolle, tolle!*' quod another, and toek of kene thornes
> And bigan of grene thorn a garlond to make
> And sette hit sore on his heved, and sethe saide in envye,
> '*Ave, raby*', quod that ribaud, and redes shotte up his yes;
> And nayled hym with three nayles naked upon a rode
> And, with a pole, poysen potten up to his lippes
> And beden hym drynke, his deth to lette and his dayes lenghe...
>   C.XX..46-53

Although Langland does not dwell on Christ's sufferings,[128] the enormity of Christ's sacrifice is conveyed by the contrast between the vigour of a knight galloping towards a joust and the passive figure who lays down his power and becomes the object of active verbs. Langland stresses Christ's human vulnerability by placing 'heved', 'yes', 'naked upon a rode', and 'lippes' at the stress-point at the end of each clause. The cruelty of the catchpoll and ribald is accentuated by the harsh alliteration on 'c', 't' and 'g'; by the contrast between the springtime imagery of a 'garland' of green thorn and the harshness of 'sore on his heved'; by the alliteration and violent imagery of the phrases 'reeds shot up at his yes', 'nayled

---

[127] As Warner observes, he replaces the lady of romance with Mankind (p.132).
[128] Pearsall, *C-text*, XX.50 n; Aers, 'Christ's Humanity', p.121.

hym with three nayles naked upon a rode', and 'with a pole, poysen potten up to his lippes'.

Langland's account of Christ's death is, nevertheless, understated:

> '*Consummatum est,*' quod Crist, and comsed for to swoene,
> Pitousliche and pale, as a prisoun that deyeth;
> The lord of lyf and of liht then leyde his eyes togederes.
> The daye for drede therof withdrouh and derke bicam the sonne.
> The wal of the temple to-cleyef evene al in two peces,
> The hard roch al to-roef, and riht derk nyht hit semede.
> The earth to-quasche and quoek as hit quyk were
> And dede men for that dene came oute of depe graves.
>
> C.XX.57-64

Christ makes no reproach or appeal from the Cross; there is only the poignancy of the single utterance '*Consummatum est*', the swoon, the pallor, and the closing eyes. The passage is like a triptych, with the figure of Christ in the central position, flanked by the torturers' cruel responses and nature's vigorous and sympathetic response.

Following Christ to the underworld, Will sees two debates about justice and mercy: the first between the Four Daughters of God – Mercy, Truth, Rightwiseness and Peace – and the second between Lucifer and Christ. Most versions of the Debate take place *before* the Incarnation: Truth and Justice, following the satisfaction theory,[129] argue that Man's sin is too great for him to deserve salvation, and insist that satisfaction must be made before mercy is granted. This position, though harsh, is not ridiculous. In *Piers Plowman*, however, the Debate takes place *after* the Incarnation, and Truth and Rightwiseness adopt the untenable position that Christ *cannot* save Man (C.XX.144-51;192-206). Truth and Righteousness are ludicrous figures who rudely accuse their sisters of raving and drunkenness. In *Piers Plowman*, the claims of Truth and Righteousness are not met. Rather they are dismissed by Christ. The sisters are finally reconciled because, as Peace says in a telling C-revision, 'Crist hath converted the kynde of rihtwisnesse/ Into pees and pyte, of his puyr grace' (C.XX.188-9). Truth and Justice change their very nature in Langland's version of the Redemption.

Langland discredits the claims of Truth and Righteousness by placing them in Lucifer's mouth (Milton places them in God the Father's):

> Yf he reve me of my rihte, a robbeth me of his maistrie;
> For by riht and by resoun the renkes that ben here
> Body and soule beth myne, bothe gode and ille.
> For hymselve said hit, that sire is of hevene,
> That Adam and Eve and alle his issue
> Sholde deye with doel and here dwelle evere,
> Yf that they touched a tre or toek therof an appul.
>
> C.XX.299-305

---

[129] Godden, pp.138-44.

Lucifer here follows the heroic theory of Redemption – the idea that the Devil has rights and that God cannot justly use his power to rescue Man. As is usual in the heroic theory, he is defeated by the love and mercy of God-in-Christ.

Christ vindicates the views of Mercy and Peace,[130] sweeping aside the Devil's rights and the claims of Righteousness and Truth: he comes to save 'alle synfole soules' (C.XX.371), a considerably stronger claim than B's 'tho that ben worthi' (B.XVIII.329). He shows that Lucifer's claim is invalidated because he deceived Adam and Eve 'agaynes alle resoun': since the Old Law demands 'That gylours be begiled and in here gyle falle', Christ can 'through right and through resoun raunsome here my lege' (C.XX.377-95). He institutes the New Law of grace and love:

> So that lyf shal lyf lete there lyf hath lyf anyentised,
> So that lyf quyte lyf – the Olde Lawe hit asketh.
> Ergo soule shal soule quyte and synne to synne wende,
> And all that man mysdede, Y man to amenden hit;
> And that Deth fordede my dethe to releve,
> And both quykie and quyte that queynte was thorw synne;
> And gyle be bigyled thorw grace at the laste...
> So that with gyle was gete, thorw grace is now ywonne.
> And as Adam and alle thorwe a tre deyede,
> Adam and alle thorw a tre shal turne to lyve.
>
> C.XX.386-98

Christ's speech attains great lyric power: the alliterative lines are reinforced by repetition ('life', 'guile', 'grace', 'tree'); parallel structures are intensified by the antitheses between the Death inflicted by Lucifer and Christ's restorative death, between misdeeds and amends, guile and grace, death and life. Christ here speaks of *amending* Man's misdeed, not of *paying for* it, and dismisses Lucifer:

> The bitternesse that thou has browe, now brouk it thysulve;
> That art doctour of deth, drynke that thow madest!
> For Y that am lord of lyf, love is my drynke,
> And for that drynke today Y deyede, as hit semede,
> Ac Y wol drynke of no dische ne of deep clergyse,
> Bote of comune coppes, alle Cristene soules;
> Ac thy drynke worth deth and depe helle thy bolle.
>
> C.XX.401-7

Lines 405-7, with their implication of universal Christian salvation, are added in C. They show the C-reviser's great poetic power as he increases the force of the drink metaphor[131] with the contrasting images of the 'comune coppes, alle Cristene soules', and the bowl of deep hell.

---

[130] Davlin says that Truth and Rightwiseness rely on scriptural knowledge of justice, while Mercy and Peace rely on experiential knowledge of God's love: '*Kynde Knowyng* as a Major Theme', p.11.

[131] Ruffing shows that C strengthens the drink imagery throughout the poem (p.108).

Most critics argue that the two debates vindicate justice[132] and follow the satisfaction theory.[133] However, I believe, with Godden and Thomas Hill, that they vindicate mercy.[134] This passage deals with God's justice solely in relation to Lucifer, demonstrating Christ's right to defeat him. Langland makes no mention of God the Father as distinct from Christ,[135] no mention of God's justice in relation to Man, and no mention of making satisfaction. Having dismissed Lucifer, Christ says that his thirst for love can never be slaked until Doomsday when he will 'have oute of helle *alle* mennes soules' (C.XX.414). This stress on divine love and mercy is, as I argued in Chapter 2, typical of the heroic theory.

Up to this point Christ's tone remains triumphant: he uses declarative clauses that suggest his certainty of the truth of what he is saying, and he uses the words 'but' or 'ac' to underline the difference between Lucifer's misguided view and his own correct one. At line 415 the tone changes, as soon as Christ envisages himself, not as a kingly victor over Lucifer, but as Judge of humanity. Now he speaks, not triumphantly about the Redemption of Mankind, but more tentatively about individual salvation at Doomsday:

> Fendes and fendekynes byfore me shal stande
> And be at my biddynge, at blisse or at payne.
> Ac to be merciable to man thenne my kynde asketh,
> For we beth brethrene of o bloed, ac nat in baptisme alle.
> Ac alle that beth myn hole brethrene, in bloed and in baptisme,
> Shall nevere in helle eft come, be he ones oute.

> C.XX..415-20

Lucifer here slips out of the picture as Christ concentrates on his 'brethren'. He seems to promise that all the baptized will ultimately be saved through kinship with him, but his tone sounds tentative. Whereas the only reasons Christ gave for defeating Lucifer were Lucifer's guile and his own divine love and grace, here he searches for reasons, justifying divine mercy with examples of human mercy, and the words 'ac', 'yet', 'but', and 'for' show the fluctuations of his internal debate. On Doomsday he will judge 'fendekynes', *ac* his 'kynde' will demand mercy, *for* man and he are 'bretheren', *ac* not all are full, baptized bretheren, *ac* those who are, will never go back to hell *because* a felon who survives hanging cannot be hanged again, and *if* a king looks at a condemned man *then* 'Lawe wolde he gove hym lyf' (C.XX.425). A time will come, Christ continues, when 'doem to the deth dampneth alle wikkede', but '*if* lawe wol Y loke on hem' then it is up to his grace to decide *whether* they die or not, 'dede they nevere so ille' (C.XX.427-9).

---

[132] Stokes p.268; Bennett, pp.104-11. Marx does discuss the heroic theory, but he concentrates on the Devil's Rights, that is, on Christ's relationship with the Devil rather than his relationship with Man.

[133] Stokes, p.268; Simpson, *Piers Plowman*, p.215; Warner, p.134; Bennett, pp.95-8. Harbert shows the presence of both views in medieval liturgy: 'Langland's Easter', in Phillips, pp.57-70. None of these critics gives much textual analysis of the passage.

[134] Godden, pp.146-9; Hill, p.66.

[135] Godden, p.146.

Langland's Christ thus constructs doom and punishment, not as a judgement imposed by himself, but as a constraint that he may be able to circumvent:

> 'Be hit enythyng abouhte, the boldenesse of here synne,
> Ymay do mercy of my rihtwysnesse, and alle myn wordes trewe.
> For Holy Writ wol that Y be wreke of hem that wrouhte ille –
> As *nullum malum impunitum, et nullum bonum irremuneratum.*
> And so of alle wykkede Y wol here take veniaunce;
> And yut my kynde, in my kene ire, shal constrayne my wille –
> *Domine, ne in furore tuo arguas me* –
> To be merciable to monye of my halve-bretherne.
> For bloed may see bloed bothe afurst and acale,
> Ac bloed may nat se bloed blede, bote hym rewe.'

C.XX..430-8

He veers between the conflicting claims of justice and mercy: he '*may* do mercy of my rightwysnesse', *for* Scripture demands vengeance; *and yet* his *kynde* demands mercy on his brethren, whom he depicts, in terms that recall Langland's concern for the poor, as thirsty, cold, and bleeding. Any idea of God exacting punishment for sin is weakened by this pitiful picture and by the omission of two lines (B.XVIII.392-3) that said that sinners will be punished in Purgatory.

The final constraint on Christ is mercy, not justice:

> Ac my rihtwysnesse and rihte shal regnen in helle,
> And mercy [alle][136] mankynde bifore me in hevene.
> For Y were an unkynde kyng but Y my kyn holpe –
> And namliche at such a nede that nedes helpe asketh.

C.XX.439-43

Christ consigns his righteousness to hell on the grounds that he would be *unkynde* if he did not help his kinfolk. As Davlin remarks, the final appeal is 'to the ultimate reality – the nature of God himself... his *kynde*, being *caritas*, calls for our salvation.'[137] Langland's Christ here rejects hell as a final option for sinners: he relaxes justice by allowing sinners to repent and cry mercy in his very presence, that is, after death. Langland, however, remains doubtful about the accuracy of this prophecy:[138] Christ uses conditional and concessive clauses to indicate uncertainty, and uses scriptural texts to direct rather than to reinforce his actions (as they did in the first part of his speech).

Unlike the Mystery Plays, where mercy rules the world of time, but justice rules at the end of time, Langland here suggests that mercy will ultimately

---

[136] Pearsall and Russell give 'alle'; Schmidt gives 'and'; think 'alle' is more in the spirit of the passage.

[137] Davlin, '*Kynde Knowyng* as a Major Theme', p.15. See also White, p.109; Davlin *The Place of God*, pp.161-2.

[138] Noting some uncertainty, Evans still concludes that Langland's 'overwhelming concept of a God of infinite love and mercy is unquestionable': p.278.

rule in heaven with 'alle mankynde'.[139] This is a message that the C-revisions at this point serve to emphasize. For Langland, justice and good works are essential for this life, but, at the threshold to the next, faith in God's mercy will suffice. Christ's whole speech is ostensibly addressed to Lucifer, but the second half, with its uncertainty, is surely directed at the Dreamer. Will's heartfelt question to Holy Church, 'how may I save my soul', is here given its final, if somewhat tentative answer, as if Langland expressed what he most longed to believe about God's mercy, but at the same time feared to presume that this was God's ultimate reality. This is the moment of most intimate encounter in the poem, the climax of Will's search, a moment in which he experiences God rather than being instructed about him.

At the end of his speech, Christ binds Lucifer, the Four Daughters are reconciled, and Will's dream ends with an Easter celebration of the Resurrection, linking the salvation of humanity and the individual. Will now calls his wife and daughter to join him in reverencing the Cross: that is, he accepts his responsibilities to his family and commits himself to Christ, going to Mass to receive the Eucharist (C.XX.472-8; XXI.1-3). Here, at the climax of the poem, Will rests for a moment from the anguish of doubt, sure that Christ's merciful love has made human virtue possible.

9. The anguish of history: the failure of the just society

All the major C-revisions and many of the minor ones, as I have argued, stem from the tension between two ideas: that sinners who believe in God's mercy can always be saved; and that Christian teaching promises justice – heaven for those who do well and hell for those who do evil. This dilemma generates a strongly linear narrative: Will first observes that a corrupt society can be reformed only if individuals live virtuously, next uses his intellectual powers to discover the nature of virtue, then attempts to do well under the guidance of moral powers, and finally learns that good works are impossible without Christ and Grace. Will's encounter with Christ shows that Mankind has been redeemed and the individual can achieve salvation.

However, unlike Dante, Langland continues his poem beyond the protagonist's encounter with God. The poem's central dilemma leads to a circularity, as Langland wrestles with the problem that, despite the Redemption, human good works are not forthcoming.[140] The final vision of fourteenth-century England shows that, despite the Redemption, humanity *en masse* is as sinful as ever. The last two passus of the poem are unrevised. Although Langland may have died or run out of energy,[141] it seems to me more likely that, on reaching the end of

---

[139] Godden, pp.147-8. Godden does not observe the change of tone and syntax, nor that the speech is no longer directed to Lucifer but to Man.

[140] Aers, *Chaucer, Langland*, p.13.

[141] Russell, 'As They Read It: Some Notes on Early Responses to the C-Version of *Piers Plowman*', *Leeds Studies in English*, 20 (1989), 173-89 (p.175); Godden, p.173.

B, he was driven to revise the poem in the light of B's bitter conclusion, and thus allowed B's ending to stand.

Ricoeur spoke of the anguish of history as enabling Man to escape the self-absorbed 'anguish of Narcissus' by undertaking

> ... a work at once communal and personal, universal and subjective... We may call the new level of anguish which we have attained *historical*, for man appears herein as the protagonist – the craftsman and the sufferer – of the history of mankind on its collective level.[142]

After the climax of the Dreamer's personal quest for salvation, the last two passus return to social issues and the anguish of history – the attempt to establish a just society, and its disintegration under pressure from Antichrist, the Seven Deadly Sins, and the friars. Langland, having suggested the primacy of faith and mercy in the next world, demonstrates the primacy of works and justice in this, and his poem ends in near despair because of the failure of society to embrace the work which would give each life a meaning both 'communal and personal, universal and subjective'.

Early in the poem, Conscience prophesied a just society in which 'kynde love and Conscience' would 'maky of lawe a laborer' and

> Uche man to pley with a plogh, a pikois other a spade,
> Spynne, other speke of God, and spille no tyme.
>
> C.III.462-63

At the end of the poem, Conscience, Piers, and Grace actually try to establish this society. Conscience recapitulates Christ's life, death, and resurrection (69-182), using the indicative mood to assert the historical reality and redemptive validity of Christ's life. He then describes how Christ gave Piers the power to absolve sins, and a pardon. But this pardon, like the previous pardon, is not a final remission of sins, but an imperative that commands continued action, *redde quod debes* or 'pay what you owe' (C.XXI.183-91). Langland warns that Christ will punish those who do not pay this pardon:

> And demen hem at domesday, bothe quyke and dede –
> The gode to Godhede and to grete joye,
> The wikked to wonye in wo withouten ende.
>
> C.XXI.197-9

This harsh vision is surprising, coming so soon after Christ's speech to Lucifer: it is the only time that C depicts God as actively punishing sinners. Although the whole of this part of the poem is unrevised, the C-reviser may still have actively intended this, allowing the bleakness of B's final vision to stand. Langland's account of salvation varies according to the context: speaking of Mankind, he is confident that Redemption has already taken place; encouraging the individual, he

---

[142] Ricoeur, *History and Truth*, p.293.

stresses the availability of mercy to all who ask; when addressing society, the collection of individuals still living on this earth, he sees all around him the hell on earth that sin creates, and he stresses the possibility of damnation.

Moreover, when Grace comes to institute a new Christian society, it becomes clear that *redde quod debes* is the duty that each member of society owes to the rest – the duty to assist in harvesting the crop of truth that will feed all. At the start of his search, Will asked Holy Church to explain his vision of a corrupt society. Here, in the figure of Grace, the Holy Spirit, Langland depicts God's answer. Grace gives each man 'a grace' so that the *comune* will not be encumbered by Idleness, Envy or Pride (C.XXI.214-29). As in Truth's Pardon, these 'graces' or 'craftes' are types of virtuous labour, thus integrating the claims of grace and works. In Grace's society there are to be priests, lawyers, merchants, labourers, artists, astronomers, philosophers, and policemen,

> And some he lered to lyve in longyng to be hennes,
> In poverte and in pacience to preye for alle Cristene.
> And alle he lered to be lele, and each a craft love othere.

C.XXI.249-51

The life of patient poverty is just one among the sanctioned ways of life, but the guiding principle for all is love. Aers believes that this 'reconciliation... is unconvincing because it only functions at the ideological level.'[143] However, the whole point of this episode is that it presents an ideal society in which each member of society will, this time round, give Piers the dues of *redde quod debes* (C.XXI.260). This is an ideal that society tragically fails, yet again, to live up to.

No sooner have Grace and Piers set out to till truth by sowing the Cardinal Virtues in 'the londe of bileve' (C.XXI.334-6), than Pride attacks Unity-Holy Church. Conscience and his supporters dig a moat, filled with repentant tears, but when Conscience insists on *redde quod debes*, the Cardinal Virtues, and forgiveness as prerequisites for receiving the Eucharist, insurrection breaks out. The virtues of prudence, fortitude and justice have been turned respectively into guile, a knight's abuse of power, and a king's claim to be above the law (C.XXI.412-79).

Following this corruption of language and the sacraments, Grace's just society lapses swiftly into the corruption of fourteenth-century England. Will awakes, distressed, poor, and alone (having apparently abandoned his family).[144] He meets Need, who corrupts language further by offering Will the specious advice that if he follows 'temperance', he may, without sinning, take the necessities of life wherever he can find them.[145] Need argues that need has no law, that Christ was willfully needy, and that therefore Will should not be 'abasched to byde and to be nedy' (C.XXII.48-70). Need thus sides with Recklessness and

---

[143] Aers, *Chaucer, Langland*, p.32.

[144] Middleton points out that this suggests that he is still without proper work: 'Acts of vagrancy', p.274.

[145] Harwood calls this 'a travesty of temperance': *The Problem of Belief*, p.133.

Patience, but contradicts the teaching of Grace and all the guides who stressed that begging was not acceptable, and that one should work to meet one's own needs and those of the community.

In Will's final vision, Antichrist uproots the crop of truth, and Conscience calls for the help of Kynde, who brings disease and death. The Seven Deadly Sins return, now no longer repentant, comic, almost genial figures, but terrifying and indestructible giants. The situation degenerates into a pitched battle between good and evil. Once again, suffering turns Will towards good: attacked by Elde, he appeals to Kynde, who directs him to Unity, and tells him, in now familiar terms, that if he loves *leelly* (a concept that includes labour) he will never lack clothes or food (C.XXII.183-210). Will approaches Unity through Contrition and Confession, showing that the sacrament is still valid for the sincere individual, and contradicting Aers's suggestion that 'the only motivation for entering "into unitee", the church, is terror'.[146] However, the sacrament is not working for society as a whole: motivated by need and envy, helped by 'Hende-Speche' and flattery, the Friars corrupt this sacrament that depends upon language to function properly. When the Sins make a final assault, Conscience is forced to abandon Unity and make a final pilgrimage

> 'To seke Peres the Plouhman, that Pryde myghte destruye,
> And that freres hadde a fyndynge, that for nede flateren
> And countrepledeth me, Conscience. Now Kynde me avenge,
> And seende me hap and hele, til Y have Peres the Plouhman!'
> And sethe he gradde aftur Grace, tyl Y gan awake.
>
> C.XXII.383-7

The crop of truth is abandoned, no one is working, Piers and Grace have disappeared, the clergy are hopelessly corrupt, and society is courting the damnation that Conscience threatened. With this bleak vision the poem ends, although it avoids despair by initiating a renewed search.[147]

In the final analysis, Langland always hopes that mercy is available for the individual, just as he always doubts the possibility of perfecting society. Will's continued access to the sacraments indicates that he does not fear damnation for himself.[148] For Langland, the anguish of doubt is neither doubt of God's ultimate goodness, nor doubt that salvation is available to the soul that ardently seeks it; what he doubts is the willingness of individuals *en masse* to seek, and thus to win, salvation. The doctrine that faith in God's mercy is sufficient for salvation may be adequate on an individual level and in the next world, but it is a recipe for disaster and despair in this world.[149] In the final vision, Langland shows what happens if individuals *en masse* do not proceed to the *leel* works of justice and hope that should demonstrate, strengthen, and confirm that faith by building a just Christian society.

---

[146] Aers, *Chaucer, Langland*, p.36.
[147] Rudd, p.xiii. Aers, p.37.
[148] Cf. Schmidt, 'Langland and the Mystical Tradition', p.18.
[149] Stokes, p.278.

But the justice Langland seeks to foster is not the justice of God in any Anselmian sense. At no point in the poem does he mention any need to satisfy the claims of God's justice before his mercy can take effect. Throughout the poem, he stresses that God's mercy is always available, even, perhaps, at Doomsday, for those who ask for it. The problem is that human society is unable or unwilling to respond to the suffering mercy of God with the *leel* works of justice that will enable social redemption.

It is the tension between the individual's need to rely on faith-grace-mercy and society's need to rely on hope-works-justice (human justice) that drives the major C-revisions: Conscience's insistence on labour and communal effort in the grammatical metaphor; Reason and Conscience's indictment of the Dreamer for his failure to do work that 'to the comune nedeth'; the increased concern for the working poor in the Pardon; the omission of Piers's rejection of ploughing; the attribution of the praise of patient poverty and beggary to Recklessness rather than Trajan; the attribution of the final definition of Dowel to Piers rather than Patience; the replacement of the disreputable Hawkin-*Activa Vita* with the more reputable Active; the insistence on works rather than words in the Tree of Charity episode.

Of all the poets discussed in this book, Langland pays the greatest attention to social and moral issues. He is the one who believes most in the value of human effort, the need for free will to align itself with God's grace, and the possibility of doing well when this occurs. His imagination is rooted firmly in the historical world, and at the same time, passionately engaged with the quest for salvation. Schmidt argues that Langland's historical approach allows him to endure the proximate meaninglessness of the history of his own time while glimpsing the ultimate meaning of human history.[150] However, a linear, Christian view of history is optimistic, while a cyclical view is pessimistic, denying the possibility of anything radically new or better:[151] Langland's narrative, both linear and cyclical, arises from his struggle to endure the tension between his optimism (his faith in Christ) and his pessimism (his despair at the state of the world).

This tension creates an *aporia*, a gap in the language of the narrative. In the lyrics, the encounter with Christ was a present actuality, but in *Piers Plowman* the lyrical moment of encounter with Christ in the Harrowing of Hell recedes into the past of a *dream*, leaving the Dreamer to face the anguish of what Ricoeur calls 'the absence of eternity... felt at the heart of temporal experience... permeated through and through with negativity... raised to the level of a lamentation.'[152] It is this anguish at the heart of temporal experience that ends Langland's poem. Langland continually stresses God's mercy and love of God in the figures of Truth, Kynde, Christ, and Grace: like the lyricists, he locates the gap between God and Man in the failure of human response rather than in God's inaccessibility.

---

[150] Schmidt, '*Lele Wordes* and *Bele Paroles*: Some Aspects of Langland's Word-Play', *RES*, 34 (1983), 137-50 (p.139).

[151] Michael J. McClymond, *Encounters with God: An Approach to the Theology of Jonathan Edwards* (New York and Oxford, 1998), pp.65-6. See also, White, p.1.

[152] Ricoeur, *Time and Narrative*, pp.7, 26.

This anguish is particularly acute because of the time in which Langland wrote – a time when the Church was beginning to show the serious corruption and division that would lead to the Reformation. In both B and C, Langland expresses anguish that the clergy, who should help to perfect society, have become so corrupt that they contribute to further social corruption.[153] Nevertheless, Langland is not against the Church itself. Davlin argues that Conscience's decision to leave Unity is not a 'choice against the church', but 'a choice to be faithful to the church by rejecting corruption in some of its members and by seeking Piers, the faithful member chosen by Grace'.[154] This commitment to the ideals of the Church is enhanced in C by the moderation of heretical opinions expressed in B, and by the revision of Piers's account of the Pilgrimage to Truth to include the building of the Church (cf.B.V.605-8):

> And yf Grace graunte the to go in in this wyse
> Thow shalt se Treuthe sitte in thy sulve herte,
> And solace thy soule and save the fram payne,
> And charge Charite a churche to make
> In thyne hole herte, to herborwe alle trewe
> And fynde alle manere folk fode to here soules,
> Yef love and leute and oure lawe be trewe.
>
> C.VII.254-9

The Church, for Langland, should be for all souls the source of nourishment and the refuge from pain, but this vision fails because humans do not remain true to Truth in their practice of love, *leaute* and law.

When Langland's narrative circles back to its beginning, it is with a far bleaker tone: Holy Church, the 'lovely lady of lere in lynnene yclothed', the utterly confident foundational guide to the poem, has been replaced by the besieged barn of Unity-Holy Church; the Seven Deadly Sins, comic and venial in the second vision, have become terrifying and indestructible giants in the last; Conscience, who attempted to set up a just society with the help of the King in the first vision, who assisted Piers and Grace in their attempt to establish a Christian society in the penultimate vision, has become an isolated and imperilled seeker. For Langland, Christian Unity is on the verge of destruction, a destruction that became a historical reality before the birth of the next poet to be discussed, John Donne.

Langland's narrative of salvation history uses the past indicative to convey a certainty that Christ's Atonement has historically already taken place. Yet this certainty of the salvation of Mankind is held in constant tension with the question of whether fourteenth-century society and Will as an individual can share in the fruits of Redemption: the dominant mood of Will's personal search is the interrogative as he asks repeated variations on his two driving questions 'what does this all mean?' and 'how may I save my soul?' As the poem circles back to the beginning, these questions remain without a final answer.

---

[153] See Schmidt, 'The Inner Dreams', pp.35-6.
[154] Davlin, *The Place of God*, p.137.

Chapter 4

Donne's Seeker and the Anguish of Desire

Take mee to you, imprison mee, for I
Except you'enthrall mee, never shall be free,
Nor ever chast, except you ravish mee.

Holy Sonnet XIV

1. 'Seeke true religion. O where?'

Unlike Langland, John Donne wrote in a world marked by the complete breakdown of the unity of the Catholic Church that had been for centuries the most powerful institution in Latin Christendom. Under the Tudors, England experienced reformation, restoration, and further reformation, Catholic persecution of Protestants, and then Protestant persecutions of Catholics. Even when the active persecutions of Elizabeth I's later reign had ceased, the country remained profoundly anti-Catholic.[1] Donne was born a Catholic, a member of a persecuted minority, yet, having converted to Anglicanism, he ended his life as the Dean of St Paul's, and moved from being a marginalized member of a minority to being a key figure in the establishment.[2]

Critics have tended to doubt the sincerity of Donne's 'conversion'. John Carey speaks of Donne's 'apostasy' rather than his 'conversion', arguing that Donne

> ...could never believe that he had found in the Church of England the one true church outside which salvation was impossible...when he abandoned Catholicism he lost an irreplaceable absolute...'Show me deare Christ, thy spouse, so bright and cleare'... [shows] the lasting disorientation his apostasy entailed.[3]

---

[1] Patrick Collinson, 'English Reformations', in *A Companion to English Renaissance Literature and Culture*, ed. by Michael Hattaway (Oxford, 2003), p.27.
[2] Cummings observes that, when preaching at Whitehall and Paul's Cross, Donne commanded 'the most important audiences in English culture': p.366.
[3] *John Donne: Life, Mind and Art* (London, 1981), pp.29-30. Herbert Grierson doubts 'that he ever found his heart quite at rest': *Donne: Poetical Works* (London, 1967), p.xv. Collinson, however, sees Donne's apostasy as 'a kind of fulfilment and dénouement': p.40.

Cummings suggests that in his *Pseudo-Martyr*, Donne betrayed the martyrs within his own family 'by libelling them as *Pseudo-Martyrs* in the work which led to his own preferment and ordination'; he sees Donne's 'conversion' as symptomatic of the pressures 'catholic and protestant, devotional and opportunistic, sincere and insincere' of 'English religion in its most difficult century'.[4] Not surprisingly, Donne's poetry is marked by a sense of urgent religious conflict – 'This intermitting anguish Pietie', as he calls it in *The Litanie* (XXIV).[5]

Critics have seen evidence of both Catholicism[6] and Calvinism[7] in Donne's work. In particular, they identify a conflict between the Catholic view that the grace of the sacraments, dispensed by the Church, enabled the soul to assist its salvation through good works, and the Protestant belief in justification by faith alone. Carey argues that Protestant belief that Man was 'a hopelessly depraved and fallen creature' who could not perform good works or do anything to assist his salvation 'was a recipe for anguish'.[8] On the other hand, Patrick Collinson, suggests that Calvinism's stress on predestination has been exaggerated, and that salvation did require the effort of 'unremitting spiritual endeavour'.[9] However, the key question is not to what extent Donne was a Catholic or a Calvinist: as R.V. Young observes, the seventeenth-century devotional poets as a whole,

> ... bring to their poetic encounter with God varied experiences and draw upon a number of Christian resources – Catholic and Protestant, Medieval and Renaissance... Instead of versified theological expositions, marks of the strain exerted by competing versions of grace and salvation ought to be the quarry of the critic. For it is the poet's sensitivity to the theological tensions of the era that generates the urgency peculiar to these poems.[10]

In the context of this book, the question to be asked is, how did these conflicts affect Donne's treatment of anguish and his ability to resolve it through depicting an encounter with God?

Donne takes a far more individualistic approach to anguish than the poets who preceded him. The medieval lyricists spoke for and to Everyman in the public

---

[4] Cummings, pp.366, 373.

[5] Unless otherwise stated, references are to Grierson's edition.

[6] For example, Carey, pp.38-46; Helen Gardner, *The Divine Poems* (Oxford, 1952), pp. xxii-xxiii; p.131.

[7] For example, John Stachniewski, 'John Donne: The Despair of the "Holy Sonnets"', *English Literary History*, 48 (1981), 677-705; Donald M. Friedman, 'Christ's Image and Likeness in Donne', *JDJ*, 15 (1996) 75-95; Barbara Kiefer Lewalski, *Protestant Poetics and the Seventeenth-Century Religious Lyric* (Princeton, 1979), pp.265, 272. P.M. Oliver, however, finds a 'damning critique of Calvinist determinism': *Donne's Religious Writing* (London, 1997), pp.130-2.

[8] Carey, pp.56-7. See also Stachniewski, pp.702-3, and Martz, 'Donne and Herbert,' *JDJ*, 7 (1988), 21-34 (p.23).

[9] Collinson, p.39.

[10] R.V. Young, 'Donne's Sonnets and the Theology of Grace' in *"Bright Shootes of Everlastingnesse"*, ed. Claude J. Summers, and Ted-Larry Pebworth (Columbia, 1987) pp.20-39 (pp.38-9). See also Stachniewski, p.702, and Oliver, p.109.

context of preaching; Langland showed deep concern for the sufferings of the poor; but Donne's best-known religious poems are almost exclusively concerned with a particular individual's struggle to find God.[11]

Carey argues that Donne's 'egotism' is a source of power, and that 'his poems bear the stamp of self more deeply than those of any other English poet'.[12] Yet Donne's focus on the self is not entirely egotistical. In his Divine Poems, he tells the reader very little about himself, constructing his persona as a seeker after God rather than as a poet (I shall therefore call his persona the Seeker). His powerfully individual voice creates the impression that he is speaking directly to God, agonizing, not over the common fate of Everyman, but over his own fate. This makes the human dilemma more personal, particular, and powerful. The sense that nothing outside his own concerns matters very much, when tamed by devotion to God, enables his persona to beseech the beloved with a poetic energy rarely matched, and the sympathetic reader too is given access to this energy. Thus, in Donne's poems, both reader and persona are able to confront the anguishes of death, psychic disintegration, history, sin, and doubt with a renewed intensity.

In Donne's Divine Poems, the anguish of death is ever present, for, as Carey observes, death alone will bring him to God: 'Dead, he will at least know whether or not he is saved.'[13] This view of death is intimately bound up with the anguish of sin, which may lead to final damnation, and the anguish of doubt as to whether God's goodness will ultimately embrace the Seeker. Bypassing the anguish of history almost completely, these poems are not concerned with the trials of other people (Carey observes Donne's lack of compassion for the Spanish sailors killed at Cadiz, or for condemned criminals and beggars),[14] but only with the speaker's salvation. In both his love poems and his Divine Poems, people outside the closed circle of the speaker and his beloved hardly exist. A few, like the 'virtuous men' of 'A Valediction: forbidding mourning' or the physicians in 'Hymne to God my God, in my sicknesse' appear in support of the speaker. More often (as in 'The Canonization'), the speaker dismisses outsiders and the world in general: as he tells the Sun in 'The Sunne Rising', 'since thy duties bee/ To warme the worlde, that's done in warming us'.

But is this apparent lack of interest in the social world around him really egotism? Is Donne really impervious to the anguish of history? Although Langland agonized over the corruption of the Church and society in the fourteenth century, his allegorical characters were still able to instruct the Dreamer about the 'truth' of Christ's life and death. The apostate Donne did not feel the same assurance that he had access to the 'truth' about God.[15] He did not embark, as Langland did, on a coherent, public narrative about the intersection of salvation history with

---

[11] However, I cannot agree with Cummings that 'sometimes their only satisfactory audience is God or Donne himself': p.285.

[12] Carey, pp.97-9.

[13] Carey, p.202.

[14] Carey, pp.97-9.

[15] Raymond-Jean Frontain, Introduction to *John Donne's Religious Imagination*, ed. Frontain and Frances M. Malpezzi (Conway, AR, 1995), pp.1-2.

contemporary social history. Instead, he used short, lyric forms to focus on the individual's search for connection with God in an age when certainty and unity were lost. The intellectual and emotional difficulties involved in such an enterprise lead to an undercurrent of psychic anguish throughout Donne's work, an anguish that varies in intensity with the form that Donne chooses to express it. As Stachniewski observes, in Donne's Holy Sonnets 'the discipline of a tight verse form is brought to bear on an often disturbed psychic state... the poem's meaning lives in the tension between the argument and the emotion.'[16] Similarly, Cummings sees a tension between the diction and the syntax.[17] These tensions partly account for the diverse ways in which critics have interpreted some of Donne's poems.

Some critics have doubted whether Donne actually does create a sense of dialogue with God. P.M. Oliver complains that:

> ... the addresses to the divine person have a hollow, amplified ring, as if those speaking are not at all sure that anyone is listening... The divine voice is never heard in Donne's writing, nor does it seem to be expected to speak... if one requires sacred poetry to enact even modest contact between the human and the transcendent, then much of Donne's religious poetry will fail to qualify. However urgently his speakers call for divine intervention in their lives, there is no indication that it takes place.[18]

However, it is rare, and, as the response to Milton's Father shows,[19] problematic, for a poet to depict God (as opposed to Christ, or Herbert's 'my Lord') speaking in a poem. To attempt to do so can be to attempt to domesticate God. Nevertheless, God can still be present as what Hart calls an '*absent* presence'.[20] And, as Jennings remarks, 'this absence is not simply absolute. The longing, yearning, opening, and orienting of existence qualifies this absence as a "no longer present" or a "not-yet present"'.[21]

The poet's sense of the absence or presence of God is reflected in his use of tenses. The medieval Crucifixion lyrics use the present indicative to depict Christ as actually present and in dialogue with the Meditator. Langland's pre-Reformation narrative of the search for salvation in a chaotic historical period uses the past indicative to assert the historical reality of Christ's Redemption of Mankind. However, he uses interrogatives for Will's repeated questions about his own salvation and that of his particular society – questions that in the end turn out to be unanswerable. God's lack of response in Donne's poems may, as Lawrence Beaston suggests, represent his 'radical otherness'.[22] Like Derrida, Donne is concerned with 'what is to come, *à venir*, against the complacency of the present,'

---

[16] Stachniewski, pp.685, 691.

[17] Cummings, p.400.

[18] Oliver, pp.8-9. See also Margaret Blanchard, 'The Leap into Darkness', *Renascence*, 17 (1964), 38-50 (pp.39, 47).

[19] See Chapter 5.

[20] Hart, pp.6-7.

[21] Jennings, p.188.

[22] Lawrence Beaston, 'Talking to a Silent God', *Renascence*, 51 (1999), 95-109 (p.96).

and for him too, 'the *tout autre* can never be present'.[23] Donne represents his desired encounter in the urgent-future through the medium of imperatives and interrogatives: for him, connection with God is ardently desired, but never actual.

And yet, Donne's God is not really absent. It is worth recalling Paul Friedrich's remark that although there may be no 'actual quoted, literal dialogue' in lyric poetry, the 'deep structure is always dialogic' because 'the poet, no matter how solipsistic he intends or claims to be, is actually attempting to engage someone else, an interlocutor.'[24] As I observed in Chapter 1, the You of dialogue is always present (even if only to the writer's mind), and this is particularly true of Donne: one of the key aims of this chapter is to show that although Donne's syntax constructs God as absent, his diction, with its reliance on the Biblical imagery of salvation history, makes God a powerful presence in his poems.

Much of the tension in Donne's poetry arises from his depiction of the individual's desire to claim for himself the promises of salvation history. In many of Donne's poems, the Seeker directly addresses the God who acts, not only in Christ's life, but also in Creation and Judgement. This is an undertaking that no other major English poet attempts. Donne collapses all the anguishes into one anguished question: 'When I die, will the God who has saved the historical world forgive my sins and save me?' This question is explored in a variety of forms whose agitated tone and jerky rhythms at times display the depth of Donne's psychic anguish. It underlies 'Satyre III', the Holy Sonnets, 'Goodfriday 1613. Riding Westward', and even, though with less agitation, the Hymnes. That God is never depicted as answering the question is the very thing that ensures the poems' urgency, as Donne explores the tension between his longing for a loving God, and his fear that this God may not be accessible to him.

2. Displaced anguish and subversive form

The anguish of psychic disintegration is perhaps strongest in some of Donne's love lyrics, where he displaces religious imagery onto his treatment of human love. Raymond-Jean Frontain argues that Donne sees secular love as a religious experience that combines the erotic with the spiritual.[25] However, Carey believes that Donne's guilt over his own infidelity to his religion is behind the restless sexuality, the worries about infidelity, and the blasphemous Catholic imagery of these poems; their religious elements are subversive because they have been 'transferred to human love'.[26] Many of these poems are indeed subversive. Their ostensible subject matter is undermined by an angry, egotistical tone, by cynicism and hyperbole, by contempt for the world and its sanctions. Their specious argument and inner conflict generate metre and rhyme patterns that fight each other.

---

[23] Caputo, pp.xx, xxiv.
[24] Friedrich, p.79.
[25] Frontain and Malpezzi, pp.2-7
[26] Carey, pp.36-46.

'The Flea' sets secular against sacred love:

O stay, three lives in one flea spare,
Where wee almost, yea more than maryed are,
This flea is you and I, and this
Our mariage bed, and mariage temple is;
Though parents grudge, and you, w'are met,
And cloysterd in these living walls of Jet.
  Though use make you apt to kill mee,
  Let not to that, selfe murder added bee,
  And sacrilege, three sinnes in killing three.

The poem subverts its surface theme of seduction by its form and by its use of religious imagery. The rhyme and metre contradict each other, the rhyme moving in pairs with a triplet at the end (aabbccddd), while the metre alternates between tetrameter and pentameter (abababbb). The image of a flea as the lovers' 'marriage bed, and marriage temple' suggests the insignificance of unhallowed secular love. The idea the mistress kills three lives in one flea suggests the Trinity, while the image of the nail 'Purpled...in blood of innocence' suggests Christ. Although the poem should not be taken too seriously, its very humour reinforces the triviality of its subject, and its blasphemies open up the possibility of other readings.

One of the most blasphemous and irritable of Donne's love poems is 'The Canonization'. The poem opens with aggressive, reiterated imperatives ('hold your tongue... let me love... chide... flout... improve... Take... get... observe... Contemplate... approve' – ten in one stanza). The rhyme scheme of each stanza (quatrain, triplet, couplet – abbacccaa) again fights against the metre (the first 8 lines shift between tetrameter and pentameter, with a single trimeter at the end – abaabbabc).

This is not really a love poem at all: the stress on 'love' as the dominant rhyme at the start and close of each stanza, has a defensive, almost frantic ring.[27] The world of court and commerce, of worldly success, is the interlocutor for the first two stanzas, addressed with angry spleen by a man who suffers from 'ruin'd fortune'. The beloved herself does not appear until the end of Stanza 2. She has no individual character, and in Stanza 3 she is lost under a welter of clichéd and blasphemous sexual imagery – death, flies, tapers, Eagle, Phoenix and Dove.[28]

The poem is full of angry hostility towards the world, and an agitated (sighs, tears, colds and heats) and highly sexual account of his love. Yet the poet

---

[27] Patricia Garland Pinka, *This Dialogue of One* (University, Alabama, 1982), p.126.

[28] C.A. Patrides (ed.), *John Donne: The Complete English Poems*, 2nd edn, revised by Robin Hamilton (London, 1944), p.11. Carey calls 'die' a 'worn Elizabethan pun': p.43. Arthur L. Clements argues that the poem concerns love's power to transmute the secular into the divine: *Poetry of Contemplation* (Albany, 1990), p.50. See also James S. Baumlin, *John Donne and the Rhetorics of Renaissance Discourse* (Columbia and London, 1991) pp.226-7, and Albert C. Labriola, 'Donne's "The Canonization"', *Huntington Library Quarterly*, 36 (1973), 327-39.

claims he will 'build in sonnets pretty rooms' which will be like 'a well wrought urne'. That is, he will *bury* his love in 'sonnets' that, far from depicting the feverish pains of his love, will be 'pretty' and 'hymnes' – they will be untruthful. The 'urne', which will contain the 'greatest ashes' of the lovers, suggests a pagan funeral, and yet the lovers are to be '*Canonized*', another blasphemous Catholic image. The final stanza, equally falsely, represents *all* future people as praying to the 'reverend' lovers who were each other's hermitage, and who loved peacefully; yet this love is not after all, holy, but a mere substitute for the worldly 'Countries, Townes, Courts' that they 'epitomize'.

'The Flea' and 'The Canonization' (and other poems, such as 'The Sunne Rising') use complex and tense forms[29] to explicitly oppose secular love to the world of parents, states, and geography. By implication, they also oppose it to the eternal world whose imagery it filches. In 'The Indifferent', Donne takes these features to their extreme: the poem uses a ragged metrical pattern (varying between eight and fifteen syllables – abcdaaeee) to undercut the more regular rhyme scheme (abbacccaa); the speaker appeals to the pagan goddess Venus, and makes the untenable and desperate argument that 'I can love any, so she be not true'. The speaker of these poems is often cynical, demanding, envious, arrogant, and full of the hostility of a ruined man towards the world in which he cannot advance.[30] Their specious arguments and subversive forms show the psychic disintegration of a man driven by conflicts he cannot resolve, unable to reach what he truly loves.

The effect is completely different when, in 'A Valediction: forbidding mourning', Donne writes of an earthly love that is in harmony with divine love.[31] The poem focuses on the beloved, using gentle, extensive chains of dependent clauses, rather than the angry imperatives and interrogatives of 'The Canonization':

> As virtuous men passe mildly away
> And whisper to their soules, to goe,
> While some of their sad friends do say,
> The breath goes now, and some say, no:
>
> So let us melt, and make no noise,
> No teare-floods nor sigh-tempests move,
> T'were profanation of our joyes
> To tell the layetie oure love.

---

[29] See also: 'Song: Goe, and catche', 'Woman's Constancy', 'Loves Usury', 'Loves Exchange', 'Love's Alchymie', 'The Message', 'The Apparition', 'The Funerall', 'Farewell to Love'. Richard Radford notes the rhythmic complexity of 'The Flea', but says nothing about the rhyme: *A Linguistic History of English Poetry* (London, 1993), pp.44-5. Arnold Stein notes briefly that Donne's rhythmic patterns can vary from his rhyme patterns: *John Donne's Lyrics* (Minneapolis, 1962), pp.139, 214.

[30] Gardner suggests that in his middle years Donne was tempted 'to sins more deadly, because less generous, than those of his youth – envy, bitterness, and despair': *The Divine Poems*, p.xxi.

[31] A.B. Chambers, 'Glorified Bodies and the "Valediction: forbidding Mourning"', *JDJ*, 1 (1982), 1-20 (pp.1-2).

The complex sentence structure is reflective and thoughtful. The thought is simply expressed, for Donne, and the open-vowel rhymes and soft consonants match it with a quiet and gentle tone. Images of spheres and circles abound, suggesting perfection. The compass image suggests the compasses with which God marks out Creation.[32] The simple tetrameter quatrains carry the argument of the poem round in a circle, from the 'virtuous men' to the compass image that closes the poem with an image of justice:

> Thy firmness makes my circle just,
> And makes me end, where I begunne.

The beloved is directly addressed, and is the source of the speaker's strength and virtue. Here the analogies between the lovers and the movement of the spheres, gold, and God's compasses, suggest not so much arrogance as aspiration.

Carey suggests that Donne's desire to overcome the 'sense of separation' arising from his apostasy is a major subject of his secular and religious poems.[33] It is true that the Divine Poems display a marked fear of separation from God, and, at times, some of the same irritability as the secular poems. In these poems, however, Donne openly confronts his anguish over his sense of separation from God, appealing to God directly. Consequently, a sense of trust and peace finds a way through some of the most agonized of his Divine Poems. This ultimate trust is shown in the way these poems use coherent narratives or arguments within a variety of cohesive forms. Louis Martz sees the Ignatian meditative tradition as the basis for Donne's meditative poetry, and argues that its logical, analytical tendency:

> ... satisfied and developed a natural, fundamental tendency of the human mind – a tendency to work from a particular situation, through analysis of that situation, and finally to some sort of resolution of the problems which the situation has presented...[34]

Carey takes issue with Martz, asserting that if the sonnets 'began as calmly plotted devotional exercises, intended to extirpate fear and despair, we can only say that they failed as exercises, and so succeeded as poems'.[35] I agree that Donne's Divine Poems are more agitated than Martz suggests. They are often marked by aggressive use of verbs, especially imperatives and interrogatives. In tone, they are not so much meditations as pleas or demands. Nevertheless, the 'stories' presented in Donne's Divine Poems follow a logical order which allows Donne to represent both his religious anguish about his own spiritual state, and his sense of God as ultimately loving and trustworthy.

---

[32] Chambers, p.10.
[33] Carey, p.61.
[34] Martz, *The Poetry of Meditation*, pp.38-9.
[35] Carey, p.54.

3. 'True religion' and 'merit of strict life': faith and works in 'Satyre III'

Donne's 'Satyre III', possibly written at the time of his apostasy,[36] begins in an agitated tone, but, unlike the agitated secular poems, the Seeker appears to address himself rather than another:

> Kinde pitty chokes my spleene; brave scorn forbids
> Those teares to issue which swell my eye-lids;
> I must not laugh, nor weepe sinnes, and be wise,
> Can railing then cure these worne maladies?
>
> ll.1-4

Carey argues that 'What agitates the lines, and the whole poem, is terror of hell'.[37] It is true that anger, scorn, doubt, self-loathing, and fear of damnation are all present in the poem. Yet these emotions are worked through in a coherent argument: the flexible rhyming couplets allow Donne to develop a fluid structure in which passages of anguish alternate with passages of quiet reflection. As the Seeker struggles with his longing to find the true religion, something deeper wells up, a fundamental trust in God and the existence of true religion:

> Is not our Mistresse faire Religion,
> As worthy of all our Soules devotion,
> As vertue was to the first blinded age?
> Are not heavens joyes as valiant to asswage
> Lusts, as earths honour was to them? Alas,
> As wee do them in meanes, shall they surpasse
> Us in the end, and shall thy fathers spirit
> Meete blinde Philosophers in heaven, whose merit
> Of strict life may be imputed faith, and heare
> Thee, whom hee taught so easie wayes and neare
> To follow, damn'd?
>
> ll.5-15

Affection and trust underlie this language – 'Oure Mistresse faire Religion... worthy of all oure Soules devotion... heavens joyes... easie wayes and neare' – but the trust is thrown into stark contrast by the single word 'damn'd'. The claim that his father's ways were 'easy and near' suggests approval of the Catholic Church, and the poem takes a Catholic position on the value of works.[38] The Seeker does not fear that he will be damned for following a false religion (a lack of faith). Rather, he fears damnation because he fails to restrain his lusts and follow an 'easie... and neare' religion that is worthy of all his soul's devotion: such a failure is due to sloth or a lack of good works. The Seeker compares this sloth with 'the merit of strict life' of pagan philosophers, merit which 'may be imputed faith': that

---

[36] Carey, p.26. Paul R. Sellin argues that it was written between 1598 and 1610: 'Satyre III No Satire', *JDJ*, 10 (1991), 85-89.

[37] Carey, p.27.

[38] Oliver reads this passage as a 'joke at the expense of Calvin and Luther' (p.55).

is, good works will be taken to include right faith, but merely belonging to the true faith will not make up for a lack of works.

The poem continues with the Seeker's searing self-criticism of his adventuring and quarrelling over his mistress's beauty (ll.15-28). His diatribe comes to a sudden pause with the poem's first mention of God:

> O desperate coward, wilt thou seeme bold, and
> To thy foes and his (who made thee to stand
> Sentinell in his worlds garrison) thus yeeld
> And for forbidden warres, leave th'appointed field?
>
> ll.29-32

The tone is one of self-loathing. The Seeker confesses that his 'boldness' is in fact cowardice, contrasting his aggressive adventuring with God's intention that he should *stand*, defensively. Yet the lines also suggest longing, gentleness, and even certainty. The parenthesis after 'his' forces a reflective pause, and the pronouns 'his' and 'who' affirm that there is only one person the Seeker could mean: their central position in the line affirms God's central importance. The possessives in 'thy foes and his' connect God intimately with the Seeker, with the recognition that their foes are the same. The compressed, parenthetical syntax places the Seeker in a close grammatical relationship with God twice in one line.

The Seeker then castigates himself for loving the World, the Flesh, and the Devil when:

> ...thy faire goodly soule, which doth
> Give this flesh power to taste joy, thou dost loath.
>
> ll.41-2

The inverted, parenthetical syntax places the 'faire goodly soul' first in its clause, with a tenderness that sharpens the delayed, horrible idea of loathing it.

This is the pivot of the poem, leading to the bleak injunction and question of the next line:

> Seeke true religion. O where? Mirreus...
>
> l.43

The poem falls into three parts.[39] Up to this point, the argument has been coherent, with one idea leading directly into the next as the Seeker explores his own soul. This line is cut into three parts, a command, a question, and an isolated name, and it leads into the central fragmentary section of the poem (ll.43-69a). Here, instead of each argument leading to the next, each is kept separate, five minuscule narratives in which five men pursue five false mistresses or religious views. The language here is different from that in sections one and three: there is no direct

---

[39] Thomas Hester argues that the sections satirize failures of memory (the adventurers), intellect (the sectarians), or will (the court suitors), but his interpretation requires him to read Donne's 'thou' as plural: *Kinde Pitty and Brave Scorn* (Durham, N.C., 1982), pp.54-6, 60.

address, but it is couched in the distancing third person; there is no gentleness, but an anger which refers to sects or sectarians as 'ragges', 'plain, simple, sullen, yong,/ Contemptuous, yet unhansome', 'vile ambitious bawds', and 'whores'. None of these sects represents true religion; none offers a right way of believing.[40] The five sectarians may be aspects of the Seeker himself as he studies the various Christian sects in his effort to make up his own mind about the true religion.[41] Their misguided search for true religion is a false and emotionally easy searching for human versions of faith instead of the arduous search for God's Truth, which the Seeker urges in the next section.

The final section starts at 69b[42] – 'but unmoved thou' with a marked change in tone and content as the Seeker again addresses himself, and again follows a logical sequence, in which each idea leads to the next. The Seeker enjoins himself to 'allow' one religion,

> And the right; aske thy father which is shee,
> Let him aske his; though truth and falshood bee
> Neare twins, yet truth a little elder is;
> Be busie to seeke her, beleeve me this
> Hee's not of none nor worst, that seekes the best.
>
> 11.71-5

Although the mention of the Seeker's father suggests that Donne was still inclined to think Catholicism closest to the 'right' religion, the statement about truth and falsehood being twins suggests that he was far from certain. For the poet, born into an age of religious uncertainty, the important thing was not certainty, but the willingness to search ardently for the truth. The repetition of 'aske... aske... seeke... seekes' suggests the importance of effort in the search, and Donne goes on to suggest that doubt is wiser than a foolish certainty:

> ... doubt wisely; in strange way
> To stand inquiring right, is not to stray;
> To sleepe, or runne wrong, is...
>
> 11.77-9

To 'stand' indicates courage and faithfulness to God's purpose, for the soul was created to 'stand/ Sentinell' (11.30-1), and in the next passage Truth 'stands' on a hill:

> ... On a huge hill,
> Cragged, and steep, Truth stands, and hee that will

---

[40] Hester notes that each has one aspect of true devotion: tradition, plainness, perfection, doubt, and tolerance (*Kinde Pitty*, p.64). Oliver suggests that Donne is most sympathetic toward Mirreus, who seeks what was once a real religion, not one that is 'called Religion': pp.54-5.

[41] Carey, p.26.

[42] Hester thinks that this section starts at 1.89 with 'a portrait of the abuses of will': *Kinde Pitty*, pp.65-7. However, will is important at 1.85.

> Reach her, about must, and about must goe;
> And what the hills suddennes resists, winne so;
> Yet strive so, that before age, deaths twilight,
> Thy Soule rest, for none can worke in that night.
> To will, implies delay, therefore now doe:
> Hard deeds, the bodies paines; hard knowledge too
> The mindes indeavours reach...
>
> ll.79-87

The lines express renewed tenderness for the soul, and a willingness to make a great effort (expressed in the verbs 'goe... winne... strive... doe') to secure its comfort. Unlike Langland, Donne is not a social reformer but an intellectual, and for the Seeker, work is primarily intellectual, 'The mindes indeavours'. For him, faith is not something that God imparts at his good pleasure, but something the soul can and must strive to find.

This effort leads to the discovery of a mystery,

> ... like the Sunne, dazzling, yet plaine to all eyes.
> Keepe the truth which thou hast found...
>
> ll.88-9

These lines suggest that the individual should find truth directly in God, rather than in any particular religion. Donne speaks harshly of the religious intolerance that allows kings to think that God has given them 'blanck-charters to kill whom they hate'. On the last day, the soul will not be tried according to the 'mans lawes' dispensed by any religious leaders, Catholic or Protestant, Philip, Gregory, Harry, or Martin. These laws offer 'mere contraries/Equally strong', and to submit to their worldly power is 'idolatrie' (ll.89-102). Rather the soul should seek the true source of power:

> As streames are, Power is; those blest flowers that dwell
> At the rough streames calme head, thrive and do well,
> But having left their roots, and themselves given
> To the streames tyrannous rage, alas, are driven
> Through mills, and rockes, and woods, and at last, almost
> Consum'd in going, in the sea are lost:
> So perish Soules, which more chuse mens unjust
> Power from God claym'd, then God himselfe to trust.
>
> ll.103-10

The poem's ending blends the delightful image of the 'blest flowers' of souls thriving near God, the 'calme head' of power, with a poignant vision of those who choose the 'tyrannous rage' of 'mens unjust/ Power from God claym'd' and may, as a result, be 'lost'. The final image suggests that the Seeker, having given himself over to 'tyrannous rage' in the early parts of the poem, returns to 'the rough streames calme head', and chooses the safety of trust in God: it is 'Soules' that perish, not the Seeker's particular soul.

This poem is the one in which Donne most clearly confronts all of the anguishes: the anguish of a death that may lead to damnation; the anguish of psychic disintegration in the central section, caused by the anguish of the historical circumstances of the Reformation; the anguish of sin that leads the lover and adventurer away from God; the anguish of doubt, which nevertheless leads the soul to an ardent search for the true God. The poem stresses the need for human effort to attain salvation: the value of 'strict life'; the need to 'stand/ Sentinell' against God's foes; to ask for the truth, to 'Be busie to seeke her', to 'strive', to 'doe'; to reach 'hard knowledge' through 'The mindes indeavours'; to 'Keepe the truth which thou has found'. The soul that, rejecting the leaders of earthly sects, dwells near God, the 'calme head' of all power, will be able to 'thrive and do well'. In this vision of an ardent search for the Truth of God, a search that should issue in the ability to 'do well', Donne is very close to Langland.

4. The double tension: desire and separation in the Holy Sonnets

Although Walton believed the Holy Sonnets were written during Donne's ministry, recent scholarship dates them to 1608-10.[43] This makes sense, because of their acute anxiety about the absence or unavailability of God – as Cumming puts it, they seem to be 'Screaming for conversion'.[44] Such anxiety seems inconsistent with Donne the Preacher's belief in Christ's Real Presence in the Eucharist.[45]

Some critics see Donne's approach to God in the Holy Sonnets as fearful and despairing[46] and his God as 'a wrathful judge'[47] or 'a humanoid giant' manipulating physical objects, circumstances and events to express His variable attitude towards individuals'.[48] However, as Beaston suggests, the Sonnets' failure to reach comforting conclusions is not a sign of despair: rather, Donne follows the *via negativa* in believing that salvation can be found even in the experience of God's 'silence, his apparent absence'; this absence only heightens the speakers' 'yearning for God, as well as their sense of their own spiritual aliveness'.[49]

Donne maximizes the technical resources of the tight sonnet form to convey the anguish of this unconsummated desire for God. His arguments exploit the sonnet's divisions, developing quatrain by quatrain, usually with a strongly marked volta. He makes a vigorous use of rhyme and rhythm, alliteration and assonance, figurative imagery, word classes, syntax and rhetoric. To this he adds a dramatic use of imperatives and interrogatives, marked variations in tone and pace,

---

[43] Richard Strier, 'John Donne Awry and Squint', *Modern Philology*, 86 (1989), 357-84.
[44] Cummings, p.398.
[45] The Church of England saw the Real Presence within the receiver rather than in the bread and wine, as in the Catholic tradition: Anne Barbeau Gardiner, 'Donne and the real Presence of the Absent Lover', *JDJ*, 9 (1990) 113-24 (pp.118-19).
[46] Martz, 'Donne and Herbert', p.26.
[47] Friedman, 'Christ's Image', pp.80-1.
[48] Stachniewski, p.688.
[49] Beaston, pp.96, 104.

and sudden shifts from the third person to direct address. These formal devices allow him to convey the tension and drama of the spiritual search.

Cummings argues that the Sonnets show a constant tension

> between the eschatological doctrine which dominates the dictional surface of the poems and the prevaricating and protesting syntax which purports to justify that doctrine but eminently fails to do so.[50]

I agree that there is a constant tension between the diction, or lexis, on the one hand and the syntax on the other, but I do not think that this tension is concerned with doctrine. Rather this linguistic tension conveys a spiritual tension between the idea of God (who is present in the lexis) and the Seeker's inability to be united with him (conveyed in the syntax).

Although some critics see Donne's God as 'a wrathful judge' or 'a humanoid giant, the Sonnets do not express fear of God himself. They fear separation from a loving and lovable God. In them, Donne represents Redemption in terms of the heroic theory – as a three-way transaction in which Man is saved when the loving mercy of God-in-Christ defeats the Devil (Sonnets I, II, VI, XIV, XV, and XVII mention the Devil). Thus Sonnet XV starts by asking, 'Wilt thou love God, as he thee!' and then demonstrates the unity of love in the Godhead by describing how each member of the Trinity humbled himself in the Redemption: the Spirit made his temple in the human breast, the Father adopted lesser sons, and finally,

> The Sonne of glory came downe, and was slaine,
> Us whom he'had made, and Satan stolne, to unbinde.
> 'Twas much, that man was made like God before,
> But, that God should be made like man, much more.

The language Donne uses to describe the Redemption suggests an undivided God motivated solely by the bonds of love:

> ...O God, first I was made
> By thee, and for thee, and when I was decay'd
> Thy blood bought that, the which before was thine.
>
> Sonnet II

> But their Creator, whom sin, nor nature tyed,
> For us, his Creatures, and his foes, hath dyed.
>
> Sonnet XII

In Sonnet XVII, the Seeker asks how he can possibly ask God for more love, when God has given his own soul to woo him. God is depicted as an almost human lover, suffering a 'tender jealousy' lest the Seeker's soul should be distracted from him by the world, the flesh, and the Devil.

---

[50] Cummings, p.400.

There is little in Donne's poetry to suggest the satisfaction theory. Only once, in Sonnet XI, does he mention satisfaction in relation to Christ's death:[51]

> But by my death can not be satisfied
> My sinnes, which passe the Jewes impiety...

The poem follows the satisfaction theory in stressing human inability to make satisfaction for sin, but it avoids any sense of division between God's justice and mercy, any idea of a three-way transaction in which Christ is offered to the Father on Man's behalf. It is not the 'Son', but 'God' who, motivated by 'strange love', bears 'our punishment', and clothes himself in 'vile mans flesh' so that 'Hee might be weake enough to suffer woe', sharing, like Langland's God, his creatures' suffering. The poem makes no mention of justice: punishment is not something that God *inflicts*, but something he *suffers* on our behalf.

In Sonnet XVI, Donne does represent the Father and Son separately:

> Father, part of his double interest
> Unto thy kingdome, thy Sonne gives to mee,
> His joynture in the knottie Trinitie
> Hee keepes, and gives to me his deaths conquest.

The satisfaction theory, as I argued in Chapter 2, tends to a time-bound view of Redemption in which God's justice must be satisfied *before* his mercy can operate. Here the poet follows the heroic view, talking of Christ's 'conquest,' and saying that the Lamb 'Was from the worlds beginning slaine' – that is, his sacrifice is eternal, assured *before* the Fall. The poem asks whether a man can fulfil God's laws, but ends by concluding that God's ultimate law is love:

> Thy lawes abridgement, and thy last command
> Is all but love; Oh let this last Will stand!

Given that critics have argued that Donne dreaded damnation, it is surprising that the words 'damn' and 'damnation' occur nowhere in his poems. The passive form 'damn'd' occurs only twice in the sense of eternal damnation. The first time is in Satyre III.11-15 where the Seeker asks 'shall thy fathers spirit... heare Thee... damn'd?' The second is in Sonnet IX,[52] where he asks:

> If poysonous mineralls, and if that tree,
> Whose fruit threw death on else immortall us,
> If lecherous goats, if serpents envious
> Cannot be damn'd; Alas; why should I bee?
> Why should intent or reason, borne in mee,

---

[51] H.C. Combs and Z.R. Sullens, *A Concordance to the English Poems of John Donne* (New York, 1969), p.301.

[52] Combs and Sullens, p.69. Barry Spurr argues that Donne is nevertheless preoccupied with the issue: 'Salvation and Damnation in the *Divine Meditations* of John Donne', in *Changing Patterns of Salvation*, ed. William P. Shaw (New York, 1991), pp.165-74 (p.165).

> Make sinnes, else equall, in mee more heinous?
> And mercy being easie, and glorious
> To God, in his stern wrath, why threatens hee?
> But who am I, that dare dispute with thee
> O God? Oh! of thine onely worthy blood,
> And my teares, make a heavenly Lethean flood,
> And drowne in it my sines black memorie;
> That thou remember them, some claime as debt,
> I think it mercy, if thou wilt forget.

Cummings comments that:

> This quizzical and querulous poem torments itself with questions and conditions...
> Wishing itself in a state of inorganic oblivion in preference to the imputation of
> sin and mortality, the poem centres on the paradox of the fatal consequences of
> 'intent or reason'... the very contortions of 'intent or reason' in evidence in the
> poem's wracked speech acts seem to prove his point... The state of sin is bodied
> forth in fallen syntax. It is as if the language cannot bear grace. Propositional
> assertion is incapable of completion, constantly giving way to hypothesis or
> interrogation. There is not a single indicative in the whole poem.[53]

This interpretation misses several aspects of the poem. In the first place neither
here nor in 'Satyre III' is God specified as the agent of damnation: in both, the
reference to damning is hypothetical – a question, not a statement. There *are* many
hypothetical questions in the poem, but there is also an adverbial clause of reason –
'mercy being easie and glorious to God' – that contrasts with the Seeker's
contortions of reason and provides a rational basis for the poem.

The Seeker does suggest that God can be angry, asking 'why threatens
hee?', using the third person to distance God. But the question, coming just before
the volta, is a question from an irrational speaker, and therefore may not be
reliable. At the volta, the poem, as so often in the Holy Sonnets, takes a completely
different direction in tone and purpose. In the octave the questions, querulous as
they were, questioned God's avenging justice with the frantic 'contortions' of one
who sees himself as a sinner, more heinous because he is rational and can intend to
commit his sins. The sestet, however, starts with a different sort of question,

> But who am I that dare dispute with thee
> O God? Oh!

Cummings wonders if this is 'an exhalation, a groan, or an expletive?' and
suggests that the speaker is 'swearing at himself, or... perhaps at God,'[54] but he
misses the change of address. The three questions of the octave were directed at the
universe, challenging the justice of God's threats. The single question of the sestet
confronts and challenges the Seeker himself, and goes on to make a direct appeal
to God in the second person. The diction is calmer, focusing on the Seeker, his

---

[53] Cummings, pp.399-400.
[54] Cummings, p.400.

sins, and God, rather than on the agitated piling up of the minerals, tree, goats and serpent of the octave. The calmer tone and diction suggest that the 'Oh!' is part of a plea as the questions and conditionals of the octave give way to two plea-imperatives asking God to make the Seeker's tears drown 'my sinnes blacke memorie'.

Cummings says of the final couplet that it is:

> ...looking for a main clause, seeming to find it ('I thinke it mercy'), and then revealing a further subordination to the ultimate anti-climax of an inconclusive 'if'... The grammatical subject commits suicide in front of us, erasing himself into subordination.[55]

But the last if-clause ('I thinke it mercy, if thou wilt forget') is quite different from those of the octave. Those express a certainty that the condition has been met: mineralls, trees, goats, and even serpents cannot be damned (this use of 'if' is comparable to saying on a sunny day, 'If it is not raining, why should I take a raincoat?'). But the final if-clause expresses a request, not a certainty (as in, 'However, I will take a raincoat just in case, if you will lend me one'). Rather than committing grammatical suicide by ending on a subordinate clause, the sentence expresses the Seeker's willingness to surrender himself to God's mercy, as a Christian soul should do. Although God's merciful forgetfulness remains syntactically only a possibility, the lexis of the poem places this image of mercy at the end of the poem, in the strongest position, suggesting that God's mercy is the reality. Cummings points out that in his sermon for New Year's Day in 1625, Donne spoke of that 'Execrable and Damnable Monosyllable, *Why*' which questions God's goodness, power and wisdom.[56] The 'why' questions of the octave construct the Seeker as an argumentative and recalcitrant sinner, but the request of the sestet expresses submission, trust, and desire for God.

Other Sonnets also show a move from fear to trust. In Sonnet VI, Donne speaks of Doomsday, when his soul 'shall see that face,/ Whose feare already shakes my every joynt', but immediately the poem's volta turns to the image of his soul taking flight to heaven. In Sonnet XIX, the Seeker speaks of his 'true feare' of God's rod, yet, recognizing that this fear stimulates his inconstant virtue, he concludes that 'Those are my best dayes, when I shake with feare.' Sonnet XIII introduces images of fear only to negate them with a strongly marked volta ('No, no; but...') and the claim that Christ's beauty 'assures a pitious minde'.

The Sonnets thus depict a loving God whose motivation for Atonement is love, pity, and mercy: his role as Judge is mentioned only to be denied. Almost all the Sonnets close with an image of the Seeker's separation from sin and death, or of union with God: God's adamant draws 'mine iron heart' (I); Satan loses 'mee' (II); Christ's blood dyes the red soul white (IV); God's fire heals the soul (V); the Seeker leaves 'the world, the flesh, the devill' (VI); Christ seals 'my pardon' with his blood (VII); God put true grief in 'my breast' (VIII); God forgets sins (IX);

---

[55] Cummings, p.400.
[56] Cummings, p.402.

death dies (X); God shows his 'strange love' by suffering woe on behalf of sinners (XI); the Creator dies on behalf of his creatures (XII); Christ's beauty offers assurance of his pity (XIII); God ravishes 'mee' (XIV); God made Man like himself, and then made himself like Man (XV); God confirms the Will of love (XVI); God fears that the world, the flesh and the Devil might usurp his place in the Seeker's heart (XVII); Christ's church is most pleasing to him when open to most men (XVIII). Although these final images are not always represented in the indicative mood, as an actuality, the lexis powerfully suggests the loving God whom the Seeker desires to encounter.

And yet, despite this view of a loving God, the 'note of anguish' remains, as Gardner observes, 'almost histrionic':

> No other religious poems make us feel so acutely the predicament of the natural man called to be the spiritual man. None present more vividly man's recognition of the gulf that divides him from God and the effort of faith to lay hold on the miracle by which Christianity declares that the gulf has been bridged.[57]

The Sonnets' final images of union with God do not necessarily include the Seeker. In four, the ending expresses a positive outcome for humanity: Death will die (X); God has become man in order to save Mankind (XI, XII, XV). Only in three does the Seeker claim the fruits of Redemption for himself, stating, in the indicative mood, that he leaves 'the world, the flesh, the devill' (VI), that God has put 'true griefe' into his breast (VIII), that Christ has a 'pitious minde' and therefore will not condemn him to hell (XIII). In the majority (I, II, IV, V, VII, IX, XIV, XVI, XVIII), the final hopeful image is expressed as a plea or command to God, or as a future possibility. These endings create a tension between the image of an overwhelmingly loving God, and the anxiety of a Seeker who doubts whether that love can save him.

What may prevent the individual soul's participation in Redemption is sin. Unlike Langland, Donne does not tend to represent sin as something the sinner does, something that has consequences in the world. Rather, he represents sin as a force outside the sinner's control, something that he cannot escape. In several Sonnets he represents the Devil as his own personal enemy, a force outside himself who tempts him (I), usurps and steals God's rights in him (II), and to whom he has been betrothed against his will (XIV). For a poet whose verbs are as strong as Donne's generally are, he offers a curiously passive account of sin: sin is *in* his flesh and weighs it towards Hell (I); his sins were sins of suffering rather than action (III); sin has betrayed him to endless night (V); sins abound in him (VII). In Sonnet IX the Seeker uses the quite extraordinary image of the Tree in Eden *throwing* 'death on else imortall us', as if human agency had no part in the catastrophe.[58] This approach to sin is a mark of Protestantism: William Halewood notes that 'Typically, Protestantism concerned itself with sin in the singular, as

---

[57] Gardner, *The Divine Poems*, p.xxxi.

[58] Stachniewski, p.695. Beaston notes that the speaker seems powerless against sin: p.96.

something associated with self and defined as opposition to God; *sins* in the plural were a Catholic matter.'[59]

Sonnet XIX shows the effects of this objectifying of sin:

Oh, to vex me, contraryes meet in one:
Inconstancy unnaturally hath begott
A constant habit; that when I would not
I change in vowes, and in devotione,
As humorous is my contritione
As my prophane Love, and as soone forgott:
As ridlingly distemper'd, cold and hott,
As praying, as mute; as infinite, as none.
I durst not view heaven yesterday; and to day
In prayers, and flattering speaches I court God:
To morrow I quake with true feare of his rod.
So my devout fitts come and go away
Like a fantastique Ague: save that here
Those are my best dayes, when I shake with feare.

In its form, this is one of the weaker Sonnets: the quatrains are not used to mark divisions of the argument; there is no volta, and no marked use of the final couplet; the vocabulary is unusually abstract, and there are more adjectives and adverbs than usual; the verbs are weaker, and they are not used, as they are in Sonnets VII and XIV, to urge the argument along with strong enjambments. Unlike Langland's Dreamer, who could confess to the serious sin of failing to work for the common good, this Seeker's sense of sin is remote from the world: there is no agonized sense, for example, that he may have drawn his mistresses into sin. Sin is not something that the Seeker really *does*. It is as if the Seeker's egotism, his lack of interest in a real world where others suffer as a consequence of his actions, weakens his ability to deal with sin, and increases his separation from a God whom he can approach only with 'flattering speaches' or in fear; there is nothing in this poem about God's love.

Similar effects are apparent in Sonnet III, which does not mention God at all, which treats other people's sins far more vividly than the Seeker's ('Th'hydroptique drunkard, and night-scouting thiefe,/ The itchy Lecher'), and which laments his sin of 'vehement griefe' in very solipsistic terms;

To (poore) me is allow'd
No ease; for, long, yet vehement griefe hath beene
Th'effect and cause, the punishment and sinne.

Sonnet V displays a similar attitude to sin:

I am a little world made cunningly
Of Elements, and an Angelike spright,
But black sinne hath betraid to endlesse night

---

[59] 'The Predicament of the Westward Rider', *SP*, 93 (1996) 218-28 (p.219).

My worlds both parts, and (oh) both parts must die.
You which beyond that heaven which was most high
Have found new sphears, and of new lands can write,
Powre new seas in mine eyes, that so I might
Drowne my world with my weeping earnestly,
Or wash it, if it must be drown'd no more:
But oh it must be burnt! alas the fire
Of lust and envie have burnt it heretofore,
And made it fouler; Let their flames retire,
And burn me ô Lord, with a fiery zeale
Of thee and thy house, which doth in eating heale.

Again, the Seeker's sin is abstract, an external thing, a 'black sinne' that acts on him, not an action he performs. The first quatrain ends with an outburst of feeling, but any strength is dissipated by a spiritual weakness in the following suggestion that one can weep 'earnestly' when one has to ask others to pour salt water into one's eyes so that one can weep at all. This weakness is underlined by formal weaknesses: the argument of the second quatrain spilling over into five lines, delaying the volta; the weak and clichéd adjectives – '*black* sinne', '*endlesse* night', '*most* high' and the thrice repeated 'new'. Again, God is absent from the poem, until, after reflecting that 'the fire of lust and envie' (still objectified) have burnt his world, the Seeker suddenly, in the final couplet, makes a direct appeal to God to act, driving out the fire of sin with his own healing fire.

Carey suggests that, in the Sonnets, Donne's anguish arises from the Protestant elevation of faith at the expense of works, leaving the soul unable to help itself.[60] In the Sonnets just discussed, the Seeker's dwelling on sin, as an objectified force beyond his control, does seem to have a numbing effect on his relationship with God. However, the Sonnets do not, as a whole, depict the soul as completely incapable of good. If God assists him, the Seeker is able to look towards God and 'rise againe' (I); to make himself black with holy mourning, and to wash himself in Christ's blood (IV); to ask the grace to repent (VII); to valiantly overstride 'hels wide mouth' because of his 'mindes white truth' and the 'true griefe' that God has put in his heart (VIII); he loves God dearly (XIV, XV, XVIII) and seeks him with 'a holy thirsty dropsy' (XVII).

Sonnet I illustrates the different dynamic achieved when the Seeker concentrates, not so much on sin itself, but on the way it separates the soul from God, and the need for God's help to overcome that separation:

Thou hast made me, And shall thy worke decay?
Repaire me now, for now mine end doth haste,
I runne to death, and death meets me as fast,
And all my pleasures are like yesterday;
I dare not move my dimme eyes any way,
Despaire behind, and death before doth cast
Such terrour, and my feeble flesh doth waste
By sinne in it, which it t'wards hell doth weigh.

---

[60] Carey, pp.55-7.

Here Donne expresses, not so much the anguish of sin, as the anguishes of death and doubt, with the poignant question 'And shalt thy worke decay?' and the appeal to God to repair him. Without God, the Seeker is helpless, even his 'dimme eyes' immobilized by despair, death, and sin. Yet his very helplessness saves him: the directional words in the poem form a cross, 'Despaire behind' and 'death before' form the horizontal arms, and 't'wards hell' the downward shaft. The Seeker cannot bear to look in these directions, and so the sources of his anguish force his thought upwards to God (the upward shaft of the cross):

> Onely thou art above, and when towards thee
> By thy leave I can looke, I rise againe;
> But our old subtle foe so tempteth me,
> That not one houre myself I can sustaine;
> Thy Grace may wing me to prevent his art,
> And thou like Adamant draw mine iron heart.

Ronald Bond notes the second volta ('But our old subtle foe...'), and argues that these lines suggest the sinner's inability to assist his redemption.[61] However, despite the syntactic uncertainty of 'By thy leave' and 'may',[62] the actual word choice of the sestet suggests that with God's grace the Seeker can act, looking upwards, rising, and even growing wings that will enable him to prevent Satan's art and fly to heaven.[63]

Sonnet II also expresses the anguish of doubt:

> As due by many titles I resigne
> My selfe to thee, O God, first I was made
> By thee, and for thee, and when I was decay'd
> Thy blood bought that, the which before was thine,
> I am thy sonne, made with thy selfe to shine,
> Thy servant, whose paines thou hast still repaid,
> Thy sheep, thine Image, and till I betray'd
> My selfe, a temple of thy Spirit divine.

The octave creates a tension between connection with God and movement away from God. In the first quatrain the b-rhymes suggest a motion away from God: God *made* the Seeker, who then *decayed* from virtue. The quatrain contains these negative movements: original sin was redeemed by the blood of Christ, and the a-rhymes suggest the Seeker's movement towards God, describing how he *resigns* himself to God, and ending with *thine*. In the second quatrain, the movement is away from God: the Seeker used to *shine* with God's light, and his service was *repaid*, but then he *betrayed* his true self, and is no longer 'a temple of the Spirit *divine*'.

---

[61] 'John Donne and the Problem of "Knowing Faith"', *Mosaic*, 14 (1981), 25-35 (pp.32-3).
[62] Spurr, pp.168-9.
[63] See also Antony F. Bellette, '"Little Worlds Made Cunningly"', *SP*, 72 (1975), 322-47 (p.335).

The same tension is apparent in the tense structure. God's gifts are in the past, that is, they have already been given: God made the Seeker, redeemed him, made him shine, and repaid his service. In the present, the Seeker's sense of connection to God seems strong ('I resigne/ My selfe to thee... I am thy sonne'), but as Thomas Hester observes, the analogies (son-servant-sheep-image-temple) become increasingly remote.[64] So too, the tense structure moves from connection to distance: the present in which the Seeker is God's son recedes into the past, as he has 'betray'd' this connection. This initiates a new present in which the devil usurps God's place:

> Why doth the devill then usurpe on mee?
> Why doth he steale, nay ravish that's thy right?
> Except thou rise and for thine owne worke fight,
> Oh I shall soon despaire, when I doe see
> That thou lov'st mankind well, yet wilt'not chuse me,
> And Satan hates me, yet is loth to lose mee.

The sestet is full of doubt and questioning. Susan Linville points out the Sonnet's extensive use of line-onset rhyme, with 'I/Thy' dominating the octave, the repeated 'Why' in the sestet creating a vortex as he describes 'his own alienation, internal division and disorder'.[65] Whereas the Seeker used positive statements to express God's actions in the octave, here he uses interrogatives, the conditional clause, 'Except thou rise', and the negative 'wilt not chuse'. This linguistic uncertainty expresses his loss of firm connection with God.[66] The sestet is bounded by the operations of the devil who usurps God's position in the first line and is loath to loose the sinner in the last. The tense structure again demonstrates a motion away from God: the Seeker says that he *will* 'soon' despair, and immediately does so, for he now *sees* that God will not choose him personally. This is the same sin of despair that is the last to be resolved in 'A Hymne to God the Father'.[67] Although the octave asserts that God has already, in the past, chosen the Seeker, the Seeker's betrayal of himself means that this choosing can be undone, and he can still be claimed by the Devil.[68]

Although the poem ends with an image of the Devil, the sense of connection with God remains very strong. In the octave, God is largely represented by verbs, acting on the Seeker who is largely represented by nouns:[69] God made him, bought him, and made him shine; the Seeker is a sun, a servant, a sheep, an image, and a temple. When he betrays himself through sin, he becomes inert,

---

[64] Hester, 'Re-signing the Text of the Self', in Summers and Pebworth, pp.59-71 (pp.63-5).

[65] Susan Linville 'Contrary Faith', *Papers on Language and Literature*, 20 (1984), 141-53 (pp.150-1).

[66] Bellette notes that the sestet contains 'isolated elements at war with themselves': p.329.

[67] Stachniewski thinks that the poem ends with despair (p.701). See also Spurr, p.171.

[68] See also Spurr, p.171, and John N. Wall, Jr., 'Donne's Wit of Redemption', *SP*, 73 (1976), 189-203 (pp.193-4).

[69] Heather Asals, 'John Donne and the Grammar of Redemption', *English Studies in Canada*, 5 (1979), 125-39 (p.128).

capable only of despair: Satan becomes the agent, usurping, stealing, ravishing, and hating. And yet, paradoxically, it is this very sin of betrayal that brings the Seeker closer to God. In the octave he was a representative man, made, as all humans were, by God, redeemed, as all humans potentially were, by Christ. When he betrays this Redemption by individual sin, he puts himself, as an individual, into Satan's power, and must, as an individual, implore God to choose him again – with an urgency underlined by the repeated 'me' rhymes of the sestet.[70] While the sense of the last line is that Satan will try to hold onto the Seeker's soul, the poem ends with the words 'lose mee', which, reinforced by the double rhyme 'chuse me', suggests that God in fact may choose the Seeker, while Satan loses him. Thus, sin both separates a sinner from God and forces the sinner to rely on the God who alone can save him.

Many of the Sonnets start with a vocabulary that stresses sin, and yet the syntactic movement of the poem is towards God (I, IV, V, VI, VII, IX, XII, XIII, XIV). On the other hand, while the vocabulary largely represents a loving God, the grammar often expresses this love as uncertain: in the future tense, as a hypothesis or a plea. Thus the semantics of the vocabulary conflict with the semantics of the syntax, creating a double tension between a man, alienated by sin, who yet is constantly seeking God, and a God, constantly spoken of in terms of love, who yet holds himself distant. This double tension arises because, in the demand function of dialogue, which Donne uses in many of the Sonnets, there is a tension between the Seeker's request and his uncertainty as to whether God will grant it.

Sonnet VII, for example, opens with a representation of the Last Day in traditional terms:

> At the round earths imagin'd corners, blow
> Your trumpets, Angells, and arise, arise
> From death, you numberlesse infinities
> Of soules, and to your scattred bodies goe...

The first quatrain is vigorous and triumphant: the inverted syntax gives the imperatives 'blow... arise, arise... goe' prominence at the end of lines, and the hard initial consonants and open vowels of 'blow' and 'goe' mimics the force of a trumpet blast. In the second quatrain the mood changes markedly as the soft consonants of 'o'erthrow... woe', make the long 'o' rhymes mournful:

> All whom the flood did, and fire shall o'erthrow,
> All whom warre, dearth, age, agues, tyrannies,
> Despaire, law, chance, hath slaine, and you whose eyes,
> Shall behold God and never tast deaths woe.

The second quatrain starts with a relative clause dependent on the energetic main clauses of the first quatrain. Here humans cease to be agents, becoming passive goals of the action. The compressed force of 'All whom flood did, and fire shall o'erthrow' allows the Seeker to place into a single clause the past

---

[70] Hester reads these as a sign of egotism and despair: 'Re-Signing', p.68.

and future cataclysms that overthrow humanity. There is no concept here of death as a process one might willingly undergo. Instead there is a desperation in the piling up of multiple subjects ('warre, dearth, age, agues, tyrannies,/ Despaire, law, chance') with their stark single verb ('hath slaine') directed against the simple object ('All whom'). The octave ends with a sudden shift of tense from the past ('hath slaine') to the future ('and you whose eyes/ Shall behold God, and never taste deaths woe'): on earth human souls are hapless creatures beset by hostile forces, but after death, facing the eternal future, they should become active, summoned to arise, resume their bodies, and behold God.

In the Judgement plays of the mystery cycles, Christ becomes an implacable judge who damns sinners, but Donne avoids such a cosmic account. As if unwilling to contemplate God in the role of angry judge, the poet here turns from the cosmic story to the individual plane. The tense structure, which has moved between the future and past tenses, embracing the whole of Christian history, changes to the simple present tense as the anguish of death and possible damnation drives the Seeker to turn to the God who can save him:

> But let them sleepe, Lord, and mee mourne a space,
> For, if above all these, my sinnes abound,
> 'Tis late to aske abundance of thy grace,
> When wee are there; here on this lowly ground,
> Teach me how to repent; for that's as good
> As if thou'hadst seal'd my pardon, with thy blood.

With the change from a cosmic 'there' to a homely 'here on this lowly ground', there is a striking change from triumph and fear to gentleness as the Seeker directly addresses God. The thought of his sins abounding above all the sins of the world leads him, not to fear and despair, but to trust in God. The first quatrain was full of a restless energy conveyed by powerful verbs, prominently placed at line endings. The compressed syntax of the second quatrain directed this energy against humanity. In the sestet, however, only one line ends with a verb ('abound'), and as the line is end-stopped, there is no enjambment, no forcing through of syntax and idea. Yet there is a higher proportion of verbs (nine in six lines, as opposed to eight in the octave), as the Seeker pictures himself as being enabled to act by the loving actions of God. The complete, reflective and flowing syntax gives the imperatives ('let them sleepe... and mee mourne... teach me how to repent') the status of requests rather than commands,[71] and places God and the Seeker in intimate connection. The last couplet, with its rhyme on 'good' and 'blood' suggests that Christ's death, unlike the deaths in the second quatrain, is a positive force, bringing pardon. Beverly Flanigan argues that the 'as if' of the last line is clearly ironic, since Christ's blood has already sealed the pardon, and the Sonnet thus expresses 'the faith of the Seeker in a system of accepted certainties'.[72] I would suggest that the construction is only partially ironic: humanity's pardon is sealed, but the

---

[71] Beverley Flanigan, 'Donne's "Holy Sonnet VII" as Speech Act', *Language & Style*, 19 (1986), 49-57 (p.54).
[72] Flanigan, p.27.

individual may still fail to claim it. In this Sonnet too, the sense of sin and separation from God is the very thing that drives the Seeker to trust in God.

The Sonnet that expresses the most ardent desire for connection with God is Sonnet XIV:

> Batter my heart, three person'd God; for, you
> As yet but knocke, breathe, shine, and seeke to mend;
> That I may rise, and stand, o'erthrow mee,'and bend
> Your force, to breake, blowe, burn and make me new.

There are several tensions in the grammar of this poem, especially in its use of verbs. Donne's poems have more verbs than the average for English poetry,[73]and this is one of his most verbal. It has thirty-one processes,[74] more than two per line, and fourteen of these are in the first quatrain. Since God is the subject of most of them, the poem appears at first sight to represent him as a very active force. Yet several of these verbs depend on bald imperatives ('Batter... o'erthrow... bend') that are addressed to God, and the tone suggests that these are commands, not prayers.[75] The Seeker complains that God, when left to his own devices, is too gentle: 'for, you/ As yet but knocke, breathe, shine, and seeke to mend': the first four of these verbs are intransitive, not acting directly on an object. If the Seeker is to become capable of the actions of rising and standing, God must act more vigorously, actually *mending* with the transitive verbs [76] that the Seeker now enjoins: 'bend Your force, to breake, blowe, burn and make me new.'

Cummings argues that the poem is 'blasphemous in its strident command, bullying God to take the dominating role in the partnership with self-consciously masochistic bravado'.[77] However, Ernest B. Gilman points out that this imagery follows the English Reformation's iconoclasm, echoing the passage which Donne used in a sermon against idolatrous images,

> And ye shall overthrow their altars, and break their pillars, and burn their groves with fire; and ye shall hew down the graven images of their gods, and destroy the names of them out of that place. (Deut.12:3)

Gilman comments

> Hence... even the Christian mended by the Reformation ('a faint discontinuing of idolatry') if he would 'rise, and stand' must compel God to more radical acts of

---

[73] Josephine Miles, 'Ifs, Ands, Buts for the Reader of John Donne', in *Just So Much Honour*, ed. Peter A. Fiore (University Park and London, 1972), pp.273-91 (p.275).

[74]Michael Gregory, 'A Theory for Stylistics – Exemplified', *Language and Style*, 7 (1974), 108-18 (p.116).

[75] Martin Coyle, 'The Subject and the Sonnet', *English*, 43 (1994), 139-50 (p.144).

[76] Radford notes 'the use of transitive verbs to present God as active and the speaker as passive': p.49. He does not distinguish between the transitive and intransitive verbs predicated of God.

[77] Cummings, p.397.

> destruction... the work of iconoclasm... must be completed morally in the heart still drawn to the lure of '*their images*'.[78]

If he is made new, he will become once again the true image of God.

The second quatrain explains the need for this more urgent action:

> I, like an usurpt towne, to'another due,
> Labour to'admit you, but Oh, to no end,
> Reason your viceroy in mee, mee should defend,
> But is captiv'd, and proves weake or untrue.

There are fewer verbs in this quatrain, as the Seeker pictures his inability to act while 'usurpt' by the devil: he labours, but 'to no end'; the Reason that should defend him is 'captiv'd... weake or untrue'. The passive forms, 'usurpt... captiv'd... betroth'd' suggest again that sin is something forced on the soul rather than something it does. Cummings comments that: 'No amount of good works (Labour to'admit you') can possibly be fruitful.'[79]

However, as in many of the Sonnets, the very helplessness induced by the consciousness of sin propels the soul towards God with renewed vehemence. There is a marked turn at the volta, where the Seeker claims that he is the one who loves, and this action of the soul unleashes a further flurry of verbs, urging God into action:

> Yet dearely'I love you,'and would be loved faine,
> But am betroth'd unto your enemie:
> Divorce mee,'untie, or breake that knot againe,
> Take mee to you, imprison mee, for I
> Except you'enthrall mee, never shall be free,
> Nor ever chast, except you ravish mee.

Interpreting Donne's imperatives (rather strangely, since they so clearly address God) as 'solipsistic', Cummings argues that:

> ... it is hard to perceive the poem as being within God's hearing: these are shouts in the dark, with a strangely directionless and unmotivated energy of articulation. The violence is over-determined, as if in compensation for the marked absence of the violent intervention of grace.[80]

It is true that there is a great tension in the syntax of this poem, arising from the frequent changes of direction (but... But... Yet... But... Except... except) and the Seeker's repeated pleas to God to act, which suggest that God has so far declined to do so. Yet the imagery places God in positions of ever increasing intimacy with

---

[78] Ernest B. Gilman, *Iconoclasm and Poetry in the English Reformation* (Chicago and London, 1986), pp.128-9.

[79] Cummings, p.398.

[80] Cummings, p.397. See also Mary Ann Koory, ' "England's Second Austine"', *JDJ*, 17 (1998), 137-61 (p.156).

the soul: in the first quatrain, he is a blacksmith (or glassblower)[81] trying to mend an inanimate object; in the second, a general who is begged to relieve a town whose populace longs to admit him; in the sestet a master enthralling a slave; and finally a lover ravishing a woman.

Cummings accuses the poem of 'raucous sexuality',[82] but Gilman notes that 'The tangled snare coupling idolatry with adultery and fornication is both traditional in the literature of iconoclasm and deeply personal for Donne.'[83] Although the word 'ravish' can mean 'rape', it can also mean 'To transport *in spirit* without bodily removal... to carry away with rapture, to entrance' (*OED* 2a). It is the word that Donne's younger contemporary, Frances Quarles, uses in 'On Zacheus' to describe Zacheus's response to Christ:

> Down came *Zacheus*, ravisht from the Tree;
> Bird that was shot ne're dropt so quicke as he.

The double meaning of the word and its soft consonants allow Donne to mute the shocking image of God as a rapist.

Like the imagery, the sound patterns also show a movement towards intimacy. Noting the poem's irregular metre, Craig Payne says that the pure iambic metre of the final couplet 'reflects the peace found as the poem finds its spiritual resolution',[84] and other sound patterns reinforce this. While the a-rhymes of the octave are on an open vowel, the b-rhymes end with a harsh 'd'. In the first quatrain the hard consonants, b, p, g, k, d, and the listing of monosyllabic verbs mimic the imagery of smith and forge. In the second quatrain, clusters of consonants break up the lines into a jerky rhythm, mimicking the labour of the soul: 'usurpt towne', 'to'admit you' 'should defend,/ But is captiv'd.' However, in the sestet, while there are still some hard consonants, many of the verbal phrases start with softer consonants or vowels: 'love', 'would be loved', 'untie', 'imprison mee', 'enthrall mee', 'shall be free', 'ravish mee'. Two of the rhyme pairs are on open vowels, and the other ends on the gentler 'n' sound. There is a particular openness in the last three lines which all end on an open vowel.

These last three lines place the soul in intimate connection with God:[85] there are no participants except the soul and God, and no nouns, only the intimacy of pronouns: 'mee... you... mee... I... you... mee... you... mee' – eight pronouns (plus two more implied in the imperatives) in three lines.[86] The hammer-like blows of the verbs in the first quatrain and the choppy syntax of the second are replaced

---

[81] Tunis Romein, 'Donne's "Holy Sonnet XIV"', *Explicator*, 42 (1984), 12-14 (pp.13-14). David K. Cornelius suggests a progression from the Father's power, to the Son's wisdom, to the Spirit's love: 'Donne's Holy Sonnet XIV', *Explicator* 24 (1965), Item 25.

[82] Cummings, p.397.

[83] Gilman, p.130.

[84] Craig Payne, 'Donne's Holy Sonnet XIV', *Explicator*, 54 (1996), 209-13 (p.212).

[85] Stachniewski says that the lines follow the Calvinist doctrine of irresistible grace: p.689. However, Hester cites Donne's Sermon V: 'God saves no man without or against his will': 'Re-Signing', p.65.

[86] See also Gregory, p.115.

by full clauses in which the subject, verb, and object are fully expressed (except for one compression in 'Nor ever chast'). Donne does not attempt to convey a vision of God: rather he seeks to portray the dynamics and direction of the soul's relationship with God through an intimate web of connectives,[87] pronouns[88] and verbs. The sestet's intimate imagery, its connected syntax, and its gentleness of sound and tone, all suggest trust in God's final response.

In the Sonnets, all the anguishes – the fear of death and damnation due to sin, the fear of psychic disintegration shown in the tensions of language and syntax, the doubt as to whether the individual can claim the promises of salvation history – are subsumed into one overwhelming anguish – the anguished desire for a loving God who is always just out of reach.

Yet at the same time, in Sonnet after Sonnet, the anguish of doubt, the Seeker's sense of separation from God engendered by his sinfulness, his fear that God may not choose him as an individual, provides the very force that impels him to seek God. As Beaston says, although even the hopeful Sonnets 'never attain the certainty of God's favour',[89] this only increases the sense of the Seeker's longing:

> ...by juxtaposing the speaker's cries for God's grace with God's silence, Donne intensifies the desire of the speaker in the face of his inability to do or say anything to fulfil that desire... In fact, in all the sonnets addressed to God, God is present in the very words of the pray-er... The very turning of the speaker to God, therefore, is a sign and symptom of God's working in the life of the speaker.[90]

The syntax of the Sonnets presents encounter with God as being just out of reach, in some future or hypothetical time, and yet the narrative direction of these poems is overwhelmingly towards God, and the 'story' of each, while marked by tension and anguish, is nevertheless worked out logically. Sonnet after Sonnet issues in a dialogue with God, sometimes with a dramatic grammatical shift as the Seeker switches from the third person to the second. The tension of the syntax is counterbalanced by a vocabulary which overwhelmingly constructs God as the source of loving actions, particularly towards the end of the poems: the Spirit made his temple in the human breast, the Father adopted lesser sons, and the Son left his glory and died for 'Us whom he'had made' (XV); the Creator died for his Creatures who had made themselves his foes (XII); God gave his own soul to woo the Seeker's and suffers a 'tender jealousy' lest the soul should not respond (XVII); God is a liberator and a lover who mercifully forgets sins (IX) and imprisons the soul from bondage to freedom, and ravishes it from lust to chastity (XIV) and whose grace draws the heart and soul away from the devil (I, VI); the burning zeal of the Lord is healing (V) and he puts true (healing) grief in the breast (VIII); Christ's 'beauteous forme assures a piteous minde' (XIII), and he has

---

[87] Miles notes that Donne averages 24 connectives in ten lines, other English poets 12-18: p.275.
[88] Radford notes the 'almost obsessive emphasis upon personal pronouns' in 'The Flea': p.42.
[89] Beaston, p.98.
[90] Beaston, pp.103-5.

sealed our pardon with his blood (VII) and dyed red souls to white (IV); God clothed himself in man's flesh so as to be weak enough to suffer woe (XI), and his law and command are summed up in love (XVI). Thus, while the syntax of the Sonnets often expresses doubt whether the Seeker can access God's love and mercy, the narrative direction of the poems, moving towards closing lines which emphasize God's goodness, suggests that faith and desire are ultimately stronger than fear and doubt.

5. 'Goodfriday, 1613. Riding Westward': the journey towards encounter

In 'Goodfriday, 1613. Riding Westward', the tone and feeling are quite different from the Sonnets. After the tensions of the tight sonnet form, the easier form of rhymed couplets allows a slower, more reflective approach to the topic. There is anguish in the poem, but, unlike the anguish of the Sonnets, this anguish is centred more on God's suffering in the Incarnation than on Donne's personal anguish. There is less sense of a religious crisis and a greater sense of encounter with Christ.

The Crucifixion is perhaps the most difficult topic of all for a Christian poet, since for full expression it requires a balancing of Christ's godhead with his humanity. Although they touched on Christ's divinity, the medieval lyrics emphasized his human suffering; although Langland portrayed Christ's suffering, he emphasized his divinity. In 'Goodfriday, 1613' Donne attempts to place the individual soul in direct relationship with a crucified Christ who is equally human and divine, and the difficulty of this task is shown by his tentative, oblique method.

Unlike the Sonnets, the poem opens in an erudite, intellectual tone:

> Let mans Soule be a Spheare, and then, in this,
> The intelligence that moves, devotion is,
> And as the other Spheares, by being growne
> Subject to forraigne motions, lose their owne,
> And being by others hurried every day,
> Scarce in a yeare their naturall forme obey:
> Pleasure or businesse, so, our Soules admit
> For their first mover, and are whirld by it.
>
> ll.1-8

These lines form a single sentence, a complex chain of clauses teasing out a puzzling cosmological image,[91] as if calmly working out a mathematical problem. The Seeker is not made present in these lines, and God, since he does not act as 'first mover' here, is both suggested and kept distant by this abstract term.[92]

---

[91] For a discussion of this image see Patrides, p.356, and Carol M. Sicherman, 'Donne's Discoveries,' *SEL*, 11 (1971), 69-88.

[92] For possible sources of Donne's 'prime mover', see Gardner, *The Divine Poems*, pp.99, 156-7.

Gilman sees 'a kind of Euclidean arrogance' in this opening,[93] but the feeling of a merely intellectual exploration dissipates on a closer reading. The opening starts in the third person, proposing that 'mans Soule' should be considered as a sphere, but when the Seeker leaves his description of the spheres and reaches the second part of the proposition, he uses the first person plural to include himself in the analogy: 'Pleasure or businesse, so, our Soules admit'. The idea of *souls* taking 'Pleasure or businesse' as their 'first mover' and the object of their 'devotion', is shocking. The lines display an understated but terrifying sense of the powerlessness that comes from this unnatural choice: souls lose their own motion, becoming passive, 'hurried' by others, unable to obey 'their naturall forme', and 'whirld' by their false Prime Mover. The opening is essentially a confession of the Seeker's weakness and loss of control, and leads directly to the 'Hence' that opens the next section, in which he expands on his own inadequacy.

After the linguistic and technical complexity of the opening sentence, the next couplet offers a stark contrast. The Seeker uses simple language to make two simple statements about himself, linked by a simple conjunction, 'when':

> Hence is't, that I am carryed towards the West
> This day, when my Soules forme bends toward the East.

ll.9-10

The Seeker, having submitted to the wrong Prime Mover, is powerless and passive, 'carried' westward, against his soul's natural bent. By contrast with the indeterminate 'every day' and 'a year' of the opening lines, 'This day' suggests that Good Friday is the only day in the whole of time that matters; the words are stressed by being placed at the beginning of the line, with an early caesura afterwards. The words assert both the timelessness of the First Good Friday and its continuing significance to each Christian soul who must grasp its meaning.[94]

Although the Seeker is moving westward, the couplet moves eastward, to an imagined vision of what the Seeker cannot see:

> There I should see a Sunne, by rising set,
> And by that setting endlesse day beget;
> But that Christ on this Crosse, did rise and fall,
> Sinne had eternally benighted all.

ll.11-14

The lines seem curiously lacking in passion for Donne: there is no enjambment, no spilling over of meaning and feeling. The opening conditional verb excludes the Seeker from the action: he cannot see the saving action described. In Sonnet XV, the sharp image, '*the* Sonne of glory came downe, and was slaine', renews the old pun with touching force. Here *a* Sun remains symbolic, prevented from fully

---

[93] Gilman, p.146. See also Friedman, 'Memory and the Art of Salvation in Donne's Good Friday Poem', *English Literary Renaissance*, 3 (1973), 420-37.

[94] Frances Malpezzi, 'Donne's Transcendent Imagination', in Frontain and Malpezzi, pp.141-61 (p.152).

transmuting into a human Christ by the strong pause between the couplets. Christ is presented in the distancing third person, in theological rather than human terms: first by the punning reference to rising and falling; secondly by his function as the one who saves 'all' from sin. Yet the word 'benighted' suggests, with particular poignancy, the Seeker's situation: as a traveller, he is away from a safe haven, and may still be benighted, eternally excluded from the salvation Christ has won.

The next lines suggest that the Seeker remains caught by sin, unwilling or unable to face the sight that would lead, not to physical death, but to the death of the self and the beginning of spiritual life:

> Yet dare I'almost be glad, I do not see
> That spectacle of too much weight for mee.
> Who sees Gods face, that is selfe life, must dye;
> What a death were it then to see God dye?

ll.15-18

With this first, pivotal question of the poem, the Seeker places into stark juxtaposition the humanity and the divinity of Christ: one who is God and yet can die. At this point, the poem comes to life. From being measured, abstract, and theological, it now reverts to the passionate and concrete language of the Sonnets, with the vigorous and harshly monosyllabic verbs of the next couplet:

> It made his owne Lieutenant Nature shrinke,
> It made his footstoole crack, and the Sunne winke.

ll.19-20

These lines put God into relationship with nature, and the Seeker begins to respond:

> Could I behold those hands which span the Poles,
> And turne[95] all spheares at once, pierc'd with those holes?
> Could I behold that endlesse height which is
> Zenith to us, and our Antipodes,
> Humbled below us? or that blood which is
> The seat of all our Soules, if not of his,
> Made durt of dust, or that flesh which was worne
> By God, for his apparell, rag'd and torne?

ll.21-8

---

[95] Grierson's reading. Gardner prefers 'tune' as well attested and the more difficult reading: *The Divine Poems*, p.99. Patrides also has 'tune' – a tempting musical analogy if there were any other musical imagery in the poem. However 'turne' emphasizes God's power and enhances the use of 'turne' in lines 37 and 42. Helen B. Brooks notes the importance of turning in the poem, but accepts 'tune' without comment: 'Donne's "Goodfriday, 1613. Riding Westward" and Augustine's Psychology of Time', in Frontain and Malpezzi, pp.284-305 (pp.294-7).

Gilman suggests that the tension between the vividness of the imagery and the speaker's inability to look at what he imagines is

> ... a terrifying exercise in negative theology, stunning [the Meditator] with the sense of God's incomprehensibleness rather than bringing [the Meditator] closer to him in imaginative participation with his suffering.[96]

But surely this central passage of the poem involves 'imaginative participation' with Christ's suffering with an unusual power, just because it is so incomprehensible that one who is God could also be subject to mortal suffering. The lines are full of a passionate tension between the desire to look and the dread of what that look might reveal. Lines 19-20 placed the Crucifixion firmly in the past, but lines 21-8 use the present tense for the divine activities (span... turne... is Zenith... is the seat'), and passive past participles for the assumption of humanity ('pierc'd... Humbled... made durt... rag'd'). This develops a powerful tension between God's eternally present power and his entry into the world of time. The division between the couplets breaks up as meaning and energy spill over the line breaks. The pace increases as the Seeker first repeats the question, 'Could I behold...' and then omits it, compressing the syntax. The interrogative allows him both to claim that he is overwhelmed, unable to look at the Crucifixion,[97] and at the same time to intersperse images of Christ's suffering, clause by clause, with powerfully visual images of his divine power. Unlike the generalized image of 'a Sunne', these images are sharpened by the demonstrative pronouns – 'those hands... that endlesse height... that blood... that flesh'. The parallel grammatical structure reinforces the force of the passive participles that depict God, the source of action and power, as suffering rather than acting. The sense of anguish is increased by the movement from the powerful metaphor of 'hands' that can turn the whole universe to the humbler, literal images of 'that blood... that flesh'. The last image is given an acute poignancy by the intimacy of the idea of God wearing our flesh as 'his apparell', and the double passives, 'rag'd and torne'.

The next lines introduce the Virgin:

> If on these things I durst not looke, durst I
> Upon his miserable mother cast mine eye,
> Who was Gods partner here, and furnish'd thus
> Halfe of that Sacrifice, which ransom'd us?

> ll.29-32

Donne here reinforces Christ's humanity by mentioning his mother.[98] As a human agent who *is* looking at Christ she prepares the Seeker to look as well:

---

[96] Gilman, pp.144-5. See also Oliver (p.38) and Julia J. Smith, 'Donne and the Crucifixion', *Modern Language Review*, 79 (1984), 513-25.

[97] Terry G. Sherwood suggests that he is awed by the cosmic scope of his sin: *Fulfilling the Circle* (Toronto, 1984), p.167.

[98] Patrides considers that these lines Mariolatrous: p.357). But see George Klawitter: 'John Donne's Attitude toward the Virgin Mary', in Frontain and Malpezzi, pp.122-40 (pp.133-4).

Though these things, as I ride, be from mine eye,
They'are present yet unto my memory,
For that looks towards them...

                                                          ll.33-5

As soon as the Seeker admits that 'these things' are present in his memory, and that he *does* look at this death, Christ enters into relationship with him, with a sudden shift from the third to the second person:

                    ... and thou look'st towards mee,
O Saviour, as thou hang'st upon the tree;
I turne my backe to thee, but to receive
Corrections, till thy mercies bid thee leave.

O thinke mee worth thine anger, punish mee,
Burne off my rusts, and my deformity,
Restore thine Image, so much, by thy grace,
That thou may'st know mee, and I'll turne my face.

                                                          ll.35-42

Friedman sees these lines as Calvinistic, stressing punishment 'even though the meaning of the crucifixion was the forgiveness of sins'.[99] This overlooks the fact that it is the movement of the Seeker's will, consenting to look at Christ through his memory, that allows Christ to relate to him, *looking* at him in return. It misreads, I think, the tone of the lines: the Seeker speaks of *receiving* corrections, of willingly participating in a punishment that is governed by mercy,[100] the pain of correction turning the soul back towards Christ, where it can find true comfort.[101]

Here Christ is no longer represented in the third person and the past tense, but in the intimacy of the second-person and the immediacy of the present tense. This brings him into the same time as the Seeker. For the first time in the poems discussed, it is Christ who approaches the Seeker, not the Seeker who attempts to approach God. In the last four lines the pace builds up with a simple coordinate structure in which the Seeker appeals directly to Christ, in demand function, imploring him to punish, burn, and restore him. As always in demand function, the desired actions are not yet an actuality. However, the poet's description of Christ's cleansing actions lead to another dramatic grammatical shift, as, in the poem's only future construction, the Seeker promises to return to his natural motion and to *look* at Christ: 'I'll turne my face'. This verb, however, is a promise, not an actuality. Here the Seeker's anguish is the anguish of sin, the sin that prevents him from responding fully to Christ: the Seeker can only act if Christ acts first, purging his sin, and Christ's action remains hypothetical.

Gilman sees the poem as following a circular motion, from the soul's failure to follow its 'natural forme' to the 'deformity' of the closing lines. He

---

[99] Friedman, 'Christ's Image and Likeness', pp.80-1.
[100] Sherwood, pp.158-9, and Gilman, p.146.
[101] Malpezzi, pp.144-6.

suggests that 'the image of Christ formed by the poet must itself be regarded as a deformity, a scum of rust that must be burned off'; he thinks the future tense of the last line breaks the circle of the poem, marring it, and thus destroying the the the poet's idolatrous image of Christ.[102] This is an interesting suggestion: the future tense avoids closure and the presumption of claiming a present encounter with Christ.

However, as in the close of 'Batter my heart', there is a great sense of intimacy created by the large number of personal pronouns and imperatives placing Christ and the soul in continual connection (Gilman comments, 'how strongly the voltage of Donne's piety flows across the gap between "I" and "thee"').[103] And once again, although the syntax of the ending suggests delay, doubt, and imperfection, the lexis concludes the poem with images of a restored image, grace, Christ's recognition, and the Seeker's response. In this poem, the final clause is an indicative, a firm promise of the Seeker's commitment: the Seeker who makes that promise already has his heart turned towards Christ, and has in some sense already encountered him there.

6. The Hymnes: uncertain certainties

In the Holy Sonnets, Donne exploited all the technical resources of the form in order to convey the tension between the Seeker's vision of a loving God, and his doubt as to whether that love would finally embrace him. In 'Satyre III' and 'Goodfriday, 1613', he chose flexible pentameter couplets to explore, in a more narrative and reflective style, the soul's journey towards Christ. In the 'Hymnes', with their relatively simple stanza forms, their flowing syntax, and a gentler use of imperatives, he conveys a greater assurance that he can find peace in God's love: yet even here a note of uncertainty remains.

In 'A Hymne to Christ, at the Authors last going into Germany', the Seeker calmly accepts the possibility of death at sea, speaking of God's anger only to negate it:

> Though thou with clouds of anger do disguise
> Thy face; yet through that maske I knowe those eyes,
>   Which, though they turne away sometimes,
>   They never will despise.

ll.5-8

The use of the indicative mood and the flowing syntax convey a sense of assurance. The poem has only three imperatives:

> Put thou thy sea betwixt my sinnes and thee...

l.12

> Seale then this bill of my Divorce to All...

---

[102] Gilman, pp.146-7.
[103] Gilman, p.147.

Marry those loves, which in youth scattered bee
On Fame, Wit, Hopes (false mistresses) to thee.

ll.25-8

These are very different from the multiple imperatives packed together in 'Batter my heart' or the last lines of 'Goodfriday, 1613'; with their extended clauses, they have the tone of polite requests rather than agitated commands.

However, the poem retains a muted echo of Donne's wrestling with the pain of sin.[104] He deals with the possibility of death, the sacrifice of 'all whom I lov'd there' (l.10), and the sudden bursting out of doubt:

O, if thou car'st not whom I love,
Alas, thou lov'st not mee.

ll.23-4

He chooses 'God only' in order 'to scape stormy dayes': it is still pain that leads him to God.

Joseph Duncan claims that 'A Hymne to God the Father' displays the Seeker's 'confidence that his sins are forgiven'.[105] I agree that the sense of forgiveness is strong: while the Sonnets talk of the need for repentance, this poem repeats the word 'forgive' four times, the only such use of the word in Donne's religious poetry.[106] Nevertheless, Duncan's seems to me too confident a reading. Although the continued questions in the first two stanzas are measured in comparison with the agonized questions of the earlier poems, the repetition gives them urgency:

Wilt thou forgive that sinne where I begunne,
  Which was my sin, though it were done before?
Wilt thou forgive that sinne; through which I runne,
  And do run still: though still I do deplore?
When thou hast done, thou hast not done,
        For, I have more.

Wilt thou forgive that sinne which I have wonne
        Others to sinne? and, made my sinne their doore?
Wilt thou forgive that sinne which I did shunne
        A yeare, or two: but wallowed in, a score?
When thou hast done, thou hast not done,
        For I have more.

ll.1-12

---

[104] John J. Pollock, 'Donne's A Hymne to Christ', *Explicator*, 38 (1980), 20-22.

[105] Joseph Duncan, 'Resurrections in Donne's "A Hymne to God the Father" and "Hymne to God my God in my sicknesse"', *JDJ*, 7 (1988), 183-9.

[106] Combs and Sullens, p.127. In Sonnet XIII, Christ 'pray'd forgiveness for his foes fierce spight', but the poet did not ask for forgiveness.

There is a strong feeling of alarm in the idea of persistent sin and of winning others to sin. Any sense of security implied by the repetition of 'forgive' is prevented when the Seeker negates the effectiveness of God's forgiveness in the last two lines of each stanza.

In the third stanza, the syntax and the tone change. The questions of the first two stanzas give way to a statement which is much sharper than the first two stanzas, since it specifies the sin:

> I have a sinne of feare, that when I have spunne
> My last thred, I shall perish on the shore;
> But sweare by thy selfe, that at my death thy sonne
> Shall shine as he shines now, and heretofore...

ll.13-16

Whereas the other sins were expressed in the same breath as the idea of forgiveness, this one is expressed in the same breath as the idea of perishing, and with the use of the future tense, as Cummings notes, 'for the first occasion in the poem, the threat of real time looms over the sinner'.[107] Instead of the questions, there is an imperative, reminiscent of the tone of the Sonnets. And yet, despite this increase in fear and tension, the poem ends with a statement of trust:

> And having done that, Thou hast done,
> I feare no more.

ll.17-18

Once again, it is the confrontation with the anguish of sin that brings the Seeker closer to God in the final stanza. And yet, this closeness is still not absolute: the verbs in the penultimate line, given the imperative of line 15, should not be read as past perfect, as an action already complete, but rather, as hypothetical, as an action still to be desired. Yet, as Cummings observes of the alternative last line, 'I have no more', this line is 'a miniature indication of grace': both these final lines are in the indicative, a statement of faith rather than a request.

'Hymne to God my God, in my sicknesse' is unique among Donne's poems for its expression of full harmony with God and its peaceful tone:

> Since I am comming to that Holy roome,
>   Where, with thy Quire of Saints for evermore,
> I shall be made thy Musique; As I come
>   I tune the Instrument here at the dore,
>   And what I must doe then, thinke here before.

ll.1-5

The poem is largely expressed in the indicative mood, and its questions – 'What shall my West hurt me... Is the Pacifique Sea my home? (ll.13, 16-17) – are without urgency. There is no mention of sin, no mention of fear, no questions

---

[107] Cummings, pp.415-16.

directed at God, no commands. Instead there is a calm acceptance of God's will that he should die 'by these streights' and joy that 'death doth touch the Resurrection' (ll.10-15). Yet the last two stanzas still stress that it is through pain and trial that the soul comes to God:

> We thinke that *Paradise* and *Calvarie*,
>   *Christs* Crosse, and *Adams* tree, stood in one place;
> Looke Lord, and finde both *Adams* met in me;
>   As the first *Adams* seat surrounds my face,
>   May the last *Adams* blood my soule embrace.
>
> So, in his purple wrapp'd receive mee Lord,
>   By these his thornes give me his other Crowne;
> And as to others soules I preach'd thy word,
>   Be this my Text, my Sermon to mine owne,
>   Therfore that he may raise the Lord throws down.
>
>   ll.21-30

The imperatives ('Looke', 'May the last *Adams* blood my soule embrace', 'receive mee', 'give me'), like the imperatives of 'A Hymne to Christ, at the Authors last going into Germany', are polite requests, rather than agitated demands. The final imperative ('be this my Text') addressed to the Seeker's self, has a triumphant ring to it as the Seeker commands himself to trust that God will finally answer the plea in Sonnet XIV, 'That I may rise, and stand, o'erthrow mee'. Yet the syntactic inversion, in both cases, places the idea of being thrown down *after* the idea of rising: until the final throwing down and the final rising have occurred, the Seeker dares not express complete certainty, but merely a strong hope.

In the 'Hymnes' as well as in 'Satyre III', the Holy Sonnets, and 'Goodfriday 1613', Donne avoids closure. Linville argues that problems arise when a poet is tempted to end a poem with 'a too easy pietism or self-righteous affirmation of ready-made, orthodox belief', and goes on to argue that Donne in fact 'revivifies faith' by presenting his search for God as an 'arduous struggle toward an inevitably elusive ideal'.[108] In Donne's Divine Poems, anguish is never actually, but only potentially resolved. The anguish of death with its threat of damnation is partly transcended by the knowledge that death will at least bring the soul face to face with God, for good or ill. The anguish of psychic disintegration is apparent, even in the Hymnes, in the tension between the Seeker's desire for a loving God and the possibility that this desire may never be consummated. The anguish of history is encapsulated in the possibility that the Seeker may not be able to claim the promises of salvation history for himself. As for the anguish of sin, in contrast to medieval writers, Donne lays less emphasis on individual responsibility for sins and their consequences in the world, and more on sin as a force that the sinner cannot escape and that may separate him from God. Drawing all these anguishes together is the anguish of doubt – doubt not as to God's goodness, but as to the sinner's right, after death, to claim that goodness for himself.

---

[108] 'Contrary Faith', pp.142-3.

These anguishes are worked out in a variety of forms in which a linear narrative progression is strong, but never absolute. The poems discussed in this chapter chart the soul's search for God, but never depict its ultimate arrival: for Donne, there is always a gap between the Seeker's desire for God and certainty of God's response – encounter is always just out of reach, but all the more to be desired for that. Unlike the lyricists and Langland, who depict encounter with Christ as a *present* or *past* reality that humans may fail to respond to, Donne constructs it as a possibility in the *urgent-future*: the gap for him lies not so much in the Seeker's failure of response, for the Seeker is always ardently seeking God, but in an uncertainty about when or if God will respond to this particular Seeker.

Nevertheless, while the Divine Poems express fear of separation from God, or frustration at God's delay, the language they use depicts God largely in terms of love, a God who punishes only in order to redeem. In this, Donne is like Langland. On the other hand, although Donne thinks that some effort on the part of the soul is possible and necessary, he does not discuss the nature of human virtue at any length: he gives no examples of it, he makes no stories about it. In this, Donne looks forward to Milton. Yet the central figure in his poems, like Langland's Will, is predominantly a Seeker after God. The overwhelming message of the Divine Poems, the story that Donne consistently tells, is that the anguishes of death and sin that might lead to separation from God are the very forces that drive the soul towards God. In *Paradise Lost*, the picture is bleaker: Milton's poem has sin rather than salvation at its centre, and whereas Langland and Donne start with a sinful soul and bring it closer to encounter with God, Milton's Adam and Eve start their poetic life in harmony with God, and end it excluded from Paradise.

Chapter 5

Alienation from God in *Paradise Lost*

> No more of talk where God or angel guest
> With man, as with his friend, familiar used
> To sit indulgent, and with him partake
> Rural repast, permitting him the while
> Venial discourse unblamed: I now must change
> Those notes to tragic; foul distrust, and breach
> Disloyal on the part of man, revolt,
> And disobedience: on the part of heaven
> Now alienated, distance and distaste,
> Anger and just rebuke, and judgement given,
> That brought into this world a world of woe...

IX.1-11

1. Poet and Believer: Milton's double voice

In *Paradise Lost*, Milton's approach to the Christian story is radically different in two main respects from the Crucifixion lyricists', Langland's, or Donne's. Unlike them, he does not write himself into the action of his poem, but constructs his persona as outside his story, a self-conscious poet who narrates the action. Unlike any other major English poet, Milton makes God the Father a character in his poem; many readers, finding his Father repellent, have considered the poem flawed as a result.[1]

Unlike the medieval lyrics or Donne's Divine Poems, *Paradise Lost* and *Piers Plowman* both represent their personae as poets. However, the role of these two poetic personae is different in each poem. The stated purpose of Langland's poetic persona is satirical – to 'make' poems that criticize 'lollares of London and lewede ermytes' (C.V.4) and 'publish' the corrupt doings of the friars (C.XII.23-42). Apart from its climactic visions of Easter and Pentecost, *Piers Plowman* is set in Langland's own historical period, and its narrative is concerned with the social and spiritual ills that beset the Folk of fourteenth-century England. In order to redeem this society, Langland stresses the need for individuals to respond to God's mercy with human justice. His persona attempts to fulfil this requirement in his own life, and the Dreamer is not primarily a poet, but rather the ardent yet

---

[1] For example, John Peter, *A Critique of Paradise Lost* (New York, 1960); William Empson, *Milton's God*, 2nd edn (Cambridge, 1981); Terry Eagleton, 'The God that Failed', in *Remembering Milton*, ed. Mary Nyquist and Margaret Ferguson (New York, 1987), pp.342-9; J. Allan Mitchell, 'Reading God Reading "Man"', *MiltonQ*, 35 (2) May 2001, 72-86.

recalcitrant Will whose personal quest for social and spiritual salvation drives the action of the poem. He is more concerned with human justice than with God's justice.

Milton, on the other hand, constructs his persona primarily as a Poet. This poet has a double stated intention: first, to write an 'adventurous song' that will pursue 'Things unattempted yet in prose or rhyme'; and second, to 'justify the ways of God to men' (I.11-26). His narrative is not ostensibly concerned with the history of seventeenth-century England,[2] but, like the lyricists and Donne, focuses almost exclusively on salvation history. Milton places his Poet outside his story rather than within it, and the narrative of *Paradise Lost* is not determined by the Poet's spiritual search. Thus he cannot encounter Christ in the same way that the personae of the lyricists, Langland, and Donne all do. The Poet is not apparently concerned with his own spiritual state, nor with that of the historical world that surrounds him: he is concerned with God's justice rather than human justice.

Both aspects of the Poet's stated intention – the process and the content of his writing – are problematic. Citing an anonymous Elizabethan sermon, Gilman points out that the iconoclasts of the English Reformation attacked poetry as well as images:

> [the mind] *full as it is of pride and boldness, tries to imagine a god according to its own capacity, whence a new wickedness joins itself, that man tries to express in his work the sort of god he has inwardly conceived. Therefore, the mind begets an idol; the hand gives it birth...* If the 'factory of idols' is located not in the choice of pigment over language but in the very mind behind the work, and if no man can trust his own motives, then every poem risks becoming a strange god even if the poet's declared intention is to 'plainly say, *My God, My King.*'[3]

Although Gilman says very little about Milton's treatment of God in *Paradise Lost*,[4] his suggestion that in 'Goodfriday, 1613. Riding Westward' Donne both makes and mars the circular structure of the poem in order to '"hew down" the idolatrous "images" within the self'[5] seems to me to apply to Milton as well. One of the key aims of this chapter is to show the process whereby Milton's Poet both makes and mars the poem he depicts himself as creating, suggesting that Milton feared that his own poetic endeavour was potentially idolatrous.

The Poet's intention to 'justify the ways of God to men' is also problematic. As Cummings shows, the problems of Luther's conversion centred on his reading of Romans 1:17: '*Iustitia enim dei in eo revelatur ex fide in fidem sicut*

---

[2] The history of his own time does not enter his poem on the level of story. However, critics such as Andrew Milner have demonstrated its influence on theme and character: *John Milton and the English Revolution* (London and Basingstoke, 1981). See also Michael Wilding, *Dragon's Teeth* (Oxford, 1987); J. Martin Evans, *Milton's Imperial Epic* (Ithaca and London, 1996).

[3] Gilman, p.42.

[4] He talks of the importance of seeing and light, and of the movement from vision to hearing in Books XI and XII (pp.151-70)

[5] Gilman, pp.146-7.

scriptum est: Iustus autem ex fide vivit.' Initially, Luther interpreted this *iustitia* as 'the justice by which a just God punishes wrongdoers'. Believing that since no one is just, man must be born to a life of inevitable crime and inevitable eternal punishment, Luther hated God, until he began to understand *iustitia* as '*that passive justice, with which the merciful God justifies us*'.[6] Cummings says that much of sixteenth- and early seventeenth-century theology was 'a collective act of recoil' against Luther's 'terrifying sentence':

> God so orders this corporeal world in its external affairs that if you respect and follow the judgement of human reason, you are bound to say either that there is no God or that God is unjust.[7]

Writing of Milton's intention to 'justify the ways of God to men', Cummings says:

> In this phrase the Reformation comes full circle. What begins with the promise of justification for men ends with a promise of justification for God. As well as brazen or even boastful, the word 'justify' is strangely vulnerable... a God who needs justifying is one who seems on the face of things less than perfectly justified, possibly not altogether justifiable... Milton sets himself the task of bringing the best possible or least indefensible defence against Paul's scandalous charge, 'Is there then unrighteousness with God?'[8]

Milton's use of the word 'justify' is further suspect, because the only other time it occurs in *Paradise Lost* is when Adam is trying to justify himself by blaming Eve and God:[9]

> This woman that thou madest to be my help,
> And gavest me as thy perfect gift, so good,
> So fit, so acceptable, so divine,
> That from her hand I could suspect no ill,
> And what she did, whatever in it self,
> Her doing seemed to justify the deed;
> She gave me of the tree, and I did eat.

X.137-43

The tone of Adam's speech is sarcastic, irresponsible, and untruthful: he clearly did suspect ill from Eve, knew she was lost, and consciously decided to die with her (X.896-907). Adam's fallen use of the word to describe a false (seeming) moral position casts into doubt the Poet's whole enterprise.

This chapter will explore the tensions apparent in Milton's treatment of God's justice, particularly in Book III of *Paradise Lost*. I suggest that Milton's awareness of the potential 'idolatry' of his poetic ambitions leads him to deliberately create some of the 'flaws' he has been criticized for. Perhaps his

---

[6] Cummings, pp.63-6.
[7] Luther, *De servo arbitrio* (WA 18.784.36); Cummings, pp.404-5.
[8] Cummings, p.421.
[9] John Bradshaw, *A Concordance to the Poetical Works of John Milton* (Boston, 1977).

fascinating but repellent Father is intended to be *the view of a sinner*, and therefore distorted. If this is the case, then the Poet is not actually outside the action of the poem: rather, the poem includes an exploration (and not just in the invocations) of the spiritual dangers of Milton's potentially sinful undertaking.

Some critics have taken Milton's stated poetic intentions very seriously. Barbara Lewalski suggests that Milton sees the overwhelming task of writing 'the true epic story of our fallen world,' as 'one model of the Christian heroism the poem explores': his poem must 'contain, subsume, and endeavour to surpass the greatest poems we know'.[10] Milton's overwhelmingly self-conscious artistry might thus be read as his own heroic feat of arms.

For Michael Fixler, on the other hand, Milton's poem is unlike meditational poetry with its 'self-absorbed communion with God'; rather it is 'the most perfect *public* [my italics] expression of his faith... a song of praise' that involves its readers in a kind of liturgical service.[11] Such a purpose would suggest a greater religious self-confidence than either Langland or Donne displays: while it may, I think, be a part of Milton's surface meaning for the poem, it coexists with a strong undercurrent of personal anxiety.

More provocatively, Stanley Fish argues that Milton recreates the drama of the Fall by a deliberate tension between what he shows and what he says. He continually invites 'fallen' readings, and then uses the narrative voice to rebuke the reader, with the aim of bringing him to self-knowledge, contrition, and grace.[12] Fish overlooks both the dangers of evoking 'fallen' responses to God, and the egotism that his reading implies. For a pastor to rebuke his flock is one thing; for a poet to continually 'harass'[13] his readers by manipulating them into 'sinful' readings and then rebuking them, is quite another. This reading assumes a great degree of spiritual confidence in Milton. Whereas Langland and Donne invite the reader to share their personae's anguished searches for God, Milton assumes, if Fish is correct, that he understands God well enough to explain him to everyone else: rather than seeking, through his poem, to understand and accept, he seeks primarily to instruct.

Other critics have not been so sure about Milton's confidence. Northrop Frye suggests that the crisis of Milton's life was the choosing of his epic subject.[14] This crisis does not seem, on the surface, to have been a religious one. Unlike Langland and Donne, who constructed their personae as believers rather than poets, Milton chronicles the struggles of the poet rather than the believer.

[10] Lewalski, *Paradise Lost and the Rhetoric of Literary Forms* (Princeton, 1985) pp.28-31.

[11] Michael Fixler, 'Milton's Passionate Epic', *MiltonS*, 1 (1969), 167-92, pp.168, 172. See also Thomas F. Merrill, 'Miltonic God-Talk', *Language and Style*, 16 (1983), 296-312 (p.299).

[12] Stanley Fish, *Surprised by Sin*, 2nd edn (London, 1997), pp.1-22, 37-8. Fish implies that the reader should prefer what he is told to what he is shown.

[13] Fish, p.4.

[14] Northrop Frye, *Five Essays on Milton's Epics* (London, 1966), p.x.

But what if the struggles of the poet *are* the struggles of the believer? What if Milton intends to construct himself as a poet who is not merely fallen,[15] but who, bound up in poetic ambition rather than in the search for salvation, is in the process of falling? What if Milton's Father is deliberately flawed, the vision of a fallen man who has 'wisdom at one entrance quite shut out' (III.50), and who must write in 'fallen language'?[16]

As some critics have noted, Milton's stated purpose is highly egotistical. William G. Riggs shows some of the ironic parallels between the poet's invocations and Satan's speeches and actions. But then he argues that the poet avoids 'blasphemous pride' by the humility and 'dependence on God' shown in the invocations.[17] However, I would argue that the invocations are more concerned with artistic endeavour than with dependence on God, and that they are not always humble.

Noting that invocations were traditionally seen as evidence of pride, Walter Schindler suggests that Milton wishes his audience to realize that, in writing an epic about the Fall, he may be enacting his own fall. Schindler believes that Milton's 'one hope lies in the reality of inspiration', and that the invocations show him fulfilling this hope, 'overcoming the crisis', and progressing 'towards a more secure inspiration'.[18] Similarly, Robert McMahon argues that there are in fact two poets – Milton, and 'the Bard' who eventually abandons his overweening ambitions.[19]

On the contrary, I believe that the invocations dramatize an increasing distance between the poet and God, and that Milton uses his persona to enact what he fears may be his own fall, securing his poem at the cost of endangering his relationship with God. In *Piers Plowman* B, Imaginative rebuked Will for meddling with poetry when he would be better occupied in praying (B.XII.16-17); Milton too constructs his persona as a spiritual being who should be concerned, as Langland's and Donne's personae are, with his spiritual relationship with God rather than with his artistic endeavours.

Milton's fallen persona has two largely distinct roles, that of 'the Poet' and that of 'the Believer'. In the invocations Milton uses the voice of the self-conscious and bombastic 'Poet' who stands aside from the action of the story and *overtly* uses the first person to discuss *publicly* his own successes and difficulties in writing the poem. The Poet is concerned almost exclusively with poetic endeavour and has little awareness of his sinful state and the spiritual danger of his enterprise.

When the persona is relating the action of the poem, his voice is less obtrusive, with no use of first person pronouns, but he is *covertly* there: in the

---

[15] See Lewalski, *Paradise Lost*, pp.28-31. Lewalski does not pursue this suggestion.

[16] Clare Regan Kinney, *Strategies of Poetic Narrative* (Cambridge, 1992), p.134; see also Ricks, *Milton's Grand Style*, p.109; Fish, p.103; Cummings, pp.430-1.

[17] William G. Riggs, 'The Poet and Satan in *Paradise Lost*', *MiltonS*, 2 (1970), 59-82 (pp.63, 80).

[18] Walter Schindler, *Voice and Crisis* (Hamden, Connecticut, 1984), pp.81; 47-50; 56-8.

[19] Robert McMahon, *The Two Poets of Paradise Lost* (Baton Rouge and London, 1998), pp.1, 24, 59.

language of fear and distance with which he constructs the Father's insistence on justice; in the enthusiastic naïveté with which he depicts the Son's insistence on mercy; or in the tentative way that he slips himself into the angels' hymn at the end of the Parliament of Heaven. It is this second voice, 'the Believer', who is concerned with salvation, and who feels anguish at the possibility of separation from God.

There is an overlap between the two: they are not distinct *characters* but rather distinct *roles* or *aspects* (much as someone might say to me, 'that is the *teacher* in you speaking' or 'that is the *mother* in you'). It is not uncommon for an individual to present a confident outward persona, while feeling acutely conscious of a very different inner reality. Both sides of Milton's persona, it seems to me, are aspects of his personality that he wishes to project into his poem: as I shall argue in detail in this chapter, he uses the public voice of the Poet to chronicle his own documented obsession[20] with his epic endeavour, but at other times, when he is concerned with matters of belief, he chooses the humbler and more private voice of the Believer.[21] The Poet is a projection of Milton's ambitious self, the ego that he has come to see as sinful. The quieter voice of the Believer is, I believe, closer to Milton's own mature voice.

On one level, as Fixler suggests, Milton does want to write 'a public expression of his faith… a song of praise', but on another level he is aware of the *hubris* of this undertaking: a similar awareness led him to abandon his early poem 'The Passion', declaring that the subject 'was above the years he had when he wrote it'.[22] It is sometimes necessary to read passages of *Paradise Lost* on two levels, as a *public* expression of faith in God and/or the Poet's own prowess, and as a *private* expression of fear that this very prowess may be leading him further from God rather than closer to him.

If I am correct in identifying a tension between the roles of Poet and Believer in Milton's persona, and correct in arguing that Milton intends to represent the Poet as engaging in a potentially sinful endeavour, then the poem narrated by the Poet should bear the marks of this sin. It is the purpose of this chapter to argue that it does. An awareness of Milton's two-sided persona and his double purpose is helpful in resolving two of the dilemmas of Milton criticism: for example, the problems caused by Milton's presentation of the Father in Book III and the apparent artistic failure of Book XII.[23]

---

[20] T.J.B. Spencer discusses Milton's determination that his English epic should surpass its classical and renaissance models: '*Paradise Lost*: The Anti-Epic', in *Approaches to Paradise Lost*, ed. C.A. Patrides (London, 1968), pp.81-98.

[21] J. Martin Evans describes the persona as 'vacillating between self-erasure and self-assertion as he struggles to find a place for himself in his own text': 'The Birth of the Author', *Milton S* (2000), 47-65 (p.61).

[22] John Milton, *Complete Shorter Poems*, ed. John Carey (London, 1968), p.122. See below for a fuller discussion.

[23] See, for example, Lewis, *A Preface*, p.129.

2. The Poet and the invocations

Although the first invocation is the most confident,[24] it has disturbing aspects. The first lines are tightly focused, encapsulating the whole of Christian history in five lines:

> Of man's first disobedience, and the fruit
> Of that forbidden tree, whose mortal taste
> Brought death into the world, and all our woe,
> With loss of Eden, till one greater man
> Restore us, and regain the blissful seat,
> Sing heavenly Muse...

I.1-6

Historically speaking, both the Fall and the Redemption had occurred before the Poet writes about them; within his narrative, which starts with Satan's fall, neither has yet occurred. Thus it is curious that here the tense structure represents the Fall as already past, while Redemption lies in the future. This suggests that *Paradise Lost* concerns, not only the Redemption of Mankind (which is already, from a Christian point of view, assured), but also the future possibility of the fallen Poet's salvation.

As soon as the Poet appeals to the Muse for inspiration, foregrounding literary rather than moral matters, the tight focus of the opening blurs (I.6-16). The aspiring successor of Moses seeks inspiration in a *place*,[25] and clutters the text with the names of various places as he wonders whether his Muse will be found 'on the secret top/ Of Oreb, or of Sinai... or if Sion hill/ Delight thee more and Siloa's brook'. There is thus no firm location for his statement:

> I thence
> Invoke thy aid to my adventurous song,
> That with no middle flight intends to soar
> Above the Aonian mount, while it pursues
> Things unattempted yet in prose or rhyme.

I.12-16

As Schindler notes, 'adventurous' and 'unat*tempt*ed' suggest the possibility of a fall.[26] So does 'no middle flight': in Ovid's *Metamorphoses* both Phaeton and Icarus, warned by their fathers to take a middle way, disobey and fall to their deaths.[27] The language here is objectified: the Poet invokes 'aid', not for himself, but for his song; his song pursues not God, but 'Things'.

---

[24] Schindler, pp.50-1.

[25] Schindler, pp.49-50. See also Francis C. Blessington, *Paradise Lost and the Classical Epic* (London, 1979), p.96.

[26] Schindler points out that Eve's eating of the fruit is 'adventurous' (IX.921) and that Satan is a 'great adventurer' (X.440).

[27] McMahon discusses Icarus as a common figure for excessive poetic ambition: pp.28-33.

In the second sentence of the poem, the tone and language change completely as the speaker requests instruction from the Holy Spirit:

> And chiefly thou O Spirit, that dost prefer
> Before all temples the upright heart and pure,
> Instruct me, for thou know'st; thou from the first
> Wast present, and with mighty wings outspread
> Dove-like sat'st brooding on the vast abyss
> And madest it pregnant: what in me is dark
> Illumine, what is low raise and support;
>
> I.17-23

This sentence has much more movement and sense of connection than the opening sentence. There are more verbs (21 per cent rather than 13 per cent), so the verbal dynamism is higher. There are also fewer nouns (13 per cent rather than 25 per cent), and a corresponding increase in personal pronouns and names (12 per cent rather than 4 per cent). The repeated 'thou' and the four imperatives (instruct, illumine, raise, support) place the persona and Spirit in the intimate connection of plea-prayer. Here the Poet speaks as a believer, humbly asking for spiritual help: the confession of darkness and lowness suggests that he does not believe he has an 'upright heart and pure'. He makes the Spirit the subject of all the verbs in lines 17-23, and honours his primacy in the creative role of making the abyss 'pregnant'.

However, the Poet in him subverts this humility as soon as he begins to think of his poem:

> That to the highth of this great argument
> I may assert eternal providence,
> And justify the ways of God to men.
>
> I.24-6

At line 25 he makes himself into the grammatical subject (placing the pronoun 'I' at the stress point at the beginning of the line)[28] and asks to be made pure so that he may rise, not to heaven, but to the 'highth of this great argument'. The phrase '*justify* the ways of God to men' is surely meant ironically: God does not need a mortal to justify his ways,[29] and what right has the Poet to undertake this role?[30] Milton here demonstrates the sinful pride of the Poet's undertaking, and his portrait of God will stress the justice of a God who abhors that sin. Following the *hubris* of his invocation, the Poet does not 'soar' to any height, but instead plummets directly

---

[28] J. .Martin Evans thinks that in asking the Muse to sing, rather than saying 'I sing', Milton establishes 'a self-effacing speaker': 'The Birth of the Author', *Milton S* (2000), p.59. However, Evans' brief discussion does not seem to notice the hubris of his undertaking.

[29] Milner argues that Milton's concern to justify God's ways suggests 'an apparent injustice' in them: pp.139-40.

[30] As McMahon notes, the plural nouns suggest a 'resounding ambition' to justify *all* God's ways to *all* humanity: pp.35-6.

into hell and a vision of 'The infernal serpent' (I.33).[31] Ironically, the Poet goes on to make the abyss 'pregnant': first with *his* creature, Satan, whom he develops far beyond his Biblical foundation, and secondly with the foul pregnancies of Satan and Sin.

In the second invocation, the Poet is less close to God:

> Hail, holy Light, offspring of heaven first-born,
> Or of the eternal co-eternal beam
> May I express thee unblamed? since God is light,
> And never but in unapproached light
> Dwelt from eternity, dwelt then in thee,
> Bright effluence of bright essence increate.

III.1-6

Here, instead of directly addressing the Holy Spirit, he invokes the divine at one remove – the 'holy Light' that is the 'first-born' of heaven, the 'beam' of the eternal, the 'effluence' in which God dwells. This is the creative force that legitimately, 'at the voice/ Of God', gave form to the world, mantling the earth with waters 'Won from the void and formless infinite' (III.9-12).

The Poet's creative endeavour is more questionable. There is uneasiness in his question, 'May I express thee unblamed?' and in his reiterated assertion that he has returned safely from Hell:

> Thee I revisit now with bolder wing,
> Escaped the Stygian pool, though long detained
> In that obscure sojourn, while in my flight
> Through utter and through middle darkness borne
> With other notes than to the Orphean lyre
> I sung of Chaos and eternal Night,
> Taught by the heavenly Muse to venture down
> The dark descent, and up to reascend,
> Though hard and rare: thee I revisit safe,
> And feel thy sovereign and vital lamp...

III.13-22

In the first invocation, the plea-imperatives made the Spirit the subject of sentences and suggested intimacy; here the speaker is the subject of the processes, concerned with his own endeavours, flying, singing, venturing down and ascending. The loss of intimacy with the Spirit becomes more poignant when the Poet admits that, though he can attempt to revisit the Light,

> ... thou
> Revisit'st not these eyes, that roll in vain
> To find thy piercing ray, and find no dawn;

---

[31] Joseph Wittreich notes the blurring of Milton's persona with Satan, but thinks that the mention of Orpheus in Book VII indicates his safe return from Hell: 'Reading Milton', *MiltonS*, 38 (2000), 10-46.

> So thick a drop serene hath quenched their orbs,
> Or dim suffusion veiled. Yet not the more
> Cease I to wander where the Muses haunt
> Clear spring, or shady grove, or sunny hill,
> Smit with the love of sacred song; but chief
> Thee Sion and the flowery brooks beneath
> That wash thy hallowed feet, and warbling flow,
> Nightly I visit: nor sometimes forget
> Those other two equalled with me in fate,
> So were I equalled with them in renown,
> Blind Thamyris, and bline Maeonides,
> And Tiresias and Phineas prophets old.
>
> III.22-36

While the blind Poet ostensibly laments his loss of physical vision, he also suffers a lessening of spiritual vision (Thamyris is a particularly significant comparison, for he was blinded for his presumption in challenging the Muses).[32] The Poet's distance from God increases: he addresses himself to 'Thee Sion' rather than to God, and is 'Smit with the love of sacred song' rather than love of God (III.29-30).[33] Like Satan (IX.633-42) he *wanders*,[34] uncertain whether to find 'the Muses' in 'Clear spring, or shady grove, or sunny hill' (III.27-8). His source of inspiration no longer resides in Biblical places, and the change from a singular 'heavenly Muse' to plural 'Muses' (III.27) suggests pagan deities. Instead of comparing himself to Moses, he now compares himself to pagan prophets and poets; he prays, not for spiritual illumination, but that he might become as famous as they are.

He then laments, most movingly, his loss of sight: he cannot see the 'human face divine' that is the image of God; the book of nature's knowledge is blank to him, 'And wisdom at one entrance quite shut out' (III.40-50). His anguish and helplessness turn him to the intimacy of a direct appeal to the Divine Light, as he admits that his inner eye is also obscured:

> So much the rather thou celestial Light
> Shine inward, and the mind through all her powers
> Irradiate, there plant eyes, all mist from thence
> Purge and disperse, that I may see and tell
> Of things invisible to mortal sight.
>
> III.51-5

However, just as in the first invocation, the Poet promptly abandons humility: he attempts to turn Divine Light to the purposes of his artistic endeavour rather than to spiritual progress; and he seeks assistance for the powers of the mind, rather than

---

[32] Fowler, III.35-6n.

[33] Discussing Milton's sources, Estelle Haan observes that Virgil, by contrast, was motivated by filial love, and Vida by love of God's countenance: "'Heaven's purest Light'", *Comparative Literature Studies*, 30 (1993), 151-36 (p.122).

[34] Schindler, p.52.

the powers of the will. The lines suggest a detached capacity to observe and describe: again he wishes to 'see and tell/ *Of things*', not to relate *to God*.

He proceeds to relate a very visual picture of God (III.56-79):

> Now had the almighty Father from above,
> From the pure empyrean where he sits
> Hight throned above all highth, bent down his eye,
> His own works and their works at once to view:
> About him all the sanctities of heaven
> Stood thick as stars, and from his sight received
> Beatitude past utterance; on his right
> The radiant image of his glory sat,
> His only Son; on earth he first beheld
> Our two first parents...
>   ... he then surveyed
> Hell and the gulf between, and Satan there...
> Him God beholding from his prospect high,
> Wherein past, present, future he beholds,
> Thus to his only Son forseeing spake.
>
>   III.56-79

He reiterates verbs of seeing ('bent down his eye', 'to view', 'beheld', 'surveyed', 'beholding', 'beholds'). These, describing a non-material process, might convey a purely spiritual view of God, but for the abundance of prepositional phrases that place God in space: 'from above'; 'From the pure empyrean where he sits/ High throned above all highth'; 'About him'; 'on his right'; 'from his prospect high'. The insistence on visual details suggests forcibly the folly and *hubris* of attempting to depict 'things invisible to mortal sight'.[35] More disturbing is the Poet's confident placing of God within time; he tell his readers with assurance, but without Biblical foundation, that '*Now*' the Father sits, that 'he *first* beheld' Adam and Eve, and '*then* surveyed/ Hell'. His stress on place and time suggests that the Poet is not able to offer a clear vision of the eternal God, but rather the distorted view available from the limiting perspectives of time and space.

At the end of the Parliament of Heaven, the Poet promises that the name of the Son 'Shall be the copious matter of my song/ Henceforth', but, again, he immediately reverts to the activities of Satan (III.412-22). Not surprisingly, by the third invocation (VII.1-40), his spiritual state has declined further. He does not speak directly to God at all, but instead invokes Urania, and he even indicates that her inspiration has led him into presumption: 'Up led by thee/ Into the heaven of heavens I have presumed' (VII.12-13). When St Paul was 'caught up to the third heaven, he

> ... heard unspeakable words, which it is not lawful for a man to utter... for I will say the truth: but now I forbear, lest any man should think of me above that which he seeth me to be, or that he heareth of me. (2 Cor. 12: 2-6)

---

[35] Gilman links this passage with Milton's concern to avoid the 'new vomited Paganism of sensuall Idolatry': pp.115-3.

The Poet does not ask himself whether he should 'speak' what he has heard and seen.

The invocation is concerned with poetic endeavour rather than with the need for spiritual illumination. The language keeps the Poet at a distance from God: the Poet is led 'Into the heaven of heavens' – to a place, not a person; it is Urania, rather than the Poet, whose song pleases the Father. Although Urania is traditionally a Christian Muse,[36] it is disturbing when, at the end of the invocation, the Poet appeals to the Muse rather than to Divine Light, idolatrously elevating her to the status of a goddess (VII.38-40).[37]

The Poet no longer mentions Sion, but claims to soar 'above the Olympian hill', higher than Bellerophon on Pegasus. Now he compares himself, not with pagan poets or prophets whose blindness assisted creative achievement, but with a failed pagan hero whose presumption was punished with blindness. Instead of depending on his own wings, he now rides a dangerous 'steed', asks the Muse to return him to earth 'with like safety... Lest... I fall', and claims that on earth

> More safe I sing with mortal voice...
> ... though fallen on evil days,
> On evil days though fallen, and evil tongues;
> In darkness, and with dangers compassed round,
> And solitude; yet not alone, while thou
> Visit'st my slumbers nightly...
>
> VII.24-9

But why does he need to stress his safety by repeating it? And how can he be safe if he is encompassed with dangers? Schindler notes the resonance of the word *fall*, repeated three times in this passage.[38] Moreover, the Poet is distressed by his 'solitude', just as the last phrase of the poem describes Adam and Eve's 'solitary' journey to exile.

Far from conveying a feeling of safety, the invocation conveys fear and uncertainty: the Poet pathetically begs the Muse to find him 'fit audience... though few', and to 'drive far off' the Bacchic furies who beset Orpheus (VII.30-9). Orpheus is a disturbing comparison, not merely pagan, but, in Ovid's account (*Metamorphoses* X-XI) given to activities that Milton would have considered corrupt: after Eurydice's death and his fruitless journey to Hell, Orpheus lavishes his affections on young boys, and sings of the love of Cyparissus for a stag, of Apollo for Hyacinth, of Pygmalion for a statue; of Cinyras, who, like Satan, was seduced by his own daughter; of Hippomenes who defiled a temple by making love to his wife in the sanctuary. Orpheus is finally stoned to death by the women he has scorned. As the Poet observes, Orpheus' voice would have disarmed the rocks that killed him, but it was drowned by the women's 'savage clamour' (VII.36): Orpheus' fallen creativity is destroyed by savage voices.[39]

---

[36] Fowler, VII.1-7 n.

[37] Blessington thinks that this turning to a 'Christian' Muse may save him: pp.97-9.

[38] Schindler, pp.53-4.

[39] Catherine Gimelli Martin: *The Ruins of Allegory* (Durham, NC, and London, 1998), p.68.

The last invocation (IX.1-47) is not, strictly speaking, an invocation at all. As Schindler notes, 'the Muse... is unimplored. For she now visits him without his asking'.[40] However, while the Poet's literary status may be more assured, his spiritual status is less so. He begins bluntly:

> No more of talk where God or angel guest
> With man, as with his friend, familiar used
> To sit indulgent, and with him partake
> Rural repast, permitting him the while
> Venial discourse unblamed: I now must change
> Those notes to tragic ...
>
> IX.1-6

Now the Poet is not even able to talk about God, let alone to him. Words describing sin – 'foul distrust, and breach/ Disloyal... revolt/ And disobedience' – fall like blows; so do the words describing the response of heaven – 'alienated, distance and distaste,/ Anger and just rebuke, and judgment' – and the consequences – 'a world of woe,/ Sin and her shadow Death, and Misery/ Death's harbinger' (IX.6-13).

Yet while he laments distance from God, the Poet remains artistically self-conscious: he 'now must change/ Those notes to tragic'. He admits that this is a 'sad task' (IX.13), yet embraces it with relish, and at considerably greater length than his theological proem (IX.14-47), because it is 'Not less but more heroic than the wrath/ Of stern Achilles'. No longer does he implore spiritual illumination or even safety; instead he wishes to obtain 'answerable style' from the 'celestial patroness' who dictates his 'unpremeditated verse'. The Poet evaluates the literary merit of his subject, which 'Pleased me long choosing, and beginning late': it is a 'higher argument' that can 'raise' even the renown of the epic form. The Poet now seems to have chosen his topic, not because it will bring him closer to God, but because it will enable him to write a better epic than anyone else. He does not ask himself if a form and style developed in order to relate the 'tedious havoc' of 'fabled knights' is likely to be suited to justifying the ways of God to men; indeed, for several lines (IX.34-8) he finds himself carried away by describing the trappings of those now 'gorgeous' knights.

Schindler argues that the Poet's fear of failure 'if all be mine,/ Not hers who brings it nightly to my ear,'(IX.46-7) is calmed 'by the thought that... his inspiration will continue',[41] but the idea of a Muse who dictates ideas nightly to the ear of the slumbering poet is disturbing. Satan, in the form of a toad, has already been discovered 'close at the ear' of the sleeping Eve, pouring into her mind 'Illusions... phantasms and dreams' (IV.800-803) and tainting her pure blood with:

> Vain hopes, vain aims, inordinate desires
> Blown up with high conceits engendering pride.
>
> IV.808-9

---

[40] Schindler, p.55. See also J. Martin Evans, 'The Birth of the Author', p.61.
[41] Schindler, p.56.

The words could well apply to the Poet's ambition to outdo all previous poets.[42] Isabel MacCaffrey speaks of the Puritan 'belief that the ear, as the least sensuous of the senses, is best fitted to receive the revelations of the supernatural',[43] but it is difficult to imagine anything more sensual than the image of a toad-like Satan squatting at Eve's ear.[44] The Poet himself seems aware of this when he leaves the invocation with lines that stress his doubt whether his 'higher argument' will be able to 'raise that name', recognizing that he might be foiled by

> ... an age too late, or cold
> Climate, or years, damp my intended wing
> Depressed, and much they may, if all be mine,
> Not hers who brings it nightly to my ear.

IX.44-7

This is the bleakest moment of the invocations because it is so understated, the doubt confined to those simple words 'if all be mine/ Not hers': the invocations end with his ultimate fear that his work may be a self-seeking, and thus idolatrous, enterprise rather than divinely inspired. This fear is reinforced when, after describing the Muse in words that recall Satan, the Poet immediately relates Satan's return to Eden for the final temptation.

The invocations thus move from direct plea-prayer to alienation from God. The 'heavenly Muse' of the first invocation is falsely raised to the status of a 'goddess' in the third, and verbally linked with Satan in the fourth. The Poet's aspirations also become more limited: in the first invocation, he wishes to justify the ways of God to men; in the second, to equal the fame of pagan poets and prophets; in the third, to be spared the fate of Bellerophon and Orpheus – images of pride and corrupt creativity. Finally his ambition is restricted to finding an 'answerable style' so that he can 'raise the name' of epic poetry. The invocations show that the *hubris* of the Poet's undertaking distances him from God. Similarly, the narrative of *Paradise Lost* shows a movement from intimacy with God towards alienation.

3. Anguish, subverted narrative, and encounter: the four plots of *Paradise Lost*

If the Poet's enterprise is sinful, then it might be expected that his narrative would be flawed, and indeed Milton does subvert his own narrative in several ways. *Piers Plowman* is essentially a plea-poem, initiated by Will's questions to Holy Church, driven by his anguished quest for salvation, and leading to a powerful sense of encounter with Christ. On the other hand, *Paradise Lost*, is, in its stated intention

---

[42] See also Kinney, p.158; William Kerrigan, *The Prophetic Milton* (Charlottesville, 1974), p.143.

[43] Isabel MacCaffrey, 'The Theme of *Paradise Lost* Book III', in *New Essays on Paradise Lost*, ed. Thomas Kranidas, (Berkeley, 1969), pp.58-85 (pp.68, 70).

[44] For the sexuality of this episode, see Kent R. Lehnhof, '"Impregn'd with Reason"', *MiltonS*, 41 (2002), 38-75.

to 'justify the ways of God to men', a praise-poem. It arises from the Poet's assurance rather than his anguish, and it reaches its climax, not with an encounter between the human and the divine, but with a movement out into the fallen world. But if I am right in my reading of the invocations, then the poem's stated aim is evidence of sinful pride, and the poem's true aim is to show how the sins of all the main characters – Satan, Adam and Eve, and the Poet – alienate them from God. The poem is really a suppressed plea, motivated by a sense of distance from God.

In writing a praise-poem with a subtext of plea, Milton subverts the key categories of anguish, narrative, and encounter. In the invocations, Milton's Poet does not overtly engage with the anguishes of death, psychic disintegration, history, sin, and doubt. The true anguish of the poem – the Believer's fear that his poetic endeavour may be sinful, and that this sin may distance him from God – is not allowed to enter the narrative of his poem, but is masked by the Poet's bombastic statements about his poetic ambition.

Milton also subverts his narrative structures. Christian narrative, as I observed in Chapter 1, has a strong tendency towards linear structure.[45] The pre-eminent form of long Christian narrative is not the epic struggle of a hero, but the pilgrimage or journey of an individual soul:[46] Dante, Langland, and Bunyan use this form to describe the Christian's search for God and his attainment of enlightenment. Milton, however, uses it for the plot in which Satan, bent on avenging himself on God, leaves Hell on a journey that leads only to further alienation: Milton thus subverts this Christian genre, while his Poet embraces the originally pagan form of the epic.

Epic is unsuitable for a Christian poem, because, while the Christian story is ultimately, as Dante knew, a comedy, the epic form's most moving effects involve a tragic conclusion:[47] the *Iliad* ends, not with the victory of Achilles, but with Hector's funeral; the *Aeneid* with the death of Turnus rather than the triumph of Aeneas; *Beowulf* with the death of the hero, leaving his society vulnerable to many threats; *La Chanson de Roland* with the deaths of Roland and the twelve peers. Milton too ends his poem tragically, with the expulsion of Adam and Eve, rather than with the Son's triumph: the result is to reduce the Son's emotional impact as hero.

This effect is increased by the chronological dislocations that are common to epic, but which are far more marked in Milton than in Homer and Virgil. O.B. Hardison notes that *Paradise Lost* has two plots: the 'inclusive plot', which extends from the elevation of the Son to the Last Judgment; and the 'dramatic plot' which extends from Satan's infiltration of Paradise to the Expulsion.[48] To this, one

---

[45] See also McClymond, pp.65-6.

[46] R.W. Southern comments that 'As Europe became Christianised the epic was bound to decline, for it left out the personal and secret tie between man and God': p.214.

[47] McMahon's thesis is that the Bard discovers the unsuitability of epic. John M. Steadman notes that Dryden and Addison thought Milton's subject unsuitable because it was tragic: *Epic and Tragic Structure in Paradise Lost* (Chicago, 1976), pp.29-40. See also William P. Shaw, 'Milton's Choice of the Epic for *Paradise Lost*', *ELN*, 12 (1974), 15-20.

[48] O.B. Hardison, '*In Medias Res* in *Paradise Lost*', *MiltonS*, 17 (1983), 27-41 (p.30).

might add the plot of Satan's anti-pilgrimage. Both Satan and Adam are the heroes of linear plots based on conflicts in which both are defeated. The Son's plot, the inclusive plot, has a fragmented narrative, lacks the tension provided by the possibility of suffering or defeat, and is largely static. The only thing that the Son does in the dramatic plot of the poem is to talk: his triumph in the War in Heaven is related as a past event, the Passion and Second Coming as occurring in the distant future. Thus the poem, particularly in its anticlimactic account of the Passion in Book XII, subverts the role of the Son as hero.

Many of the difficulties that readers face in relating to Milton's God arise from the epic narrative: this not only uses tenses when talking about God, but magnifies the effect of those tenses by dislocating time, and thus creates a sense of God being subject to time. In *Paradise Lost*, salvation is remote and sin is present. In this Milton was a man of his time: medieval art concentrated on the Incarnation and Passion, but for the Reformation the Fall was central.[49] The epic structure of *Paradise Lost* allows Milton to emphasize the centrality of the Fall, from the first phrase, 'Of man's first disobedience', to the lines where Adam and Eve leave Eden at the end of the poem (XII.624-49). In between, the distance between God and Man is emphasized. Episodes in which Man and God are in a positive relationship are not part of the dramatic plot, but are related as past or future events – the Creation, God's habit of walking with Adam and Eve in the Garden, the Redemption. Thus Milton minimizes direct encounter between Man and God: there is nothing in the poem of what Frye describes as 'a direct and vertical relation between God and Man... in the present tense'.[50] These dislocations of time and denial of encounter contribute to the fourth plot – the plot that relates the Poet's fall and possible salvation.

4. Subverted speech: the problems of the divine dialogue

Flaws in the Poet's method are particularly apparent in his treatment of God. Book III of *Paradise Lost*, the most extensive account of God in the poem, has troubled many readers. I believe that this is because, in depicting a God who is distant from humanity, Milton has made three key literary choices: he uses narrative about God rather than the focused dialogue of plea-prayer; he then shows God speaking within that narrative; and finally, he depicts two persons of the Godhead speaking to each other.

As I have argued in Chapter 1, plea-prayer allows a poet to engage with God without having to describe or *explain* God. Plea focuses intensely on the interlocutor. It is rich in the first and second-person pronouns that create a sense of intimacy. Because pronouns do not attract articles and adjectives, the proportion of verbs tends to be higher. Many of these verbs are imperatives with suppressed subjects, and this further increases the verbal dynamism. The verbs are mostly in

---

[49] J.B. Broadbent, *Some Graver Subject* (London, 1960), pp.17-20.
[50] Frye, *Five Essays*, pp.109-10.

the present tense or urgent-future: this allows a sense that the relationship with God is outside time.

On the other hand, narrative gives a fuller, more reflective picture of the world. It can include a large amount of explanation and description, and it can talk about several participants. Narrative is consequently rich in the nouns that can attract articles and adjectives, slowing the language down and making it diffuse. It tends towards a greater concern with objects existing in space, and with events in time, whether past or predictive-future. Thus, to describe God as acting within a narrative is to represent him as operating within space and time.

Describing God as acting within a narrative involves the use of concrete language that can be ridiculous or even offensive.[51] In some of the medieval plays, God has merely to speak, and Lucifer falls into Hell;[52] in the York Cycle, God does not even speak – Satan's downfall is inherent in his motion of rebellion.[53] Milton's God, however, appears to rely on military hardware and a mighty body. The Father instructs the Son, 'my almighty arms/ Gird on, and sword upon thy puissant thigh' (VI. 713-14), and speaks of 'one sling/ Of thy victorious arm' (X.633-4). The Son's right hand grasps 'ten thousand thunders'; he rides over the 'shields and helms and helmed heads' of his foes, amid a tempest of arrows (VI. 834-52). Since Milton often uses military imagery to describe his evil agents,[54] such imagery is quite unsuitable for the Son's struggle with Satan. Milton himself alerts his readers to the defects of his narrative: he describes Raphael wondering how he can 'relate/ To human sense the invisible exploits/ Of warring spirits' (V.564-73). Later, Michael rebukes Adam for thinking of The Son's contest with Satan 'As of a duel, or the local wounds/ Of head or heel' (XII.386-95). Yet this is the very type of language that the Poet chooses to describe the activities of the Son.

The problems inherent in narrative are compounded when Milton allows God to speak, and, even worse, to speak about theology.[55] Milton's Father makes long speeches about complex theological issues, expressed in complicated syntax, and mixed with narrative and physical description. As John Hale observes, the Father is wordy, and Milton denies the Father's voice 'his own best style... the

---

[51] Lewis argues that Milton's use of concrete, anthropomorphic language makes 'the Divine laughter sound merely spiteful and the Divine rebukes querulous': *A Preface*, p.131. Mitchell believes that it causes a 'fundamental fissure in the text between ideological design and aesthetic achievement': he speaks of an 'irresponsible' and 'demonic side' of Milton's God (p.72).

[52] 'The Fall of Lucifer' plays in the Chester (lines 214-29) and N-Town (lines 66-82) Cycles.

[53] 'The Creation and the Fall of Lucifer', lines 89-96.

[54] Fowler, note to X.307-11.

[55] MacCaffrey argues that the Father speaks rather than acting, because doctrine is comprehended aurally: pp.68, 70. Milner, however, sees the Father as 'an unfortunate hybrid' of the anthropomorphic, personal God of Genesis and Milton's own belief in an abstract 'thoroughly impersonal God... who *is* reason' (pp.157-8).

God whom by definition no one has seen is here seen too clearly; humanly; in short, shrunken'. [56]

God's speeches create several problems. First, the effect of making God operate in time is magnified when God himself speaks. Milton may say that God looks at the universe 'from his prospect high,/ Wherein past, present, future he beholds...' (III.77-8), but it is hard for the reader to feel this imaginatively when God himself starts using tenses. Secondly, as Lewis observes, making God speak lays him open to the criticisms often made of humans who speak in the same way: the divine laughter 'arouses legitimately hostile reactions in us – as though we were dealing with an ordinary conflict of wills in which the winner ought not to ridicule the loser.'[57] Most seriously, the content of God's speech involves God in justifying himself. As Frye observes, there is a 'grotesque' contrast between the theological propriety of recognizing God as the source of goodness, and the dramatic impropriety of God saying this as a character, which merely gives 'the impression of a smirking hypocrite'.[58]

However, the most serious problems arise when Milton presents two persons of the Trinity talking to each other. This puts God in the position of *explaining* himself to himself.[59] In portraying the divine conversation, Milton took a risk that no other major English poet has taken. His Father and Son re-enact the debate between justice and mercy. This suggests that there is an argument within the Godhead, 'the strife/ Of mercy and justice in thy face discerned' (III.406-7), and that the Son, albeit with the Father's approval, *wins* this argument.

Given the critical debate aroused by the Father's speeches, it is surprising that critics on both sides of the argument have offered little analysis of what he actually says.[60] There has been almost no critical analysis of stylistic differences between the Father and Son.[61] As the analysis in the next two sections will show in detail, the Father distances Man by using judgemental modifiers and a syntax that

---

[56] 'Voicing Milton's God', *AUMLA*, 88 (1997), 59-70 (pp.62, 68). Hale suggests that this may be deliberate, but does not really explore Milton's reasons.

[57] Lewis, *A Preface*, p.95.

[58] Frye, *Five Essays*, p.105.

[59] Several critics have commented on the ill effects caused by this: Ricks, pp.18-20; Peter, p.13; John Demaray, *Milton's Theatrical Epic* (Cambridge, Massachusetts, 1980), pp.25-6.

[60] So far as I am aware, no critics have closely analysed the Father's use of vocabulary, word-classes, tense, and syntax. Little or no textual analysis is given by Peter, Empson, or Eagleton – critics who are hostile to the Father – or by Steadman in 'The God of *Paradise Lost* and the *Divina Commedia*', *Cithara*, 37 (1997), 22-39. The Father's supporters tend to concentrate on one aspect of Milton's style. George Miller concentrates on rhetoric: 'Stylistic Rhetoric and the Language of God in *Paradise Lost*, Book III', *Language and Style*, 8 (1975), 111-26. So does Blessington, 'Autotheodicy: The Father as Orator', *Cithara*, 14 (1975), 49-60. Beverley Sherry, 'Speech in *Paradise Lost*', *MiltonS*, 8 (1975), 253-5, concentrates on the rhythms of divine and fallen speech; T.N. Corns, *Milton's Language* (Oxford, 1990), on syntax.

[61] Without offering much analysis, Fish claims that 'the intrusion of personality is minimal... and one has little sense of a style apart from the thought': pp.66, 75. Kinney says that the Son lyricizes the Father's 'just but frigid statements': p.140.

isolates Man from connection with God; he uses many first-person pronouns to assert himself; he tends to use tautological modifiers such as '*high* supremacy' (III.205).[62] The Son, on the other hand, is concerned to restore connections: he uses equal proportions of first, second, and third-person pronouns in close connection; he tends to use the first person to offer his services; his speeches move faster than the Father's, using more verbs and fewer modifiers.

There are, moreover, marked fluctuations in the language of both Father and Son as the argument unfolds. Passages that express connection use the present tense and interconnected personal pronouns; they avoid words expressing time or space. At other times, both the Son and the Father seem self-concerned, more interested in power than in love, and remote from Man. This coincides with a use of the predictive-future, an increase in empty modifiers and words expressing time or space, and a change from true dialogue to narrative or explanation.

Milton's *descriptions* of God adhere to the Protestant tradition that human images of God should follow the Bible precisely.[63] However, many of the *actions* of his Father and Son are non-Biblical, and almost all of what they actually *say*. Milton cannot have been completely unaware of the dangers inherent in his portrayal of God. At the start of the poem the Poet prayed to the Spirit to raise him from the darkness and lowness of sin, and the Spirit's absence from Milton's heaven raises questions.

The main problem with Milton's representation of the Parliament of Heaven in Book III is that, like St Anselm's discussion of the satisfaction theory, it creates a sense of division between the Father, who emphasizes justice and the Son who emphasizes mercy. Like Anselm, he leaves the Spirit out of the equation. This sense that God has disparate, even conflicting attributes, is, I argued in Chapter 2, more common in narrative texts, texts that by their very nature subject God to the progressions of time. Unfallen or regenerate Man focuses on the unity or the harmony within the divine being: in Book VIII, God appears to the unfallen Adam as a single figure who is named only as 'Whom thou sought'st I am... author of all this thou seest' (VIII.316-17), as 'the universal Lord' and 'my maker' (VIII.376-80); at the end of the *Paradiso*, Dante finally sees a vision of the 'Light Eternal, that alone abidest in Thyself, alone knowest Thyself, and known to Thyself and knowing, lovest and smilest on Thyself.'[64] It is only from the point of view of the sinner that God has disparate, even conflicting aspects such as justice and mercy.

For many years, like some other critics, I regarded the problems caused by Milton's God as Milton's fault. It was only when I returned to *Paradise Lost* after a lapse of years and began to appreciate the poetic power of Milton's verse that I began to wonder if he could be capable of such fundamental errors in writing his poem. When I read his *Tractate of Education,* I became acutely aware of a

---

[62] For Milton's preference for adjectives see R.D. Emma, *Milton's Grammar* (London, 1964), p.67.
[63] Lewalski, *Paradise Lost*, p.111. Kitty Cohen, 'Milton's God in Council and War', *MiltonS*, III (1971), 159-84.
[64] Dante, *Paradiso*, XXXIII.124-6.

humane, at times almost a naïvely human tone and a generosity of spirit. The same spirit and humanity were apparent in the letter to Charles Diotati, where he wrote:

> Lately also, when it had been fallaciously reported to me... that you were in town, straightway and as if by storm I dashed to your crib; but 'twas 'the vision of a shadow', for nowhere did you appear.[65]

None of this fitted with my reading of Milton's God, as if he were a bombastic, vindictive, larger-than-life caricature of Calvinism.

At this point, I realized that it was more likely to be my mistake than Milton's, and I began to ask myself questions. Did Milton mean, by this division in the Godhead and this absence of the Holy Spirit, to suggest that the Poet's vision of God was neither raised nor illumined? Did he use non-Biblical statements and events in order to make the Protestant reader doubt whether this was a reliable account? Were the repellent details of God's physical violence intended to demonstrate the ridiculously inadequate view of a man who tries to visualize God as acting in space? Is his complex use of tenses meant to suggest both that all times are present to the eternal God, and that the human soul can only see God's actions from the warped viewpoint of time?[66] Are the repellent aspects of the Parliament of Heaven meant to create a tension between theological truths and the sinful Believer's response to these truths?

The answer that I propose is that some of the dilemmas raised by Milton's language and narrative method can be resolved if his account of the Parliament of Heaven is read on two levels: on one level it can be read as discussing the salvation of Man; on another, as dramatizing the Believer's internal debate about whether or not he personally can be redeemed. Such a reading is supported by the fact that, in *Paradise Lost*, Milton always places Redemption in the future: in the Son's offer of himself in Book III; in Michael's prophecy in Book XII; and even, and perhaps most significantly, as I have already observed, in the Poet's first invocation (I.1-5).

5. The Believer's anguish masked by the Father's hostility

From the outset, the Father views Adam and Eve 'From the pure empyrean where he sits' (III.57), that is, from a distance. The Father then speaks, drawing the Son's attention to Satan's journey:

> Only begotten Son, seest thou what rage
> Transports our adversary, whom no bounds
> Prescribed, no bars of hell, nor all the chains
> Heaped on him there, nor yet the main abyss
> Wide interrupt can hold...

> III.80-4

---

[65] Letter 6, *The Works of John Milton* (Columbia, 1936), Vol.XII, pp.20-1.
[66] Mitchell, however, suggests that the 'fissure' in Milton's representation of God arises by default and not by design': p.73.

In the first part of his speech the Father is not justifying himself, and does not use the first person at all. Here he is merely observing and interpreting what is happening, and his speech is succinct: there are few non-verbal modifiers to slow it down, and the verbal adjectives and participles ('Prescribed', 'Heaped', 'interrupt') allow for a compressed and vigorous syntax.[67]

As soon as the speech moves into the future tense, the language changes:

> ... and [Satan] shall pervert
> For man will hearken to his glozing lies,
> And easily transgress the sole command,
> Sole pledge of his obedience: so will fall,
> He and his faithless progeny: whose fault?
> Whose but his own? Ingrate, he had of me
> All he could have; I made him just and right,
> Sufficient to have stood, though free to fall.
> Such I created all the ethereal powers
> And spirits, both them who stood and them who failed;
> Freely they stood who stood, and fell who fell.
> Not free, what proof could they have given sincere
> Of true allegiance, constant faith or love,
> Where only what they needs must do appeared,
> Not what they would? What praise could they receive?
> What pleasure I from such obedience paid,
> When will and reason (reason also is choice)
> Useless and vain, of freedom both despoiled,
> Made passive both, had served necessity,
> Not me. They therefore as to right belonged,
> So were created, nor can justly accuse
> Their maker, or their making, or their fate,
> As if predestination overruled
> Their will, disposed by absolute decree
> Of high foreknowledge; they themselves decreed
> Their own revolt, not I: if I foreknew,
> Foreknowledge had no influence on their fault,
> Which had no less proved certain unforeknown.
> So without least impulse or shadow of fate,
> Or aught by me immutably foreseen,
> They trespass, authors to themselves in all
> Both what they judge and what they choose; for so
> I formed them free, and free they must remain,
> Till they enthrall themselves: I else must change
> Their nature, and revoke the high decree
> Unchangeable, eternal, which ordained
> Their freedom, they themselves ordained their fall.

III.92-128

---

[67] Whereas non-verbal adjectives tend to slow the pace, verbal adjectives can compress a great deal of action into a short space. Emma, however, observes that Milton uses considerably fewer verbal adjectives than Shakespeare or T.S. Eliot.

Now, rather than merely reporting what he sees, the Father begins to justify himself. His tone becomes hostile as he piles up judgemental and repetitive modifiers: 'glozing', 'easily', 'sole command,/ Sole pledge', 'faithless', 'Ingrate'. The term 'faithless progeny' draws attention to the doubtful justice, in human terms, of punishing the sinner's progeny. The Father seems almost to gloat over this prospect, even to command it with his use of '*shall* pervert'.[68] Yet at the same time, the grammar suggests that the Father holds Man responsible for his sin: when Man was virtuous, he was passive, 'placed' (by God) in the garden, the object of the verbs 'destroy' and 'pervert' (III.90-2); when he sins, he becomes active, the subject of the verbs 'hearken', 'transgress', 'fall'. The Father suggests that, even before the Fall, Man is not capable of independently acting well, only of independently sinning.[69]

The only morally positive words the Father applies to Man appear in hypothetical or negative constructions: 'Not free, what proof could they have given sincere... What praise could they receive... nor can justly accuse/ Their maker'.[70] His syntax places Man in relationship with sin rather than God: 'they themselves decreed/ Their own revolt... Till they enthral themselves... they themselves ordained their fall.' The only present, positive indicative verbs he applies to Man in this whole speech are 'they trespass' and 'man falls deceived' (III.122, 130). Thus, for the Father, Man's virtue is either impossible or already past, and what dominates the eternal present is his sin: and this is before Man has actually sinned within the narrative.[71]

This speech is monologue rather than dialogue. Apart from the first 'seest thou', the Father does not address the Son. Nor does he show any love for Man. He seems far more concerned with justifying himself than with the ideas of his Son or the fate of his creatures. It appears that his sole reason for creating Man was to gain 'pleasure... from... obedience paid' (line 107; at VII.45-56 his motive seems to be to thwart Satan). His repeated assertions ('I made him just and right... Such I created... I formed them free') suggest a self-righteous certainty, as do his judgemental and tautological modifiers ('false guile... useless and vain... high foreknowledge... high decree'). Yet, at the same time, there is a querulousness in his rhetorical questions,[72] and in the way he makes himself the subject of negative or hypothetical constructions: 'What pleasure I from such obedience paid... they themselves decreed/ Their own revolt, not I... if I foreknew... I else must change/ Their nature'.

The Father ends his speech by announcing mercy:

---

[68] Peter, p.11. Emma notes Milton's consistent use of 'shall' to express obligation or command: p.102. Compare Cummings, p.429.

[69] Mitchell says that 'One inevitably asks oneself whether Adam and Eve, if deceived by spiritual superpowers, were actually authors to themselves in all?': p.76.

[70] The Father also gives Satan freedom in Hell in order to increase his misery (I.209-20).

[71] See also Empson, p.116. Cummings comments, 'Self-justification... mixed liberally with blame-throwing... never sounds pleasant from someone in supreme power': p.430.

[72] See also Jeffrey S. Shoulson, 'The King and I', *MiltonS*, 36 (1998), 59-85 (p.65).

> The first sort by their own suggestion fell,
> Self-tempted, self-depraved: man falls deceived
> By the other first: man therefore shall find grace,
> The other none: in mercy and justice both,
> Through heaven and earth, so shall my glory excel,
> But mercy first and last shall brightest shine.
>
> III.129-34

His motive for granting mercy seems to be to make his 'glory excel' rather than to rescue his creatures. After the hostility and coldness of his speech, his sudden announcement of mercy seems unconvincing.

However, there is another way of reading this speech: the uncertainties of the Father's tone suggest that the debate between Father and Son may, on another level, function as an inner debate within the Believer's mind as to whether his own sins will be treated with justice or mercy. The Father's hostile tone and the suggestion that sin has already occurred may mask the Believer's abhorrence of his own sin, while the Father's sudden announcement of mercy may represent the Believer's hope that in his case mercy will prevail.

Such a reading seems the more likely because the Son's reply unmakes the Father's speech. The poem says that he mirrors 'all his Father' (III.139), but he does not in fact reflect justice, only 'Love without end, and without measure grace' (III.142). While the Father seems to take the side of justice in the Debate between justice and mercy, the Son takes the side of mercy.[73] He questions the Father's notion that God could justly condemn Man, and while the Father spoke coldly of Man, the Son speaks warmly:

> For should man finally be lost, should man
> Thy creature late so loved, thy youngest son
> Fall circumvented thus?
>
> III.150-2

If these words sound like a plea, the next sentence sounds like a protest, even a reproach:

> That be from thee far,
> That far be from thee, Father, who art judge
> Of all things made, and judgest only right.
> Or shall the adversary thus obtain
> His end, and frustrate thine, shall he fulfil
> His malice, and thy goodness bring to nought,
> Or proud return though to his heavier doom,
> Yet with revenge accomplished and to hell
> Draw after him the whole race of mankind,
> By his corrupted? Or wilt thou thy self

---

[73] Lewalski argues that the Father refrains from revealing his plans so that the Son can discover for himself the way to redeem Man: *Paradise Lost*, pp.115-23.

> Abolish thy creation, and unmake
> For him, what for thy glory thou hast made?
> So should thy goodness and thy greatness both
> Be questioned and blasphemed without defence.
>
> III.153-66

The Son here truly engages in dialogue, speaking *to* the Father: in this speech, he uses second-person pronouns continually, but no first-person ones.

The effect of representing the issue dramatically is to suggest that the Son wins the Father over, even dictates to him with the repeated imperative, 'that be from thee far'. The Son points out that for the Father to exercise justice against Man would be to abolish his creation, and even to unmake himself, allowing his goodness and greatness to be 'questioned and blasphemed'. If this happened, Satan would defeat the Father, becoming the subject of verbs ('frustrate', 'bring to nought') of which God's 'end' and 'goodness' are the objects. The Son uses future, hypothetical structures ('wilt thou thyself/ Abolish... and unmake... what... thou hast made') to distance this possibility. The brevity, urgency, and assurance of his plea contrast strongly with the Father's wordiness and uncertainty. His insistence that the Father cannot deny mercy without denying his own nature suggests the Believer's own urgent concern that this should be true. In response, the Father declares that it is:

> O Son, in whom my soul hath chief delight,
> Son of my bosom, Son who art alone
> My word, my wisdom, and effectual might,
> All hast thou spoken as my thoughts are, all
> As my eternal purpose hath decreed...
>
> III.168-72

The Father here uses second-person address and present tense, and really speaks *to* the Son, declaring their essential harmony.

It is therefore disconcerting when the Father immediately reverts to self-justification and hostility against Man, a change that once again occurs with a change to the future tense, subjecting God to time:[74]

> Man shall not quite be lost, but saved who will,
> Yet not of will in him, but grace in me
> Freely vouchsafed; once more I will renew
> His lapsed powers, though forfeit and enthralled
> By sin to foul exorbitant desires;
> Upheld by me, yet once more he shall stand
> On even ground against his mortal foe,
> By me upheld, that he may know how frail
> His fallen condition is, and to me owe
> All his deliverance, and to none but me.
>
> III.173-82

---

[74] Hale notes the change of tone at this point (p.63).

The Father's assertion that Man can be saved if he wills is immediately undercut when he says, 'Yet not of will in him, but grace in me.' The grammar removes any free agency: Man is the subject of the passive verbs 'lost', 'saved', 'upheld'; his powers are 'forfeit and enthralled... to foul exorbitant desires' until God renews them. Man is the subject of 'shall stand', but this action is only possible if he is 'Upheld by me... by me upheld', so that he may know his frailty and owe *all* his deliverance to God. No human effort seems possible. Here there is a conflict between theological and dramatic propriety. It may be theologically true that without God's grace all that Man can do is sin, that he can find happiness only when his will is in harmony with God's. However, for the Father to say so with a constant insistence on the first-person pronoun (twice placed in stress points at the end of lines), makes him sound tyrannical and egotistical. From this point until his address to the angels at the end of the speech (III.213) he uses no second-person pronouns: he does not actually seem to be talking to the Son at all.

Instead of showing the Father watching with compassion while Man does sin (which would be the logical way of suggesting that all times are present to God), Milton shows him foreseeing Man's sin. It is as if Milton deliberately begs the questions: why does the Father create a Man that he knows will sin; why does he set a test of obedience that he knows Man will fail?

The question becomes more urgent in the following lines when Milton raises the issue of predestination (III.183-202). Here the Father speaks more gently – of offering grace,[75] of clearing dark senses and softening stony hearts, of responding to the sinner's 'sincere intent', of placing his 'umpire conscience' in the soul as a guide. And yet there are disturbing features. In this passage, the Father mentions grace and mercy only in the context of limiting them: he has chosen *some* for 'peculiar grace...such is my will' (this merely makes him sound arbitrary);[76] sinners are warned 'to appease *betimes*/ The incensed Deity, *while* offered grace/ Invites'; sinners will '*never* taste' the Father's 'day of grace' as the Father will '*exclude*' them from mercy. Most serious is the Father's statement that neglectful men will be 'hardened, blind be blinded more,/ That they may stumble on, and deeper fall' (III.200-1). It is as if the Father is doing the hardening and blinding *so that* sinners may fall deeper into their sin and justify their punishment.

The Father next speaks of Man's inability to 'pay' satisfaction for his sin:

> But yet all is not done; man disobeying,
> Disloyal breaks his fealty, and sins
> Against the high supremacy of heaven,
> Affecting Godhead, and so losing all,
> To expiate his treason hath nought left,
> But to destruction sacred and devote,
> He with his whole posterity must die,

---

[75] For Milton's Arminian thought here see Dennis Danielson, *Milton's Good God* (Cambridge, 1982), p.85.
[76] See also Paul R. Sellin 'John Milton's *Paradise Lost* and *De Doctrina Christiana*', *MiltonS*, 34 (1996), 45-60 (p.53).

> Die he or justice must; unless for him
> Some other able, and as willing, pay
> The rigid satisfaction, death for death.

III.203-12

As is common with the satisfaction theory, Man here seems completely helpless.[77] The active verbs are again used to stress Man's ability to act only for evil: 'disobeying', 'breaks', 'sins', 'affecting Godhead', 'losing all'. As a result, Man becomes passive, 'to destruction sacred and devote', capable of only one action – dying. The Father describes a situation in which Man has cut himself off from God, and the grammar reflects this. There are no verbal processes in which Man and God are both participants: Man breaks his fealty, sins against heaven, affects Godhead, loses all, has nothing left to expiate his treason, and must therefore die. The placing of these speeches in time destroys any sense of connection between the Father and Mankind. The Father speaks of what he gave Man in the past (III.97-9); of Man's future fall (III.120-134); of future redemption or damnation (III.173-202); but he .never describes himself in harmony with Man in the present.

Such a view of Man is problematic: from a narrative point of view, Man has not yet sinned; from a Christian point of view, Man is already redeemed; from the eternal point of view, the Redemption rather than sin should be the strongest present reality. The dilemma is resolved, once again, if the passage is read as reflecting the Believer's anguished concern that for him the helplessness of sin is the present reality, while redemption is only a future possibility.

Again, the Father's speech ends with a sudden reversal:

> Say heavenly powers, where shall we find such love,
> Which of ye will be mortal to redeem
> Man's mortal crime, and just the unjust to save,
> Dwells in all heaven charity so dear?

III.213-16

The Father and the audience know that the merciful alternative will triumph: unlike the Father's earlier, querulous questions, these have the ring of confidence, the lines ending with the warm and positive words 'love', 'redeem', 'save', 'dear'. The interrogatives have the same urgency as imperatives, requiring an immediate response, calling forth the great charity that, as the Father knows and the Believer hopes, dwells always in heaven.

6. The Believer's enthusiasm masked by the Son's triumph

Milton emphasizes the ghastly pause before the Son's reply:

> And now without redemption all mankind

---

[77] In *Paradise Regained*, Milton's treatment of Christ suggests the exemplarist theory: John C. Ulreich, 'Milton's Doctrine of the Incarnation', *MiltonS*, 39 (2000), 101-28 (pp.116-17).

Must have been lost, adjudged to death and hell
By doom severe, had not the Son of God,
In whom the fulness dwells of love divine,
His dearest mediation thus renewed.

III.222-6

These lines are a powerful complex of opposing ideas. On the one hand, the 'now' suggests that Man is being judged before he has actually sinned; the lexis ('lost', 'death and hell', 'doom severe') stresses the severity of the penalty, and even begs the question whether it could possibly be just for all Mankind to be so severely punished for Adam's single sin. On the other hand, the syntax contradicts this harshness with its hypothetical structure, 'Must have been lost... had not': Man was not in fact lost. The 'now' makes present both the enormity of the sin, and the immediacy of the solution. Rather than Man being condemned before he has sinned, the lines demonstrate that he is redeemed before he has sinned.[78]

The Son sums up the situation:

Father, thy word is past, man shall find grace;
And shall Grace not find means, that finds her way,
The speediest of thy winged messengers,
To visit all thy creatures, and to all
Comes unprevented, unimplored, unsought,
Happy for man, so coming; he her aid
Can never seek, once dead in sins and lost;
Atonement for himself or offering meet,
Indebted and undone, hath none to bring.

III.227-35

The repeated negative participles ('unprevented, unimplored, unsought,') seem to lament the passivity of Man, who, 'once dead in sins and lost', cannot even *implore* or *seek* grace, but is 'Indebted and undone'. The processes of atoning and offering are turned into nouns, things that Man lacks. Once again, Man's sin is already present, and yet, there is a triumphant note as the Son resolves the dilemmas of time: the past ('thy word is past') and future tenses ('man shall find grace') are resolved in the eternal present in which Grace 'finds her way... to visit all thy creatures': through God's help the outcome is essentially 'Happy for man'.

The Son offers to die for Man:

Behold me then, me for him, life for life
I offer, on me let thine anger fall;
Account me man; I for his sake will leave
Thy bosom, and this glory next to thee
Freely put off, and for him lastly die
Well pleased.

III.236-41

---

[78] See also Kinney, p.143.

In these lines a prayer is interleaved with a promise. The grammar neatly reinforces both the Son's obedience to the Father, and his action on behalf of Man: he is the object of clauses in which the Father is the subject: ('Behold me'; 'on me let thine anger fall,/ Account me man') and the subject of clauses in which Man is the beneficiary ('life for life I offer'; 'I for his sake will leave'; 'and this glory... put off, and for him lastly die'). Here the Son uses the first person for the first time, to offer himself to the Father on behalf of Man.

Lines 236-8a contain one of the climaxes of the poem, a moment of intensely focused dialogue. The imperatives ('Behold', 'let... fall', 'Account'), with their unexpressed subjects, speed up and intensify the action. The lines are very high in pronouns (expressed and understood), all of them relating to the Father, Son, or Man: the Son's action grammatically restores the connection between God and Man '[Do thou] behold... me for him'; '[my] life for [his] life I offer [thee]'). His gratuitous offer of 'life for life' is a resounding reply to justice's demand for 'The rigid satisfaction, death for death' (III.212).

However, as soon the syntax moves into the future (III.238b), the connections weaken. Pronouns are replaced with noun phrases that make the language more wordy and remote: the Son does not speak of leaving *thee*, but 'Thy bosom, and this glory next to thee'. Milton minimizes the idea of Christ's human suffering: the human reality implied by 'die' is quickly distanced by the change to a personified 'Death' with whom the Son must contend.[79]

The passage changes from the demand to the information-giving function of dialogue, from plea to spoken narrative, as the Son goes on to describe, not his rescue of Man, but his victory over Death in the predictive-future:

> ... on me let Death wreak all his rage;
> Under his gloomy power I shall not long
> Lie vanquished; thou hast given me to possess
> Life in my self forever, by thee I live,
> Though now to Death I yield, and am his due
> All of me that can die, yet that debt paid,
> Thou wilt not leave me in the loathsome grave
> His prey, nor suffer my unspotted soul
> For ever with corruption there to dwell;
> But I shall rise victorious, and subdue
> My vanquisher, spoiled of his vaunted spoil;
> Death his death's wound shall then receive, and stoop
> Inglorious, of his mortal sting disarmed.
> I through the ample air in triumph high
> Shall lead hell captive maugre hell, and show
> The powers of darkness bound. Thou at the sight
> Pleased, out of heaven shall look down and smile,
> While by thee raised I ruin all my foes,
> Death last, and with his carcase glut the grave.

III.241-59

---

[79] As Empson notes, no one here mentions 'that the Son is to die by torture' (p.128).

Again the poetry weakens, with many auxiliary verbs and empty modifiers ('[Death's] gloomy power', 'loathsome grave', 'stoop/ Inglorious', 'ample air', 'triumph high'). Again the language becomes bound by time ('then', 'Then', 'Thenceforth', 'long absent'), and space ('through the ample air'; 'Thou... out of heaven shalt look down'; 'enter heaven'). In the Son's first speech, he did not use the first person at all; in the first part of this speech (III.227-41a) he used it only to offer himself; here he uses it to revel in his future triumph in the temporal world. In this speech the Father also seems self-concerned: he is pleased, not by Man's Redemption, but by the defeat of the enemy, smiling while the Son ruins his foes.

However, when the Son describes his entry to heaven, he again becomes centred on the Father, and his use of the first person immediately lapses:

> Then with the multitude of my redeemed
> Shall enter heaven long absent, and return,
> Father, to see thy face, wherein no cloud
> Of anger shall remain, but peace assured,
> And reconcilement; wrath shall be no more
> Thenceforth, but in thy presence joy entire.
>
> III.260-5

Although the Son's last words stress 'joy entire', the image of anger is stronger. It is unfortunate that anger is again associated with the Father: it has clouded his face, and the peace, and joy that fill his presence are brought there by the Son.

Milton treats the Redemption with a curious mix of the heroic theory (which is motivated by God-in-Christ's love and mercy and stresses Christ's divinity) and the satisfaction theory (which is motivated by the need to placate God's justice and stresses Christ's human suffering).[80] The Son's martial victory is heroic,[81] but the Father earlier insisted on 'rigid satisfaction'. Langland got the best of both worlds: first, he gave a brief but moving account of Christ's human sufferings; secondly, Christ's triumphant speech outside Hell stunned Lucifer into silence; this minimized the need for a physical account of Christ's victory. Here Milton gets the worst of both worlds: first, he minimizes The Son's human suffering; secondly he writes a concrete narrative about his spiritual conquest ('with his carcass glut the grave' seems particularly offensive). Moreover, Milton's use of the satisfaction theory causes a separation in the Godhead, requiring the Son to pay satisfaction to the Father. As Broadbent observes,

> ... the divine sacrifice is vicarious, not the self-sacrifice of the Father-in-the-Son... All the psycho-mythic power of the gospel depends on its being God who suffers and rises again from the penalty of death that his own justice requires.

---

[80] Calvin and Luther used both doctrines: McClendon, p.206. James E. Johnston notes the critical consensus that Milton preferred the satisfaction theory: 'Milton on the Doctrine of the Atonement', *Renascence*, 38 (1985), 40-53 (pp.40-2).

[81] William J. Rewak, 'Book III of *Paradise Lost*', *MiltonQ*, 11:4 (1977), .97-102 (p.100).

> Without this identity of judicial with suffering God, the Father is not more remarkable than Abraham offering Isaac, and the Son no more than a martyr.[82]

If the speech is read as the Son's declaration of triumph, it lacks emotional and poetic power and raises disturbing questions about God's motivation for Atonement.

However, once again, if the speech is read on another level, as the Believer's appropriation of the Son's voice,[83] it has a completely different ring: the future tense now expresses the Believer's faith in his own future salvation; the objectification of 'Death' indicates that the natural human fear of dying has been replaced by a Christian confidence in victory over death; the concrete details and empty modifiers merely suggest that the Believer is carried away by his enthusiasm for the offer of salvation; finally, under cover of the Son's voice, he allows himself to address the Father, stressing that anger is past and peace present.

The Father responds with his warmest speech of the poem:

> O thou in heaven and earth the only peace
> Found out for mankind under wrath, O thou
> My sole complacence! well thou knowest how dear,
> To me are all my works, nor man the least
> Though last created, that for him I spare
> Thee from my bosom and right hand, to save,
> By losing thee awhile, the whole race lost.
> Thou therefore whom thou only canst redeem,
> Their nature also to thy nature join;
> And be thy self man among men on earth,
> Made flesh, when time shall be, of virgin seed,
> By wondrous birth: be thou in Adam's room
> The head of all mankind, though Adam's son.

                                                        III.274-86

This passage is true dialogue: the passage is in the present tense, with 'when time shall be' and 'shall be restored' expressing a promise rather than describing a temporal future. It is tightly focused on the three participants. For the first time, the Father uses second-person more frequently than first-person pronouns. For the first and only time, the Father applies a positive modifier, 'dear', to Man, and uses Adam's name.

However, this mood does not last long: the Father casually declares that the Son will restore 'As many as are restored, without thee none' (III.289), as if it does not much matter how many will be restored. The Father then reverts to Man's sinfulness:

> His crime makes guilty all his sons, thy merit
> Imputed shall absolve them who renounce
> Their own both righteous and unrighteous deeds,

---

[82] Broadbent, pp.154-5.

[83] McMahon suggests that Books III and VI 'ring with the Bard's piety': p.151.

And live in thee transplanted, and from thee
Receive new life. So man, as is most just,
Shall satisfy for man, be judged and die,
And dying rise, and rising with him raise
His brethren ransomed with his own dear life.
So heavenly love shall outdo hellish hate
Giving to death, and dying to redeem,
So dearly to redeem what hellish hate
So easily destroyed, and still destroys
In those who, when they may, accept not grace.

III.290-302

Here there is a tension in the language, shown in the opposing pairs of line endings: die/raise; life/hate; redeem/hate; destroys/grace. Man's weakness is stressed: even his 'righteous deeds' are worthless; he can still be destroyed by 'hellish hate'. Yet at the same time, the rising verb phrases ('dying rise, and rising with him raise'; 'dying to redeem') have a note of triumph; for the first time, the Father places Man into intimate relationship with the divine, talking of the Son's 'brethren'.

The Father follows this brief account of the Son's love with an extensive account of his future glory:

Because thou hast, though throned in highest bliss
Equal to God, and equally enjoying
Godlike fruition, quitted all to save
A world from utter loss, and hast been found
By merit more than birthright Son of God,
Found worthiest to be so by being good,
Far more than great or high; because in thee
Love hath abounded more than glory abounds,
Therefore thy humiliation shall exalt
With thee thy manhood also to this throne,
Here shalt thou sit incarnate, here shalt reign
Both God and man, Son both of God and man,
Anointed universal king, all power
I give thee, reign forever, and assume
Thy merits; under thee as head supreme
Thrones, princes, powers, dominions I reduce:
All knees to thee shall bow, of them that bide
In heaven, or earth, or under earth in hell,
When thou attended gloriously from heaven
Shalt in the sky appear, and from thee send
The summoning archangels to proclaim
Thy dread tribunal: forthwith from all winds
The living, and forthwith the cited dead
Of all past ages to the general doom
Shall hasten, such a peal shall rouse their sleep.
Then all thy saints assembled, thou shalt judge
Bad men and angels, they arraigned shall sink
Beneath thy sentence; hell her numbers full,

Thenceforth shall be forever shut. Mean while
The world shall burn, and from her ashes spring
New heaven and earth, wherein the just shall dwell,
And after all their tribulations long
See golden days, fruitful of golden deeds,
With joy and love triumphing, and fair truth.
Then thou thy regal sceptre shalt lay by,
For regal sceptre then no more shall need,
God shall be all in all. But all ye gods,
Adore him, who to compass all this dies,
Adore the Son, and honour him as me.

III.305-43

The Father's interest in the Son's future glory makes it hard to believe his assertion that 'in thee/ Love has abounded more than glory abounds' (III.311-12).[84] Again the pace is slowed by compound verbs ('Here shalt thou sit incarnate, here shalt reign') and empty modifiers ('head supreme', 'summoning archangels to proclaim', 'fair truth', 'regal sceptre'). Again there is a strong sense of temporal ('When', 'Then', 'Thenceforth', 'Mean while', 'Then') and spatial relationships ('to this throne', 'Here thou shalt sit', 'here shalt reign', 'in the sky'). The Father closes by asking the angels to 'honour him as me': again he is concerned with divine status, although, as he welcomes the Son, first-person pronouns are replaced by second-person ones.

It sounds unpleasantly smug for Father and Son to talk to each other about the Son's future glory, undermining the idea that for God all times are present. They repeat each other, telling the story twice and prolonging it beyond its climax. This weakens the immediacy of the Son's offer to redeem Man. However, the passage has a different ring if read as the Believer's enthusiastic assent to the Son's triumph, his warning of the final 'dread tribunal', and a statement of faith in the 'New heaven and earth, wherein the just shall dwell' and 'God shall be all in all' (III.325-43).[85]

It may be helpful here to summarize the discussion of the heavenly conversation. Its language sets up tensions between the Father and Son: the Father's lexis and syntax emphasize sin and alienation, while the Son's emphasize connection; the Father appears to be on the side of justice and death, the Son on the side of mercy and life; the Father appears self-asserting, the Son self-denying; the Father can sound uncertain, the Son always speaks with assurance. Problems arise when either speaks in the predictive-future tense, contradicting the idea that all times are present to God, suggesting that Man is condemned before he has sinned, and making both Persons sound self-concerned.

These dilemmas can be resolved if the episode is read on two levels: as Milton's *public* and theologically sound account of Redemption; and as the Believer's anguished but *private* debate about his own spiritual status. Whereas

---

[84] Empson says that 'the passage turns from generosity to pride of power': pp.137-8.
[85] Robert M. Myers argues that Milton suggests either the dissolution of hell or universal salvation: '"God Shall Be All in All"', *Seventeenth Century*, 5 (1990), 43-53.

Mankind's sin is past and redeemed already, the Believer's sin continues as he continues to narrate the poem. The future passages then can be read as the Believer's over-enthusiastic expressions of faith and hope that God's mercy, already granted to Mankind, will, in the future, be granted to him as an individual.

7. The Believer's covert encounter

At the end of the Parliament is a passage that indicates the presence of a humble narrative voice in *Paradise Lost*, a voice that is distinct from the public voice of the Poet, a voice that I have been calling 'the Believer'. The angels sing a hymn to both Father and Son, which Milton reports in indirect speech:

> Thee Father first they sung omnipotent,
> Immutable, immortal, infinite,
> Eternal king; thee author of all being,
> Fountain of light, thy self invisible
> Amidst the glorious brightness where thou sit'st
> Throned inaccessible, but when thou shadest
> The full blaze of thy beams, and through a cloud
> Drawn round about thee like a radiant shrine,
> Dark with excessive bright thy skirts appear,
> Yet dazzle heaven, that the brightest seraphim
> Approach not, but with both wings veil their eyes.
>
> III.372-82

The pronoun 'Thee' is in the objective case, the object of 'sung'. However, the angels must actually have used the vocative case and sung, '*Thou*, Father omnipotent... *thou* author of all being', and later, '*Thou*... of all creation first,/ Begotten Son' (III.383-4). It is thus the persona who addresses the Father (and later the Son) directly, telling him that the angels 'sung thee'.

This puts the whole hymn in the Believer's own mouth, but humbly: he does not use the first-person pronouns that would clearly place himself in the text, but slips unobtrusively into the song; like the seraphim, he dares not approach God directly, but veils the eyes of his imagination. There is a compelling tension between the intimacy implied by his use of second-person pronouns and the distance implied by his failure to use first-person ones. In contrast with the Poet's ambitious prayers for poetic inspiration in the invocations, the Believer here is concerned only with God's glory, asks nothing for himself, and effaces himself almost completely.

In this passage, the Father is the subject of only two verbs ('sit'st' and 'shadest', both in the present tense): rather than using verbs to describe the Father's temporal actions in relation to his creatures, the persona here uses the negative abstract nouns and adjectives of the *via negativa* ('Immutable, immortal, infinite,/ Eternal king', 'author of all being,/ Fountain of light', 'invisible', 'inaccessible') approaching God as a mystic might.[86] He next uses the present tense to describe the eternal essence of the Son

> In whose conspicuous countenance, without cloud
> Made visible, the almighty Father shines...
>
> III.385-6

However, as soon as the voice leaves simple praise and returns to the *via positiva* and to narrative, *hubris* returns. The narrator starts using language that associates God with physical violence, relating in the past tense how the Father 'threw down/ The aspiring dominations', and the Son drove his flaming chariot, 'o'er the necks... of warring angels', intending 'To execute fierce vengeance on his foes'(III.390-9). Although the narrator stresses that the Father's mercy and grace incline him to pity Man, he also represents the Son as appeasing the Father's wrath, and ending 'the strife/ Of mercy and justice in thy face discerned' (III.400-407). This makes the Father subject to time, and unable to resolve the conflict between mercy and justice without the Son's help. The Believer's vision in the hymn thus declines from eternal transcendence to a concrete, spatial, and temporal view as his voice merges back into the voice of the Poet.

At the end of this time-bound passage, the hubristic voice of the Poet returns, using the first person, once again, to draw attention to himself and his artistic endeavour:[87]

> Hail, Son of God, saviour of men, thy name
> Shall be the copious matter of my song
> Henceforth, and never shall my harp thy praise
> Forget, nor from thy Father's praise disjoin.
>
> III.412-15

An interesting comparison to this passage is George Herbert's 'Praise II':

> Wherefore with my utmost art
>   I will sing thee,
> And the cream of all my heart
>   I will bring thee...
>
> Sev'n whole dayes, not one in seven,
>   I will praise thee.
> In my heart, though not in heaven,
>   I can raise thee.

---

[86] Mitchell thinks that this passage is not 'able to alleviate the problems of the preceding presentation of embodied deity': p.82.

[87] Fixler briefly notes the 'startling shift in pronouns': pp.170-2. See also Paul Reifelhoess, 'Milton's Pronomial Mating Dance', *MiltonQ*, 29 (1995), 106-11. Michael Lieb suggests that Milton here appropriates the angels' voice and offers 'his poem as the vehicle through which the voice of God is able to speak', but does not note the self-assurance that this implies: 'Reading God', *MiltonS*, 25 (1989), 213-43 (pp.236-7).

Here Herbert inverts the usual syntactic patterns in order to place his persona and his art in the lesser stress points at the start of clauses and/or lines, and God at the greater stress points at the end. The repeated rhyme on 'thee' reinforces the significance of God. Herbert focuses on the *process* of faith, on what he will *do*: 'sing', 'bring', 'praise', and 'raise'.

Milton's Poet, however, is concerned with the *product*: instead of Herbert's simple clause structure ('*I* will sing *thee*'), which places the Poet in a direct verbal relationship with God, he uses the wordy and nominal 'thy name/ Shall be the copious matter of my song'. This places the Father in the weaker stress position at the start of the clause and the Poet's work in the stronger position at the end. The clauses 'never shall my harp thy praise/ Forget' and 'nor from thy Father's praise disjoin' surround the divine with the Poet's activity. The negative constructions are weaker than Herbert's positive ones, allowing the possibility that the Poet *will* 'forget' and 'disjoin': the words 'forget' and 'disjoin' have a disturbing ring when placed at stress points at the ends of clauses and at the beginning and end of the line.

At the start of the poem, the persona declined from a humble request to be raised and enlightened by the Spirit to a prideful attempt to 'justify the ways of God to men' (I.1-25); his narrative, instead of soaring to heaven, immediately descended into hell. Here the persona starts humbly, avoiding the first-person and concentrating on God, concludes with a fulsome statement of his own poetic aims, and immediately breaks his promise of focusing on the Father and Son by returning to the activities of Satan, who is like a vulture intent on his prey (III.417ff.)

Before the Parliament of Heaven, the Poet appealed to the divine light for inward vision with which to see 'things invisible to mortal sight'. This closing hymn stresses that the brightest seraphim dare not approach the Father's light. In between, the narrator starts the Parliament with a visual description of the spatial relationships in heaven; he puts words into God's mouth; his poetry looks, through the Son's speeches and the angelic hymn, at the very face of the Father, describing it as obscured by a 'cloud of anger' (III.262-3) and contorted with 'the strife/ Of mercy and justice' (III.406-7). His poetry has attempted to make the invisible God visible and audible, and has subjected the eternal God to the fluctuations of time.

Here is the heart of the poem's tensions: the Parliament both affirms God's love as shown in the Redemption, and demonstrates the Poet's sinfulness in attempting to convey eternal verities through the warping and idolatrous medium of a time-bound narrative. The public voice of the Poet, self-concerned and self-satisfied, is not aware of the dangers of this enterprise. The narrative movement of the rest of the poem takes him further and further away from God: as I have already argued, the invocations clearly demonstrate his decline.

However, the covert, humble voice of the Believer, the voice that is primarily concerned with spiritual matters, becomes stronger as the poem continues: in the tone of anguish with which he narrates Adam's fall, a fall that has parallels to his own; in the tone of enthusiasm with which he relates Christ's redemption; and in the subdued, but nonetheless hopeful tone in which he relates the final scene.

8. Adam's encounter: from dialogue to silence

In *Paradise Lost*, whenever the narrator mentions God in relation to sin, he depicts him as distant, hostile, concrete, and time-bound – the view of the unregenerate sinner. This type of representation dominates the narrator's account of God's relationship with his creatures. Milton may say that God 'With man, as with his friend, familiar used/ To sit indulgent' (IX.1-3), but he does not actually show this happening.

Man's only innocent encounter with God in the poem is depicted as a past event that Adam relates to Raphael (VIII.311-499). Even here, God barely introduces himself to Adam before warning him not to eat the Fruit, threatening him with the 'bitter consequence' of death and 'a world/ Of woe and sorrow' (VIII.316-33). The only time that God and Man meet in the dramatic plot is after the Fall, when the Father sends the Son to judge the fallen Adam and Eve. Neither the Father nor the Son mentions love, nor expresses any sorrow at Man's defection; instead, Milton considerably extends the Biblical rebukes (X.103-56). Only at the end of the interview does the Son feel pity and clothe Adam and Eve. However, he still sees them as 'his enemies' (X 219), and leaves them without offering them a final word of comfort. It is in Heaven, not in the Garden, that the Son mixes 'intercession sweet' with his report to the Father (X 225-8).

Yet Milton's dramatization of the loss of encounter would not be so powerful if he never suggested what present encounter might involve. Milton does convey the possibility of an unfallen, warm relationship between God and Creation in its pure state in his magnificent accounts of Creation and in the Father's commendation of Abdiel (VI.29-43). The sense of a positive encounter is also especially strong in the delightful intimacy of the second part of God's reported dialogue with Adam. This dialogue turns largely upon speech. Having warned Adam of the Tree, God calls him to claim lordship over the animals by naming them (VIII.336-48). He encourages Adam to talk, smiling when Adam dares to complain of his solitude (VIII.357-68), teasing him by suggesting that he could speak to the animals, and praising him for recognizing that he is above them:

> Expressing well the spirit within thee free,
> My image, not imparted to the brute,
> Whose fellowship therefore unmeet for thee
> Good reason was thou freely shouldst dislike.
>
> VIII.440-3

This passage suggests Man's natural capacity, when raised by God, for intimate, even bold, conversation with him.

However, when Adam is put to the test, he fails to preserve God's pattern for rational dialogue. When Adam hears Eve's 'blithe' and glib account of eating the fruit, he responds with silence:

> On the other side, Adam, soon as he heard
> The fatal trespass done by Eve, amazed,

> Astonied stood and blank, while horror chill
> Ran through his veins, and all his joints relaxed;
> From his slack hand the garland wreathed for Eve
> Down dropped, and all the faded roses shed:
> Speechless he stood, and pale, till thus at length
> First to himself he inward silence broke.
>
> IX.888-95

While Adam remains silent, he remains unfallen, aware of the full enormity of sin, but when he speaks, as Valerie Carnes notes, he 'finds himself unable to distinguish between true and false speech and reason'.[88]

In this crisis, a direct and immediate appeal to God might have saved both Adam and Eve. Eve's fall lies not so much in eating the fruit as in asserting her will against Adam's and insisting on leaving him: she is compared as she does so to pagan goddesses (IX.385-96). Similarly, Adam falls in the inner monologue in which he addresses himself not to God, but to Eve:

> O fairest of creation, last and best
> Of all God's works, creature in whom excelled
> Whatever can to sight or thought be formed,
> Holy, divine, good, aimiable or sweet!
> How art thou lost, how on a sudden lost,
> Defaced, deflowered, and now to death devote?
>
> IX.896-901

Forgetting that God's command was given directly to him (VIII.323-33), not to Eve, forgetting that he is Eve's superior, formed for God (IV.295-6), he laments the deflowering of her beauty. Adam is privileging sight:[89] to him Eve is the 'fairest' and thus the 'best' of 'God's works'. The words 'works', 'formed' and 'defaced' suggest that Eve is a work of art, a sculpture, almost his own creation, 'flesh of flesh/ Bone of my bone'. In placing the creature (even one formed by God) above the Creator, he is idolatrous. He tells himself that he cannot 'forgo/ Thy sweet converse and love so dearly joined' to 'live again… forlorn' (forgetting that God would still be visiting him). He is drawn by the link of 'flesh of flesh/ Bone of my bone', and resolves never to be parted from Eve (IX.896-916). Adam thus places the love of Eve above the love of God, converse with her above converse with God, the bond of the flesh above the dictates of reason. He fails to take responsibility for what has happened and to ask God for the help he needs to sort it out. In failing to trust to God's mercy, asking for forgiveness in this crisis, he constructs God as a God only of justice and punishment, and destroys the possibility of human dialogue with God. He responds to God in the judgement scene, not with repentance and humility, but, 'sore beset', with lying self-justification and counter-accusation: he claims that he 'could suspect no ill'

---

[88] Valerie Carnes, 'Time and Language in Milton's *Paradise Lost*', *ELH*, 37 (1970), 517-39 (p.534).

[89] Carnes notes that Eve's account of her experience 'stresses the visual effects': p.534.

(although clearly he did) of the woman God gave him; he sarcastically describes her as 'thy perfect gift, so good/ So fit, so acceptable, so divine... Her doing seemed to justify the deed' (X.125-43).

Adam use of the word 'justify' in this context, recalls the Poet's ambition to 'justify the ways of God to man' and suggests that he too may have been trying to justify the unjustifiable (the making of a poem whose style and form was 'So fit, so acceptable, so divine' as to 'justify' his writing such a potentially idolatrous work).

God's rebuke makes it clear that Adam has sinned in privileging sight above hearing:

> Was she thy God, that her thou didst obey
> Before his voice, or was she made thy guide,
> Superior, or but equal, that to her
> Thou dist resign thy manhood, and the place
> Wherein God set thee above her made of thee,
> And for thee, whose perfection far excelled
> Hers in all real dignity: adorned
> She was indeed, and lovely to attract
> Thy love, not thy subjection, and her gifts
> Were such as under government well seemed,
> Unseemly to bear rule, which was thy part
> And person, hadst thou known thy self aright.
>
> X.145-56

God's tone here is reasonable – a father explaining, in detail, the mistake the child has made. Adam has valued Eve's physical charms above God's voice, and love above a rational rule in obedience to God. His sin is idolatry, making Eve his God. Adam requires this lengthy response because of the evasive and specious rationality of his own self-justification and blaming, but the sound of the Son's voice penetrates his soul, and he later remembers the 'mild/ And gracious temper' of this speech (X.1046-7).

It is significant that when the Son challenges Eve, she '*confesses soon*' meekly using the simple biblical words, 'The serpent me beguiled and I did eat', without further blame or self-justification, and the Son, instead of rebuking her further, turns to the serpent (X.159-65), and curses him.

In between the Son's uttering the curse upon the serpent and the curse upon Eve, Milton inserts a passage that asserts that the curse was 'verified' when

> ... Jesus son of Mary second Eve...
>   ...rising from his grave
> Spoiled principalities and powers...
> Captivity led captive through the air,
> The realm it self of Satan long usurped,
> Whom he shall tread at last under our feet.
>
> X.182-92

Unlike the other accounts of Redemption in the poem, which are in the future tense (I.4-5; III.238-51, 283-9; XII.375-445),[90] this is in the past, as if at this point the quiet voice of the Believer asserts the validity of the Redemption, confident in what he is saying because he is relying on Biblical language and faith in God's mercy rather than on his own imagination.

Adam's response to God's judgement is not a cry for mercy, but a sullen silence. Only after an interval of 500 lines does he begin to respond, questioning God's justice in making him without his request, seeing God as mocking him with death, hearing God's 'dreadful' voice 'thunder in my ears', fearing a 'horrid' continuation of the spirit in a 'living death' after the bodily death, fearing that God's anger and rigour will never be satisfied, asking the very vexing question 'why should all mankind/ For one man's fault thus guiltless be condemned', fearing that he will be reviled by his progeny, but finally accepting that the blame lights 'On me, me only' (X.720-844).[91] Nevertheless, when Eve attempts to soften him, he reproaches her harshly, vilifying her as a 'serpent', describing her as if she were indeed an idol (not recognizing that the idolatry is in worshipping the 'idol', rather than in the thing itself):

> Out of my sight, thou serpent, that name best
> Befits thee with him leagued, thy self as false
> And hateful; nothing wants, but that thy shape,
> Like his, and colour serpentine may show
> Thy inward fraud, to warn all creatures from thee
> Henceforth; lest that too heavenly form, pretended
> To hellish falsehood, snare them.
>
> X.867-73

First Adam blames Eve as the source of his woes, 'had not thy pride... rejected my forewarning'; then he begins to objectify her as 'but a show... a rib/Crooked by nature, bent... supernumerary... This novelty on earth, this fair defect/ Of nature'. He then distances her even further by extrapolating general misery to men at the hands of women, foretelling various misfortunes that will prevent a man from finding a 'fit mate', including that the woman of his choice may be previously married 'To a fell adversary' (X.895-908). In constructing woman as bound to an 'adversary', in seeking to break the connection of love with her, and in pitilessly blaming Eve for what he has made of her, Adam takes a similar position to the Father in Book III.

Carnes, showing how Eve uses 'fallen' language and 'bland words' as she describes her fall, and how Adam falls 'into a totally new language system' suggests that 'The Fall has deranged the intellect'.[92] However, Golda Werman

---

[90] Michael does break into the historic present at the climax of his story (XII.415-20).

[91] Desmond M. Hamlet suggests that Adam is only able to take this step 'because he has been judged earlier by the Son': 'Recalcitrance, Damnation, and the Justice of God', *MiltonS*, 8 (1975), 267-91 (p.275).

[92] Carnes, pp.533-6.

suggests that, in showing how Adam and Eve 'atone in Book X... before Adam has been educated as a Christian', Milton

> ...does not deny the need for a profound faith in Christ... But in his passionate advocacy of unrestricted free will and the individual's responsibility for his own moral life, even including atonement, he emphasizes and dramatizes the role of choice in the developing personalities and characters of Adam and Eve ... Instead of depending on Jesus to be their intermediary in heaven and to help them on earth, they rely on each other for support and inspiration. Milton asserts the centrality of Christ's sacrifice as a prerequisite for redemption, but he has the affirmation of Christ's role take place in heaven, unknown to the sinners in Eden at the time that they strengthen each other in their struggle back to God.[93]

If this is so, Eve is the first to bring about atonement, and her repentant speech, in her desire to restore connection with Adam, recalls the Son's in Book III.

> Forsake me not thus, Adam, witness heaven
> What love sincere, and reverence in my heart
> I bear thee, and unweeting have offended,
> Unhappily deceived; thy suppliant
> I beg, and clasp thy knees; bereave me not,
> Whereon I live, thy gentle looks, thy aid,
> Thy counsel in this uttermost distress,
> My only strength and stay: forlorn of thee,
> Whither shall I betake me, where subsist?
> While yet we live, scarce one short hour perhaps,
> Between us two let there be peace, both joining,
> As joined in injuries, one enmity
> Against a foe by doom express assigned us,
> That cruel serpent: on me exercise not
> Thy hatred for this misery befallen,
> On me already lost, me than thy self
> More miserable; both have sinned, but thou
> Against God only, I against God and thee,
> And to the place of judgement will return,
> There with my cries importune heaven, that all
> The sentence from thy head removed may light
> On me, sole cause to thee of all this woe,
> Me me only just object of his ire.

X.914-36

Eve's appeals are centred on Adam, using the plea-imperatives and pronouns of plea prayer, using Adam's name. Her offer to sacrifice herself, asking God that his ire 'may light/ On me... Me me only', echoes the Son's request in the Parliament of Heaven:

---

[93] Golda Werman, 'Repentance in *Paradise Lost*', *MiltonS*, 22 (1986), 121-39 (pp.127-8, 133).

Behold me then, me for him, life for life
I offer, on me let thine anger fall...

III.236-7

She speaks of Adam's virtues, 'gentle looks... aid... counsel... strength'. In so doing she recalls him to his better self and thus, in a sense, redeems him: she enables him to restore his connection with her and to take responsibility for himself, admitting that her 'frailty and infirmer sex' was 'To me committed and by me exposed' (X.952-7). As in Book III where 'charity so dear' and the 'fulness... of love divine' (III.216-25) restores Man to harmony with God, so here Eve's 'love sincere' restores her to harmony with Adam, and her language, in so far as it is repentant and seeks reconnection, is not entirely fallen.

Although Eve's repentant speech moves Adam to compassion and repentance (X.909-46),[94] the possibility for direct speech with God is lost. Whereas Milton reported in direct speech the unanimous words of praise-prayer spoken by the unfallen Adam and Eve (IV.720-39), he reports their plea-prayer in indirect speech:

...they forthwith to the place
Repairing where he judged them prostrate fell
Before him reverent, and both confessed
Humbly their faults, and pardon begged, with tears
Watering the ground, and with their sighs the air
Frequenting, sent from hearts contrite, in sign
Of sorrow unfeigned, and humiliation meek.

X.1098-104

In a plea-prayer, God may not actually speak, but the speaker's urgent requests powerfully suggest God's potential response. A Donne Sonnet, for example, uses many pronouns and verbs to stress the processes in which both God and Man participate. Here Milton relates only the sinner's side of the exchange: confession, begging of pardon, tears, sighs, sorrow, humiliation; there are no processes in which God and Man relate directly to each other.

The prayers of Adam and Eve do not reach God directly: turned into things rather than actions, they fly to heaven where the Son mixes them in a golden censer before presenting them (XI.14-44) – Man's prayers can no longer reach the Father without the Son's intercession. The Father sends Michael to expel Adam and Eve from Paradise and to comfort them by foretelling the Redemption (XI.99-125), but he does not himself respond directly to their prayers.

The poem's narrative thus demonstrates that direct dialogue with God is only possible for the unfallen Adam and Eve in Eden. Yet the Poet had the *hubris* to attempt to depict what the divine Persons say to each other in Heaven. Book IX shows that direct dialogue with God is lost when Adam chooses to look at Eve rather than appeal to God, and to trust in the creature rather than in the Creator. In

---

[94] Cheryl H. Fresch, 'Human and Divine Reconciliation in *Paradise Lost*, X-XI', in *Praise Disjoined*, ed. William P. Shaw (New York, 1991), pp. 259-71.

Book X, Milton, in the voice of the Son, clearly identifies this sin as an idolatrous elevating of the beloved to the status of 'thy God'. From this point on, the voice of the Poet, who has been more concerned with his own creation than with his Creator, is also silenced, and the rest of the poem is narrated in the unobtrusive voice of the Believer with no further invocations or interruptions from the Poet. Moreover, as Adam and Eve are unable to pray directly to God, so the Poet is unable to overhear and exactly repeat their prayers. The poetry itself begins to lose power, and in the last two books, as if in repentance for the idolatrous hubris of his undertaking, Milton mars the poetry of the ending of his epic.

9. The anguish of sin and the silencing of the Poet

All of Ricoeur's anguishes are present in *Paradise Lost*: the anguish of death in Adam and Eve's speeches after the Fall; psychic disintegration in the corruption of language and reason in the fallen speeches; the anguish of history in Michael's speech; the anguish of doubt in the questioning of God's goodness by Satan, Adam, and even the Son. Yet it is the anguish of sin that predominates. It informs the most profound moments of tragedy, when the reader can most appreciate the protagonists' potential nobility: Satan's recognition of his own malice and his admission that God could still redeem him, before he chooses obduracy (IV.32-113); Eve's repentant speech to Adam (X.909-36); Adam's anguish at Eve's sin (IX.896-16) and his acceptance of responsibility for his own (X.947-65).

Milton abandons the linear narrative of most Christian stories: he allows Satan to subvert the Christian form of the pilgrimage; he chooses and then exaggerates the convolutions of the epic form. This allows him to emphasize distance from God: to place sin in the beginning, middle, and end of his work; to render moments of positive connection with God in the past or future tense; to set Redemption in the remote future of the inclusive plot. Whereas the other poets treated so far depict a movement from sin towards virtue and encounter with God, Milton dramatizes three motions away from God – those of Satan, Adam and Eve, and the Poet.

To a large extent all of these sins involve language, but none of them is resolved, within the poem, through the medium of language. Open confession of sin to God and subsequent reconciliation does not seem to be an option for Milton. Thus Satan, instead of using language to confess his sin, uses it to deceive his peers and Eve; he is punished by losing the power of language (X.517-19), and by being divided from God forever. Adam and Eve, having entered into Satan's deceit, lose their power of innocent speech, and make their 'solitary way' out of Eden, never more to talk directly to God. The Poet, having used the invocations to declare his poetic purposes rather than to talk to God, is also silenced after the invocation of Book IX.

In the course of dramatizing the Poet's sinfulness, Milton does irreparable harm to the fabric of his chosen form, the epic. M.M. Bakhtin argues that the epic, as we know it, is 'an absolutely completed and finished' genre: 'congealed and half moribund', it is concerned with 'an absolute past of national beginnings and peak times'. Epic, he says, is isolated from personal experience; it lacks any temporal connection with the 'times in which the singer and his listeners are located'; it has 'no loopholes... through which we glimpse the future'; it demands 'a pious attitude towards itself' and can be destroyed through laughter:

> Laughter has the remarkable power of making an object come up close... where one can... turn it upside down, inside out, peer at it from above and below, break open its external shell, look into its center, doubt it, take it apart, dismember it, lay it bare and expose it, examine it freely and experiment with it. Laughter demolishes fear and piety before an object, before a world, making of it an object of familiar contact and thus clearing the ground for an absolutely free investigation of it.[95]

This is precisely what Milton does, albeit with a very grim humour: he deconstructs the epic form, ridiculing its heroic conventions; he makes his story relevant to his hearers who are still in the middle of salvation history; and he puts his own perspectives and problems into the invocations. At the end of the poem he magnifies the form's temporal dislocations even further by opening a large window onto the future of salvation history in Book XII.

Later writers complain that Milton exhausted the possibilities of the epic. Keats gave up writing *The Fall of Hyperion*, remarking that 'Miltonic verse cannot be written but in an artful or rather artist's humour'; that is, the epic style had stopped being natural for the poet.[96] T.S. Eliot believed that 'Milton made a great epic impossible for succeeding generations'[97] because every poet exhausts some possibility of the language.[98] But perhaps this depletion of the epic form was not merely a result of Milton's mastery. Perhaps he deliberately found and magnified flaws in the epic form as if to show that his ambition to write an epic to rival 'Maeonides' (III.35) was in itself sinful. This is suggested by the poor quality of poetic writing in Books XI and XII, particularly in Milton's account of the Passion.

By writing in the first person, the medieval lyrics, Langland, and Donne invite their readers to share a moment of encounter with God through a heartfelt response to the Passion. Using the past or present tense, they depict the Passion as having already happened, or as actually happening in front of the reader's eyes. All of them express, in different degrees, both awe at Christ's divinity and compassion for his human suffering. Milton, however, distances the Passion at three removes: he relates, in the third person, how Michael relates to Adam events that God has related to him. These events are also set at two temporal removes: from Michael's perspective they will occur in the distant future; from the reader's, they occurred in the distant past.

---

[95] M.M. Bakhtin, *The Dialogic Imagination*, ed. Michael Holquist, tr. Caryl Emerson and Michael Holquist (Austin and London, 1981), pp.15-17, 23.
[96] John Keats, Letter to Reynolds, September 21, 1819: see M.H. Abrams (ed.), *The Norton Anthology of English Literature*, Sixth Edn, Vol.II (New York and London, 1993), p.816.
[97] T.S. Eliot, 'Milton II', in *On Poetry and Poets* (London, 1957), p.150.
[98] Eliot, 'What is a Classic', pp.64-5, cf. 'The Music of Poetry', *Ibid.*, pp.34-5. Bakhtin makes a similar point (p.3).

Furthermore, in depicting the Passion, Milton emphasizes The Son's divinity and minimizes his humanity. Michael warns Adam not to think of the Son's fight with Satan in concrete terms, 'As of a duel, or the local wounds/ Of head or heel' (XII.387-8). He stresses that the Son conquers

> Not by destroying Satan, but his works
> In thee and in thy seed: nor can this be
> But by fulfilling that which thou didst want,
> Obedience to the law of God...
>
> XII.394-7

Michael treats the physical reality of the Son's death with cursory brevity:

> ... thy punishment
> He shall endure by coming in the flesh
> To a reproachful life and cursed death,
> Proclaiming life to all who shall believe
> In his redemption, and that his obedience
> Imputed becomes theirs by faith, his merits
> To save them, not their own, though legal works.
> For this he shall live hated, be blasphemed,
> Seized on by force, judged, and to death condemned
> A shameful and accurst, nailed to the cross
> By his own nation, slain for bringing life;
> But to the cross he nails thy enemies,
> The law that is against thee, and the sins
> Of all mankind, with him there crucified,
> Never to hurt them more who rightly trust
> In this his satisfaction; so he dies,
> But soon revives...
>
> XII.404-20

The pain of the Crucifixion is removed, treated briefly in almost dismissive terms: 'nailed to the cross', and 'so he dies/ But soon revives'. Milton's conscious rhetoric ('slain for bringing life... to the cross he nails thy enemies') and theological abstractions ('his obedience/ Imputed becomes theirs by faith... who rightly trust/ In this his satisfaction') overwhelm the human reality.

Moreover, despite Michael's warning, the poem treats the spiritual reality of the Son's victory in concrete spatial and temporal terms:

> Then to the heaven of heavens he shall ascend
> With victory, triumphing through the air
> Over his foes and thine; there shall surprise
> The serpent, prince of air, and drag in chains
> Through all his realm, and there confounded leave;
> Then enter into glory, and resume
> His seat at God's right hand, exalted high...
>
> XII.451-8

In minimizing the Son's humanity, the narrator avoids any sense of Christ's anguish. He also avoids the anguish of human response. Adam does not himself see the Passion in a vision, but hears it foretold as a future event. Making no pause for Adam's response, Michael continues his story, ending with the Last Judgment when the earth 'Shall be all paradise'. Adam, 'replete with joy and wonder', responds, not to the Son's suffering, but to his triumph 'That all this good of evil shall produce' (XII.464-78).

Lewis considers Books XI and XII an artistic failure, 'an untransmuted lump of futurity' that is written so badly that the reader sometimes feels that 'the story cannot possibly be told in a manner that shall make less impression on the mind'.[99] But perhaps this coldness and apparent failure is deliberate. Perhaps it displays, as Kinney suggests, both the entropy of fallen time, and Milton's refusal 'to make a good story out of fallen history'.[100] Books XI and XII seem to me to dramatize both Milton's doubts about portraying the Passion at all, and the distance between the Poet and God.

Milton's doubts about portraying the Passion are apparent in his early, unfinished poem 'The Passion', to which he appended a statement that the topic 'was above the years he had when he wrote it'. Michael Grossman argues that, whereas Herbert could describe the events leading to Christ's death, for Milton the precise moment that mattered was the moment of Christ's death, 'the still point at which history and eternity are joined', and that this could not be expressed in 'the necessarily temporalizing process' of language:

> The significance of the Passion, as Milton understood it, could only be written inwardly on the softened stone of the heart... Thus the one moment of true pathos in 'The Passion' depicts not the suffering of Christ, but the frustration of the poet... confronting his inability to speak outwardly a necessarily inward grief...[101]

Similarly, R. Paul Yoder argues that 'The Passion' is a poem about writing a poem, that Milton creates a persona and then shows his humiliation 'as he struggles... with an impossible task – that of elegizing the Saviour.'[102] He argues that there is 'a parallel but opposing movement in the poem':

> ... while Jesus becomes most heroic when he rejects his own self-interest by accepting death, the persona becomes more unheroic as he becomes increasingly self-interested and self-absorbed in his search for an image that will satisfy his own poetic aspirations.[103]

---

[99] Lewis, *A Preface*, p.129.
[100] Kinney, pp.149-50.
[101] Michael Grossman, '"In Pensive Trance"', in *A Fine Tuning*, ed. Mary A. Maleski (Binghampton, New York, 1989), pp.205-20 (pp.214-15).
[102] R. Paul Yoder, 'Milton's *The Passion*', *MiltonS*, 27 (1991), 3-19 (p.4).
[103] Yoder, p.6.

Yoder argues that in breaking off the poem the persona surrenders his selfish ambition and becomes 'like the Christ who underwent the humiliation of the Passion'; he thinks that Milton reprinted the poem as a reminder 'of his vanity'.[104]

It seems to me that *Paradise Lost* too demonstrates a simulated failure of art. Although Langland and Donne are highly individual writers, their personae show little consciousness of themselves as writers. Rather, these personae enter the action of their poems, confessing their sins and finding resolution within the world of the poem. Milton's artistic self-consciousness is far stronger: it is seen both in the huge range of his poetic forms and devices, and in the invocations' suppressed but anguished consciousness that his artistic ambition may lead him into pride and division from God.

Unlike the personae of Langland, and Donne, Milton's Poet does not openly confess his sin, but masks it under positive descriptions of his epic endeavour. As I have already argued, the invocations display a spiritual decline in the Poet as the invocations move from direct plea-prayer to the Spirit (I.17) to distance from a 'heaven now alienated' (IX.8-9). The Poet's aspirations also become more limited: in the first invocation, he wishes to justify the ways of God to men, but in the fourth, he wishes only to find an 'answerable style' so that he can 'raise the name' of epic poetry. Yet the invocations end on a final note of bleak fear, as the Poet wonders 'if all be mine/ Not hers who brings it nightly to my ear' (IX.46-7).

That the Poet has become entrenched in the sin of pride through writing his poem is suggested by the quality of the last four books that follow this final invocation. Whereas Books IX and X, in which the Poet narrates the Fall and its immediate consequences, contain some of the most moving and magnificent poetry in *Paradise Lost*, Books XI and XII contain some of its worst: the sinful Poet is able to depict sin successfully, but he cannot depict Redemption successfully (This may be a further reason why Milton denies the Father's voice 'his own best style').[105]

By confining the Poet's overt voice to the invocations, Milton keeps the issue of whether or not his attempt to 'justify the ways of God to men' might be sinful out of the action of the poem. Thus the persona cannot depict himself as resolving his sin and finding salvation within the poem. In relegating the Passion to the distant future, the persona declines to bring his own sinfulness to the Cross, not daring to claim its validity for himself. After a very brief encounter with the Spirit in the first invocation, the Poet moves further and further away from encounter with God.

After allowing the Poet to speak at length in four invocations, Milton silences him completely at the end of the poem:

> In either hand the hastening angel caught
> Our lingering parents, and to the eastern gate

---

[104] Yoder, pp.9-12; 15.
[105] Hale, 'Voicing Milton's God', *AUMLA*, 88 (1997), 59-70 (pp.62, 68). Hale thinks this may be deliberate, but does not really explore Milton's reasons.

Led them direct, and down the cliff as fast
To the subjected plain; then disappeared.
They looking back, all the eastern side beheld
Of Paradise, so late their happy seat,
Waved over by that flaming brand, the gate
With dreadful faces thronged and fiery arms:
Some natural tears they dropped, but wiped them soon;
The world was all before them, where to choose
Their place of rest, and providence their guide:
They hand in hand with wandering steps and slow,
Through Eden took their solitary way.

XII.637-49

Although the invocations might lead the reader to expect it, the poem does not end with the Poet's assessment of his achievement, or even with his gratitude for completing his poem. It is as if, in his deliberately flawed account of the Redemption, Milton's persona has rooted out the Poet and hewn down the idolatrous images in himself, leaving space only for the Believer.

But if the Poet does not achieve encounter in the poem, I think that the Believer does – in his covert joining in with the angels' prayer to the Father and Son, and also in his powerful portrayal of the Son's offer to redeem Man. Through the voices of Adam and Eve as they wrestle with their sin, he also achieves some degree of acceptance of his own sinfulness and some hope of redemption; through their pleas for reconciliation with each other and with God, he makes his own plea for redemption. Here, at the end of the poem, the use of the first person plural, 'Our parents', presents the persona here as one who speaks, not for himself alone, but on behalf of all humanity. Despite the 'flaming brand... dreadful faces... fiery arms' the tone of the last lines is muted and accepting. Immediately after the Fall, Adam and Eve shed stormy tears:

They sat them down to weep, nor only tears
Rained at their eyes, but high winds worse within
Began to rise, high passions, anger, hate,
Mistrust, suspicion, discord, and shook sore
Their inward state of mind, calm region once
And full of peace, now tossed and turbulent:
For understanding ruled not, and the will
Heard not her lore, both in subjection now
To sensual appetite.

IX.1121-9

But as they leave Eden, Adam and Eve have regained the use of reason: they shed 'natural tears', but soon wipe them. There is a strong note of hope as they see 'The world... all before them' and think of choosing a 'place or rest' with providence to guide them. There is sorrow as they take their solitary way slowly through Eden, but also comfort as they wander away 'hand in hand'.

The narrative voice here is gentle, accepting. There is no prideful sense of egoistic endeavour, and there is no anguish or struggle. It is as if the Believer, having finally ousted the Poet, is able to see his own sinfulness in the characters of Adam and Eve, to accept and understand it, but also to take comfort that as their sin was redeemed, so too his sinfulness may also find redemption. And yet for them, and for him, that Redemption remains a distant future promise. In withdrawing from Eden, and making himself remote (in Adam's future and in Milton's past) Milton's God has made himself inaccessible to a present encounter with his creatures: he is 'invisible... inaccessible... through a cloud/ Drawn round about thee.../ Dark with excessive bright' (III.375-80). For Milton, the gap between God and himself lies in God's unavailability rather than in the Poet/Believer himself who focuses his attention on God and seeks, however idolatrously, to 'justify the ways of God to man', and to join his praise with that of the angels.

Conclusion

Go, litel bok, go, litel myn tragedye,
Ther God thi makere yet, er that he dye,
So sende myght to make in some comedye!
But litel book, no makyng thow n'envie,
But subgit be to alle poesye;
And kis the steppes, where as thow seest pace
Virgile, Ovide, Omer, Lucan, and Stace.

Chaucer, Troilus and Criseyde, V.1786-92

Part of the purpose of this book has been to 'kiss the steps' of Langland, Donne, Milton, and even the anonymous authors of the lyrics – that is, to pay the deepest attention that I was capable of to what they wrote about encounter with God and how they wrote it. However, I have chosen this passage from Chaucer to end with because it also suggests that this whole book is in some sense a tragedy that charts – in these poems at least – a movement away from poetic encounter with God.

The key threads of this tragic narrative of encounter are a growing remoteness from the Church – the community of believers – counterbalanced by a growing emphasis on the individual, and a corresponding growth in doubt as to whether that individual can attain salvation through direct encounter with God.

As I said at the outset, the poets discussed – the lyricists, Langland, Donne and Milton – are the only major English poets who depict an encounter between a single stable persona and the God or Christ of salvation history. But unless a great gap is left in salvation history between Pentecost and the Last Days, then that history includes the history of the institutional Church – whether that Church is seen as holy or corrupt.

The Church was the great unifying force of Latin Christendom for a thousand years – from the Fall of Rome to the Reformation. Through the monasteries, universities and cathedrals, it was the main source of education and culture. Aquinas wrote that

> The Church has four marks, being one, holy, catholic or universal, and strong or lasting... This unity... comes from... faith, for all Christians who belong to the body of the Church believe the same truths... hope, for all are comforted by the same confidence of coming to life eternal... charity, for all are bound together in the love of God and of one another... The genuineness of this love is shown when the members of the Church care for one another... each should serve his neighbour; nobody should be despised, nobody should be treated as an outcast, for the Church is like the Ark of Noah, outside which nobody can be saved. Then the Church is holy: *know you not that you are the temple of God...* The Church is catholic, that is, universal... nobody is rejected, whether they be masters or slaves, men or women... it began with Abel and will last even to the end of the world...

And even after, for the Church remains in heaven. Fourthly, the Church is firm, solid as a house on massive foundations... The Church can never be brought down. Indeed it grows under persecution, and those who attack it are destroyed... Nor can the Church be destroyed by errors... nor by the temptations of demons, for the Church will stand, a secure place of refuge: *the name of the Lord is a strong tower.*[1]

Given the intermittent conflict between the Church and those it construed as 'heretics', this magnificent account must always have represented an ideal rather than the reality. But within a century even the ideal was acutely threatened by the corruption and division that led up to the shattering of the Church in the Reformation.

This period of religious flux and tension, with its growing emphasis on individual conscience rather than on the traditional teachings of the Church, presented problems for Langland, Donne, and Milton. Poets such as Herbert or Hopkins could continue to write *mystical* or *spiritual* poetry that depicts a deeply personal encounter with their 'Lord', set in the *private* realm of the poet's study, or his heart, or in his personal experience of the natural world. But Langland, Donne, and Milton write *religious* poetry that depicts the poet's personal encounter with God as Creator, Redeemer, or Judge in the *public* or *communal* realm of salvation history. These poems have to deal, not merely with the *private, emotional truth* that a mystic can feel in his own heart and soul, but also with the *public, intellectual, theological Truth* that binds a faith community together.

The Crucifixion lyrics, written by clerics as a preaching aid at the height of the Age of Faith, have little to say about the Church. The speakers of these poems represent themselves as standing outside time and outside the physical world. They are participants who witness the Crucifixion in the eternal present that makes its redemptive grace available to Everyman as soon as he responds with love and asks for it. The whole of the poem is usually focused on a direct, personal, and present encounter with Christ.

However, the poems of Langland, Donne, and Milton depict their personae's relationship with God as occurring in the world of time and space: in fourteenth-century London; on a westward journey on Good Friday in a particular year; fallen among 'evil days... and evil tongues... and with dangers compassed round' (*Paradise Lost*, VII.26-7). They show a growing alienation between the soul and the Church, the institutionalized community of Christian believers, and a corresponding uncertainty of their ability to encounter God directly.

In *Piers Plowman*, *Liberum Arbitrium*'s definition of the ideal Church is very similar to Aquinas's:

'What is Holy Churche, chere frende?' quod I. 'Charite,' he saide;
Lief and love and leutee, in o byleve a lawe

---

[1] St Thomas Aquinas, Exposition, Apostle's Creed, *Theological Texts*, ed. and tr. Thomas Gilby (London, 1955), pp.340-2.

A love-knotte of leutee and of lele byleve,
Alle kyne Cristene clevynge on o wille,
Withoute gyle and gabbyng gyve and sulle and lene.
Love-lawe without leutee, allouable was hit nevere;
God lereth no lyf to lovye withouten leel cause!'

C.XVII.125-31

This ideal is prominent at the start of the poem when Holy Church, the 'lovely lady', expounds both the nature of divine Truth and Love and the need for humans to respond with works of charity. The same connection between Truth, Charity, and the Church is apparent in Piers's description of how the Folk should attain the Castle of Truth through virtue,

And yf Grace graunte the to go in in this wyse
Thow shalt se Treuthe sitte in thy sulve herte,
And solace thy soule and save the fram payne,
And charge Charite a churche to make
In thyne hole herte, to herborwe alle trewe
And fynde alle manere folk fode to here soules,
Yef love and leute and oure lawe be trewe.

C.VII.254-9

For Langland, the Church should be the place of unity, the union of Truth and Charity, where the individual can be trained and supported by traditional wisdom and communal effort. However, by the time he reaches the end of his poem, Langland is aware that the corruption of the clergy and the failure of Christian virtue has damaged the structure of the Church itself. No sooner have Piers and Grace built the barn of Unity-Holy Church and gone together 'to tulye treuthe/ And the londe of bileue, the lawe of Holi Churche'.XXI.335-6), than Pride attacks, the virtues are corrupted, Antichrist uproots the crop of truth, the friars destroy the crucial sacrament of Confession, and the Church becomes an embattled and empty fortress in a sea of vice and hypocrisy. This threat to the Church is the main feature of Will's climactic last vision, and the poem ends in near despair.

Born amid the theological tensions of the 'English religion in its most difficult century',[2] it was impossible for Donne to feel sure that the Truth was easily accessible through the medium of the Church. For Donne the Church is meant to be the Bride of Christ, but the disunity among the human views of the Christian faith forces her into whoredom. 'Satyre III' depicts the various 'religions' as a series of undesirable mistresses (ll.43-68). In Sonnet XVIII, Donne suggests that Christ's 'spouse' is neither the 'richly painted' version of the Catholics, nor the 'rob'd and tore' version of the Protestants, but a Dove

Who is most trew, and pleasing to thee, then
When she'is embrac'd and open to most men.

---

[2] Cummings, pp.366, 373.

Christ's true Church is not to be found in any of the warring factions of the earthly churches. With the loss of one unified Church, comes uncertainty as to the truths of religion. This uncertainty is apparent in 'Satyre III' with its bleak injunction, 'Seeke true religion. O where?', its contention that 'truth and falshood bee/ Neare twins', and its image of the difficulty of climbing the 'Cragged, and steep' hill of Truth (ll.43, 72-82). For Donne, Truth cannot be found in the 'mere contraries' and 'tyrannous rage' of the disparate churches which have 'left their roots' and are guided by 'Philip... Gregory... Harry or... Martin': it is 'dazling, yet plaine to all eyes', a 'hard knowledge' that must be reached by the 'minds indeavours' of individual Christians who return to God, 'the rough streames calm head'(ll.86-110).

In *Paradise Lost*, Milton also located 'the worship... Of spirit and truth' in the individual – in the 'living temples' of 'all believers' upheld by 'faith and conscience' (XII.519-33). Michael rejects all Churchmen after the apostles as wolves

> Who all the sacred mysteries of heaven
> To their own vile advantages shall turn
> Of lucre and ambition, and the truth
> With superstitions and traditions taint,
> Left only in those written records pure,
> Though not but by the Spirit understood.

XII.509-14

Michael abhors the 'Places and titles... Secular power... carnal power' which 'feigning' churchmen shall use to force false spiritual laws 'On every conscience', persuading the masses that religion resides 'in outward rites and specious forms' (XII.515-35).

Although this disillusionment with the corruption of the Church is understandable, the decline in the role of the Church presents a problem for the poet who wishes to write *public* or *religious* poetry. During the Middle Ages, the Church sanctioned the use of 'images' as a means of teaching the Christian faith, and there were specific rules and traditions about how this faith might be represented without risking either heresy or idolatry.[3] As the individual artist moves away from the shelter of the Church's official teaching, the question of idolatry arises. If the Truth is only to be found 'in those written records pure' of the Scriptures, what business does Milton have in going beyond Scripture to write about the War and Parliament in Heaven, God's conversations with the unfallen Adam, and Michael's account of salvation history? In writing 'Things unattempted yet in prose or rhyme', is he merely an ambitious wolf, seeking his own 'vile advantages'?

The anonymous lyricists were unselfconscious artists who wrote as men of the Church, to encourage Everyman to believe in the central teachings of that Church. Langland, Donne and Milton, however, are all conscious artists. Thus they share with God an impulse towards creativity. This impulse may be idolatrous in

---

[3] Émile Mâle, *The Gothic Image* (London, 1961), pp.1-22; see also Camille, throughout.

the human, if it is directed towards selfish rather than divine ends, if, as Milton fears,

> ... all be mine,
> Not hers who brings it nightly to my ear.
>
> IX.46-7

Writing as individuals expressing their own individual searches for salvation and inspiration, Langland, Donne, and Milton all show some discomfort over the moral status of their writing, and their use of language and form shows corresponding signs of strain.

Langland is concerned by the moral and social standing of his writing: by whether he should 'publische' the evil behaviour of the friars (C.XII.23-41); whether he should write yet another book to teach men about Dowel, when he could be praying for those who give him bread (B.XII.16-18); or whether he should perform socially useful work rather than writing satire and praying for his benefactors (C.V.1-108). He does not, however, seem concerned that his poetry's more spiritual purposes may be idolatrous.[4] Like other medieval authors, he uses the form of the dream vision to suggest that he is not making up his vision of the Harrowing of Hell, but merely writing down a faithful record of what he dreamed (XXI.1). In reflecting on the meaning of Christ's life and death, Langland still has the weight of Catholic tradition behind him.

However, the unity of the Catholic Church is crumbling, and the last two visions of *Piers Plowman* depict the corruption of language: in the abuse of the names of the cardinal virtues by those who should uphold them; in the punning speech of the 'lewed vicory' who complains that the only Cardinals he knows are the corrupt and venial ones who come from the pope (C.XXI.396-484); and in the way that 'Hende-Speche' allows 'Frere Flaterare' into Unity, where he immediately corrupts Contrition, the 'sovereyne salve for alle kyne synnes' (C.XXII.372). At the end of his poem, Langland's linear narrative of Redemption, with its triumphant climax in the Harrowing of Hell, is subverted by a circular structure that stresses society's inability to profit from that Redemption. Will initially went to sleep in a softly sunny, summer season, where the carelessness of the Folk was represented by a cheerful chaos of calls for hot pies and wine. As the poem returns to its beginning, this chaos is raised to the power of ten as gigantic Sins sling 'drede of dispayr' around them (C.XXII.164). The poem ends (or rather fails to end) with the renewal of the search for Piers and Grace: now even the Tower of Truth (which has been replaced by the besieged Barn of Unity) is no longer able to guide or protect Conscience.

The same tensions in language and form are apparent in the Holy Sonnets and 'Goodfriday,1613. Riding Westward'. Apart from the 'marring' of poems and

---

[4]C adds a rough, possibly unfinished passage about 'Ydolatrie' (Pro.94-124; Pearsall 106-17n.), but this passage concerns clerical abuse and the worship of relics and 'maumettes' rather than the writing of poetry. Hudson discusses the concern with images during the Lollard period: 'Premature Reformation', pp.301-9.

the quoting from iconoclastic texts that Gilman observes, the discomfort with the process of writing religious poems is suggested by the refusal of these poems to reach closure. They reject, as Linville argues, an 'integrating vision that resolves and answers the complex problems', and their endings are 'weak, ruptured, and halting' rather than fixed and stabilized.[5] Donne's language shows the tension in his convoluted syntax, his often hectic tone, his ragged rhythms with strong enjambments, marked voltas, and multiple cesuras. Although the narrative direction of his Divine Poems, as I argued, moves towards God, they avoid idolatry by never allowing themselves to arrive.

Milton is the most concerned of the three with the possibility of idolatry and the difficulties of writing in fallen language. I have argued that the Parliament of Heaven in *Paradise Lost* needs to be read on two levels: as a public expression of faith, and as a private expression of concern about his own spiritual status. He expresses, through the persona of his Poet, his fear that his whole enterprise in writing *Paradise Lost* is sinful. He avoids or at least mitigates this idolatry by deliberately marring the last two books and by silencing the Poet at the end of his poem, not allowing him to make the self-conscious conclusion that the earlier invocations might lead us to expect. In deconstructing the heroic conventions and magnifying the temporal dislocations of the epic form, Milton left it in such a state that neither Keats nor Eliot felt able to use it.

But apart from the possibility that writing religious poetry is idolatrous, there is another problem, not so much for the Christian poet, as for the Christian soul who must live outside the Church. The central tenet of the Catholic Church is that Christ has already redeemed humanity and that individuals can gain access to this salvation through the grace provided by the Church in the sacraments, as Aquinas points out,

> Although by his death Christ sufficiently merited salvation for the whole human race, each of us must there seek his own cure... a universal cause must be applied to be effective... consequently determinate remedies need to be applied to men if they are to be brought into the blessings flowing from Christ's death. These remedies... are the sacraments of the Church.[6]

I should firmly state here that I do not believe, nor do I mean to imply, that this ever actually was the only or even the best way to achieve 'salvation', however that term is understood. Nevertheless, it was possible for Christians of the Age of Faith to take comfort in this belief, and the sense of security that this view provides underlies the medieval Crucifixion lyrics. They depict the Crucifixion as a present reality with eternal significance: the Redemption is seen as happening *now*, and the encounter of the Meditator and Christ is related in the *present tense*. This Mediator is not individualized in the way that Langland's Dreamer, Donne's Seeker, and Milton's Poet all are. Nevertheless, the lyrics' concern with whether this persona will respond as he ought to Christ's sacrifice does reinforce the importance of the

---

[5] Linville, pp.152-3.
[6] IV *Contra Gentes*, 55-6, Gilby, pp.330; 353.

individual's response. At their best, the lyrics achieve a freshness and sense of personal conviction that allows the individual reader to embrace the common experience of 'Mankind' as his or her own.

As love poems, the lyrics offer a limited view of God's nature, focusing exclusively on their belief in Christ's love and mercy. Langland, Donne, and Milton, however, lived in a period when a simple faith in the efficacy of the Church and the sacraments as a secure route to salvation was no longer possible. All of them are concerned with how or whether the individual can attain salvation, and their poems all deal with the anguish of doubt. All of them deal with the more awesome aspects of God, particularly the God who judges sinners, with a God who cannot be, in Jennings's terms, domesticated or controlled.[7] They depict the lack of or the loss of present encounter with God – a sense of the absence, distance, or alienation of God that grows more acute with each poet.

Langland, writing in the lead-up to the Reformation, depicts the Redemption as a historical reality that has occurred before the Dreamer's very eyes. However, at the end of the poem, this vision recedes into the distant *past*, as the contemporary world fails to live up to it. Donne, anguished by the breakdown of Christian unity, unsure that he has access to the truth about God, depicts an ardent desire for an encounter that is always just out of reach in the *urgent-future*. Milton displays the early Protestant focus on sin: he subverts his apparently confident justification of God's ways to Man by dramatizing the Poet's sinful movement away from encounter with God; relating the sin of Adam and Eve, he places their encounter with God in the *past*; in Michael's prophecy, he places encounter between Christ and redeemed humanity in the *distant future*. Thus Langland, Donne, and Milton avoid idolatry by creating gaps in the language, gaps that reinforce the distance between God and Man, and the fleeting or tenuous nature of encounter.

The history of encounter in the poems examined in this book displays a movement from the articulation of the presence and actuality of encounter to the articulation of the potentiality or loss of encounter. This book thus chronicles the movement of serious *public, religious* poetry away from encounter with God – a movement from certainty to alienation, a movement in which religious poetry itself, written in fallen language, seeking to express the inexpressible, and asking the questions that arise from a time-bound consciousness of sin and distance from God, is, as it were, cast out of Eden.

---

[7] Jennings, pp.93-5, 113. See above, p.8.

Bibliography

Primary Sources:

Abelard, Peter. *Commentarium super S. Pauli Epistolam ad Romanos Libri Quinque, Patralogia Latina,* 178. 787-978.

Anselm of Canterbury. *Anselm of Canterbury:The Major Works,* ed. Brian Davies and G.R. Evans, Oxford: Oxford University Press, 1998.

—*Opera Omnia,* ed. F.S. Schmitt, 6 vols, Stuttgart: Fromman, 1946.

Aquinas, Thomas. *Summa Theologica,* ed. Petri Marietti, 6 vols, Taurini: [n.pub.], 1915.

—*Theological Texts,* ed. and tr. Thomas Gilby, London: Oxford University Press, 1955.

Augustine of Hippo. *Confessions,* tr. R.S. Pine-Coffin, London: Penguin, 1961.

—*De Trinitate,* tr. Edmund Hill, *The Works of Saint Augustine,* ed. John E. Rotelle, Part 1, vol. 5, Brooklyn: New City Press, 1991.

Bernard of Clairvaux, St. *De Gratia et Libero Arbitrio* in *Opera Omnia.* ed. J. Leclerq and H.M. Rochais, Rome: Editiones Cisterciences, 1957, 7 vols., iii.155-203.

Brown, Carleton. (ed.) *English Lyrics of the XIIIth Century,* Oxford: Clarendon Press, 1932.

—*Religious Lyrics of the XIVth Century,* 2nd edn, rev. G.V. Smithers, Oxford: Clarendon Press, 1957.

—*Religious Lyrics of the XVth Century,* Oxford: Clarendon Press, 1939.

Dante Alighieri, *The Divine Comedy,* 3 vols, ed. and tr. John D. Sinclair, London: Oxford University Press, 1971.

Davies, R.T. (ed.) *Medieval English Lyrics,* London: Faber, 1963.

Donne, John, *Poetical Works,* ed. Herbert Grierson, London: Oxford University Press, 1967.

—*The Divine Poems,* ed. Helen Gardner, Oxford: Clarendon Press, 1952.

—*John Donne: The Complete English Poems,* 2nd edn, C.A. Patrides revised by Robin Hamilton, London: Everyman, 1944.

Dunbar, William. *The Poems of William Dunbar,* ed. W. Mackay Mackenzie, London: Faber, 1970.

Eliot, T.S. *Collected Poems,* London: Faber, 1963.

Gréban, Arnoul, *Le Mystére de la passion,* ed. Gaston Paris and Gaston Raynaud, (Paris, 1878), Geneva: Satkine Reprints, 1970.

Herbert, George. *The Poems of George Herbert,* with an introduction by Helen Gardner, London: Oxford University Press, 1961.

The Holy Bible: Authorized Version, London and New York: Collins, 1957.

Hopkins, Gerard Manley. *The Poems of Gerard Manley Hopkins*, 4th edn, ed. W.H. Gardner and N.H. MacKenzie, Oxford: Oxford University Press, 1970.

Langland, William. *Piers Plowman by William Langland: An Edition of the C-Text*, ed. Derek Pearsall, London: Arnold, 1978.

—*Piers Plowman: The C Version*, ed. George Russell and George Kane, London: Athlone Press, 1997.

—*Piers Plowman: A Parallel-Text Edition of the A, B, C, and Z Versions*, Vol.1, ed. A.V.C. Schmidt, London and New York: Longman, 1995.

—*The Vision of Piers Plowman: A Complete Edition of the B-Text*, ed. A.V.C. Schmidt, London: Everyman, 1978.

Milton, John. *Complete Shorter Poems*, ed. John Carey, London: Longman, 1968.

—*Paradise Lost*, ed. Alastair Fowler, London: Longman, 1968.

The Chester Mystery Cycle, ed. R.M. Lumiansky and David Mills, EETS, London, New York, Toronto: Oxford University Press, 1974.

The Early English Versions of the Gesta Romanorum, ed. S.J.H. Herrtage, EETS e.s. 33, London: Trübner, 1879 repr. 1962.

The N-town Play: Cotton Vespasian D.8, Vol 1, ed. Stephen Spector, EETS, Oxford, New York: Oxford University Press, 1991.

The Towneley Plays, Vol. 1, ed. Martin Stevens and A.C. Cawley, EETS, New York: Oxford University Press, 1994.

The York Plays, ed. Richard Beadle, London: Arnold, 1982.

Thomas, R.S. *Collected Poems*, London: Dent, 1993.

Secondary Sources

Adams, Robert. 'Langland's Theology', in Alford, *A Companion*, pp.87-114.

—'Mede and Mercede: The Evolution of the Economics of Grace in the *Piers Plowman* B and C Versions', in Kennedy et al., pp.217-32.

—'Piers' Pardon and Langland's Semi-Pelagianism', *Traditio*, 39 (1983), 367-418.

Aers, David. *Chaucer, Langland and the Creative Imagination*, London: Routledge and Kegan Paul, 1980.

—'Christ's Humanity and *Piers Plowman*: Contexts and Political Implications', *YLS*, 8 (1994), 107-25.

—*Faith, Ethics and Church: Writing in England, 1360-1409*, Cambridge: Brewer, 2000.

—*Community, Gender, and Individual Identity: English Writing, 1360-1430*, London and New York: Routledge, 1988.

Alford, John A. (ed.) *A Companion to Piers Plowman*, Berkeley, Los Angeles and London: University of California Press, 1988.

—'The Idea of Reason in *Piers Plowman*', in Kennedy et al., pp.199-215.

Allen, Hope Emily. *English Writings of Richard Rolle, Hermit of Hampole*, Oxford: Clarendon Press, 1931.

Arnold, Marilyn. 'Milton's Accessible God: The Role of the Son in Paradise Lost', *MiltonQ*, 7 (1973), 65-72.

Asals, Heather. 'John Donne and the Grammar of Redemption', *English Studies in Canada*, 5 (1979), 125-39.

Aulén, Gustaf. *Christus Victor*, tr. A.G. Herbert, new edn with introduction by Jaroslav Pelikan, New York: Macmillan, 1969.

Baker, Denise N. 'From Ploughing to Penitence', *Speculum*, 55 (1980), 715-25.

Bakhtin, M.M. *The Dialogic Imagination: Four Essays*, tr. Caryl Emerson and Michael Holquist, ed. Michael Holquist, Austin and London: University of Texas Press, 1981.

Baldwin, Anna P. 'The Double Duel in *Piers Plowman* B XVIII and C XXI'. *MÆ*, 50 (1981), 64-78.

—'The Historical Context', in Alford, *A Companion*, pp.67-87.

Baumlin, James S. *John Donne and the Rhetorics of Renaissance Discourse*, Columbia and London: University of Missouri Press, 1991.

Beaston, Lawrence. 'Talking to a Silent God: Donne's Holy Sonnets and the Via Negativa', *Renascence*, 51 (1999), 95-109.

Beckwith, Sarah. *Christ's Body: Identity, Culture and Society in Late Medieval Writings*, London and New York: Routledge, 1993.

Bellette, Antony F. '"Little Worlds Made Cunningly": Significant Form in Donne's Holy Sonnets and "Goodfriday, 1613"', *SP*, 72 (1975), 322-47.

Bennett, J.A.W. *Poetry of the Passion*, Oxford: Clarendon Press, 1982.

Benveniste, Emile. *Problems in General Linguistics*, tr. Mary Elizabeth Meek, Coral Gables, Florida: University of Miami Press, 1971.

Biggs, Frederic M. '"For God is After an Hand": *Piers Plowman* B.17.138-205', *YLS*, 5 (1991), 17-30.

Blanchard, Margaret M. 'The Leap into Darkness: Donne, Herbert, and God', *Renascence*, 17 (1964), 38-50.

Blessington, Francis C. 'Autotheodicy: The Father as Orator in *Paradise Lost*', *Cithara*, 14 (1975), 49-60.

—*Paradise Lost and the Classical Epic*, London: Routledge and Kegan Paul, 1979.

Bloomfield, Morton W. *Piers Plowman as a Fourteenth Century Apocalypse*, New Brunswick: Rutgers University Press, 1961.

—*The Seven Deadly Sins*, East Lansing: Michigan University Press, 1952.

Bond, Ronald. 'John Donne and the Problem of "Knowing Faith"', *Mosaic*, 14 (1981), 25-35.

Bowers, John M. *The Crisis of Will in Piers Plowman*, Washington: Catholic University of America Press, 1986.

—'*Piers Plowman's* William Langland: Editing the Text, Writing the Author's Life', *YLS*, 9 (1995), 65-90; with responses by Charlotte Brewer and Traugott Lawler, pp.91-8.

Bradshaw, John. *A Concordance to the Poetical Works of John Milton*, Boston: Longwood, 1977.

Broadbent, J.B. *Some Graver Subject*, London: Chatto and Windus, 1960.

Brooks, Helen B. 'Donne's "Goodfriday, 1613. Riding Westward" and Augustine's Psychology of Time', in Frontain and Malpezzi, pp.284-305.

Buber, Martin. *I and Thou*, tr. Walter Kaufmann, New York: Scribner, 1970.

Burrow, John. 'The Action of Langland's Second Vision' *Essays in Criticism*, 15 (1965), 247-68.

—*Langland's Fictions*, Oxford: Clarendon Press, 1993.

Camille, Michael. *The Gothic Idol: Ideology and Image-making in Medieval Art*, Cambridge: Cambridge University Press, 1989.

Caputo, John D. *The Prayers and Tears of Jacques Derrida: Religion without Religion*, Bloomington and Indianapolis: Indiana University Press, 1997.

Carey, John. *John Donne: Life, Mind and Art*, London: Faber, 1981.

Carlson, Paula J. 'Lady Meed and God's Meed: The Grammar of "Piers Plowman" B 3 and C 4', *Traditio*, 46 (1961).

Carnes, Valerie. 'Time and Language in Milton's *Paradise Lost*, *ELH*, 37 (1970) 517-39.

Carruthers, Mary. *The Search for St. Truth: A Study of Meaning in Piers Plowman*, Evanston: Northwestern University Press, 1973.

Carter, Ronald. *Investigating English Discourse: Language, Literacy and Literature*, London and New York: Routledge, 1997.

Chambers, A.B. 'Glorified Bodies and the "Valediction: forbidding Mourning"', *JDJ*, 1 (1982), 1-20.

Clements, Arthur L. *Poetry of Contemplation: John Donne, George Herbert, Henry Vaughan, and the Modern Period*, Albany: State University of New York Press, 1990.

Clopper, Lawrence M. 'Langland's Franciscanism', *Chaucer Review*, 25 (1990), 54-75.

—'Langland's Persona: An Anatomy of the Mendicant Orders', in Justice and Kerby-Fulton, pp.144-84.

—'The Life of the Dreamer, the Dreams of the Wanderer in *Piers Plowman*', *SP*, 86 (1989), 261-85.

Clutterbuck, Charlotte. 'Hope and Good Works: *Leaute* in the C-Text of *Piers Plowman*', *RES*, 28 (1977), 129-40.

Cohen, Kitty. 'Milton's God in Council and War', *MiltonS*, III (1971), 159-84.

Collinson, Patrick. 'English Reformations', in *A Companion to English Renaissance Literature and Culture*, ed. Michael Hattaway, Oxford: Blackwell, 2003.

Combs, H.C. and Sullens, Z.R. *A Concordance to the English Poems of John Donne*, New York: Haskell, 1969, p.301.

Cornelius, David K. 'Donne's Holy Sonnet XIV', *Explicator*, 24 (1965), Item 25.

Corns, T.N. *Milton's Language*, Oxford: Blackwell, 1990.

Coulson, John, *Religion and Imagination: 'In Aid of a Grammar of Assent'*, Oxford: Clarendon Press, 1981.

Coyle, Martin. 'The Subject and the Sonnet', *English*, 43 (1994), 139-50.

Crossan, John Dominic. *The Dark Interval: Towards a Theology of Story*, Allen, Texas: Argus Communications, 1975.

Cummings, Brian. *The Literary Culture of the Reformation: Grammar and Grace*, Oxford: Oxford University Press, 2002.

Dale, Judith. 'The Author, the Dreamer, his Wife and their Poet: Thoughts on an Essential-Ephemeral "Langland"', *YLS*, 15 (2001), 89-94.

Danielson, Dennis. *Milton's Good God: A Study in Literary Theodicy*, Cambridge: Cambridge University Press, 1982.

Davlin, Mary Clemente. '*Kynde Knowyng* as a Major Theme in *Piers Plowman* B', *RES*, ns 22: 85 (1971), 1-19.

—'*Kynde Knowyng* as a Middle English Equivalent for "Wisdom" in *Piers Plowman* B', *MÆ*, 50 (1981), 5-17.

—*The Place of God in Piers Plowman and Medieval Art*, Aldershot and Burlington: Ashgate, 2001.

Demaray, John G. *Milton's Theatrical Epic: The Invention and Design of Paradise Lost*, Cambridge, Massachussets: Harvard University Press, 1980.

Derrida, Jacques. *The Gift of Death*, tr. David Wills, Chicago and London: University of Chicago Press, 1995.

Dobson, R.B. *The Peasant's Revolt of 1381*, 2nd edn, London and Basingstoke: Macmillan, 1983.

Donaldson, E.T. *The C-Text and Its Poet*, New Haven: Yale University Press, 1949.

Donovan, Peter. *Religious Language*, London: Sheldon Press, 1976.

Dove, Mary. *The Perfect Age of Man's Life*, Cambridge: Cambridge University Press, 1986.

Dronke, Peter. *The Medieval Lyric*, London: Hutchison, 1968.

Duncan, Joseph E. 'Resurrections in Donne's "A Hymne to God the Father" and "Hymne to God my God in my sicknesse"', *JDJ*, 7 (1988), 183-9.

Eagleton, Terry. 'The God that Failed', in *Re-membering Milton: Essays on the Texts and Traditions*, ed. Mary Nyquist and Margaret Ferguson, New York: Methuen, 1987, pp.342-9

Eliot, T.S. *On Poetry and Poets*, London: Faber, 1957.

Emma, R.D. *Milton's Grammar*, London: Methuen, 1964.

Empson, William, *Milton's God*, 2nd edn, Cambridge: Cambridge University Press, 1981.

Erzgräber, Willi. *William Langlands "Piers Plowman": Eine Interpretation des C-Textes*, Heidelberg: Frankfurter Arbeiten, 1957.

Evans, J. Martin. *Milton's Imperial Epic: Paradise Lost and the Discourse of Colonialism*, Ithaca and London: Cornell University Press, 1996.

—'The Birth of the Author: Milton's Poetic Self-Construction', *MiltonS* (2000), 47-65.

Evans, W.O. 'Charity in *Piers Plowman*', in Hussey, pp.245-78.

Fein, Susanna Greer. *Moral Love Songs and Laments*, Kalamazoo, Michigan: Medieval Institute Publications, 1998.

Fish, Stanley. *Surprised by Sin*, 2nd edn, London: Macmillan, 1997.

Fixler, Michael, 'Milton's Passionate Epic', *MiltonS*, 1 (1969), 167-92.

Flanigan, Beverly Olson. 'Donne's "Holy Sonnet VII" as Speech Act', *Language and Style*, 19 (1986), 49-57.

Fletcher, Alan J. 'The Essential (Ephemeral) William Langland: Textual Revision as Ethical Process in *Piers Plowman*', *YLS*, 15 (2001), 61-84.

Frank, R.W. *Piers Plowman and the Scheme of Salvation*, New Haven: Yale University Press, 1957.

Freeborn, Dennis. *Style: Text Analysis and Linguistic Criticism*, Basingstoke and London: Macmillan, 1996.

Fresch, Cheryl H. 'Human and Divine Reconciliation in Paradise Lost, X-XI: The Strategy of Milton's Structure', in *Praise Disjoined: Changing Patterns of Salvation in 17th-Century English Literature*, ed. William P. Shaw, New York: Lang, 1991, pp.259-71.

Friedman, Donald M. 'Christ's Image and Likeness in Donne', *JDJ*, 15 (1996), 75-95.

—'Memory and the Art of Salvation in Donne's Good Friday Poem', *English Literary Renaissance*, 3 (1973), 420-37.

Friedrich, Paul. 'Dialogue in Lyric Narrative', in Macovski, ed., *Dialogue and Critical Discourse*, pp.79-98.

Frontain, Raymond-Jean and Malpezzi, Frances M. (eds.) *John Donne's Religious Imagination: Essays in Honor of John T. Shawcross*, Conway, AR: UCA Press, 1995.

Frye, Northrop. *Five Essays on Milton's Epics*, London: Routledge and Kegan Paul, 1966.

—*Words with Power: Being a Second Study of 'The Bible and Literature'*, San Diego: Harcourt Brace Jovanovich, 1992.

Fulton, Rachel. *From Judgement to Passion: Devotion to Christ and the Virgin Mary, 800-1200*, New York: Columbia University Press, 2002.

Gardiner, Anne Barbeau. 'Donne and the real Presence of the Absent Lover', *JDJ*, 9 (1990), 113-24.

Gardner, Helen. *The Composition of 'Four Quartets'*, London: Faber, 1978.

—*Religion and Literature*, London: Faber, 1971.

Gebinska, Marta. 'Some Observations on the Themes and Techniques of the Medieval English Religious Love Lyrics', *ES*, 57 (1976), 103-14.

Giachin E. and McGlashan, S. 'Spoken Language Dialogue Systems', in *Corpus Based Method in Language and Speech Processing*, ed. Steve Young and Gerrit Bloothooft, Dordrecht, Netherlands: Kluwer Academic, 1997, pp.69-117.

Gilman, Ernest B. *Iconoclasm and Poetry in the English Reformation: Down Went Dagon*, Chicago and London: University of Chicago Press, 1986.

Godden, Malcolm. *The Making of Piers Plowman*, London and New York: Longman, 1990.

Gray, Douglas. *Themes and Images in the Medieval English Religious Lyric*, London and Boston: Routledge & Kegan Paul, 1972.

Greenbaum, Sidney. *The Oxford English Grammar*, Oxford: Oxford University Press, 1996.

Gregory, Michael. 'A Theory for Stylistics – Exemplified: Donne's "Holy Sonnet XIV"', *Language and Style*, 7 (1974), 108-18.

Grossman, Michael. '"In Pensive Trance, and Anguish, and Ecstatic Fit": Milton on the Passion', in *A Fine Tuning: Studies of the Religious Poetry of Herbert and Milton*, ed. Mary A. Maleski, Binghampton, New York: Medieval and Renaissance Texts and Studies, 1989, pp.205-20.

Haan, Estelle. '"Heaven's purest Light": Milton's *Paradise Lost* 3 and Vida', *Comparative Literature Studies*, 30.2 (1993),115-36.

Hale, John K. 'Voicing Milton's God', *AUMLA*, 88 (1997), 59-70.

Halewood, William H. 'The Predicament of the Westward Rider', *SP*, 93 (1996), 218-28.

Halliday, M.A.K. *An Introduction to Functional Grammar*, 2nd edn London, Melbourne, Auckland: Arnold, 1994.

—'Language as Code and Language as Behaviour: A Systemic-Functional Interpretation of the Nature and Ontogenesis of Dialogue' in *The Semiotics of Culture and Language*, 2 vols, ed. Robin P. Fawcett, M.A.K. Halliday, Sydney M. Lamb, and Adam Makkai, London: Pinter, 1984, I.3-35.

—*Spoken and Written Language*, Deakin, Victoria: Deakin University Press, 1985.

—with Ruqaiya Hasan, *Cohesion in English*, London: Longman, 1976.

Hamlet, Desmond M. 'Recalcitrance, Damnation, and the Justice of God in *Paradise Lost*', *MiltonS*, 8 (1975), 267-91.

Hanna, Ralph. 'Will's Work', in Justice and Kerby-Fulton, pp.23-66.

Harbert, Bruce. 'A Will with a Reason: Theological Development in the C-Revision of *Piers Plowman*', in *Religion in the Poetry and Drama of the Late Middle Ages in England*, ed. Piero Boitani and Anna Torti, Cambridge: Brewer, 1990, pp.149-61.

—'Langland's Easter', in Phillips, pp.57-70.

Hardison, O.B. Jr. '*In Medias Res* in *Paradise Lost*', *MiltonS*, 17 (1983), 27-41.

Hart, Kevin. *The Trespass of the Sign*, Cambridge: Cambridge University Press, 1989.

Harwood, B.J. '*Liberum-Arbitrium* in the C-Text', *Philological Quarterly*, 52 (1973), 680-95.

—*Piers Plowman and the Problem of Belief*, Toronto: University of Toronto Press, 1992.

Haynes, John. *Introducing Stylistics*, London: Unwin Hyman, 1989.

Hester, M. Thomas, *Kinde Pitty and Brave Scorn: John Donne's Satyres*, Durham, N.C.: Duke University Press, 1982.

—'Re-signing the Text of the Self: Donne's "As Due by Many Titles"', in Summers and Pebworth, "*Bright Shootes*", pp.59-71.

Hewett-Smith, Kathleen M. 'Allegory on the Half-Acre: The Demands of History', *YLS*, 10 (1996), 1-22.

Hill, Thomas D. 'Universal Salvation and its Literary Context in *Piers Plowman* B.18', *YLS*, 5 (1991), 65-76.

Hudson, Anne. *The Premature Reformation: Wycliffite Texts and Lollard History*, Oxford: Clarendon Press, 1988.

Huisman, Rosemary. 'Who Speaks for Whom? The Search for Subjectivity in Browning's Poetry', *AUMLA*, 7 (1989), 64-87.

Hussey, S.S. (ed.) *Piers Plowman: Critical Approaches*, London: Methuen, 1969.

Jenkins, Priscilla. 'Conscience: The Frustration of Allegory', in Hussey, pp.125-42.

Jennings, Theodore. *Beyond Theism: A Grammar of God-Language*, New York, Oxford: Oxford University Press, 1985.

Johnston, James E. 'Milton on the Doctrine of the Atonement', *Renascence*, 38 (1985), 40-53.

Justice, Steven and Kathryn Kerby-Fulton. *Written Work: Langland, Labor, and Authorship*. Philadelphia: University of Pennsylvania Press, 1997.

Kaske, R.E. 'The Character Hunger in *Piers Plowman*', in Kennedy, pp.187-97.

—'Holy Church's Speech and the Stucture of *Piers Plowman*', in *Chaucer and Middle English Studies in Honour of Rossell Hope Robbins*, ed. Beryl Rowland, London: Allen & Unwin, 1974, pp.320-7.

Kean, P.M. 'Love, Law and *Lewte* in *Piers Plowman*', *RES*, ns 15 (1964), 241-61.

Kennedy, Edward Donald; Waldron, Ronald; Wittig, Joseph S. (eds.) *Medieval English Studies Presented to George Kane*, Woodbridge, U.K.: Brewer, 1988.

Kerby-Fulton, Kathryn. 'Langland and the Bibliographic Ego', in Justice and Kerby-Fulton, pp.67-143.

—*Reformist Apocalypticism and Piers Plowman*, Cambridge: Cambridge University Press, 1990.

Kerrigan, William. *The Prophetic Milton*, Charlottesville: University Press of Virginia, 1974.

Kinney, Clare Regan. *Strategies of Poetic Narrative: Chaucer, Spenser, Milton, Eliot*, Cambridge: Cambridge University Press, 1992.

Klawitter, George. 'John Donne's Attitude toward the Virgin Mary', in Frontain and Malpezzi, pp.122-40.

Kolve, V.A. *The Play Called Corpus Christi*, Stanford: Stanford University Press, 1966, p.103.

Koory, Mary Ann. '"England's Second Austine": John Donne's Resistance to Conversion', *JDJ*, 17 (1998), 137-61.

Labriola, Albert C. Donne's '"The Canonization": Its Theological Context and Its Religious Imagery', *Huntington Library Quarterly*, 36 (1973), 327-39.

Lawler, Traugott. 'The Gracious Imagining of Redemption in *Piers Plowman*', *English*, 28 (1979), 203-16.

Lawlor, John. *Piers Plowman: An Essay in Criticism*, London: Arnold, 1962.

—'"Piers Plowman": The Pardon Reconsidered', *MLR*, 45 (1950), 459-58.

Lawton, David. 'The Subject of Piers Plowman', *YLS*, 1 (1987), 1-30.

Lehnhof, Kent R. '"Impregn'd with Reason": Eve's Aural Conception in *Paradise Lost*', *MiltonS*, 41 (2002), 38-75.

Leith, Dick and Myerson, George. *The Power of Address: Explorations in Rhetoric*, London and New York: Routledge, 1989.

Lewalski, Barbara Kiefer. *Paradise Lost and the Rhetoric of Literary Forms*, Princeton: Princeton University Press, 1985.

—*Protestant Poetics and the Seventeenth-Century Religious Lyric*, Princeton: Princeton University Press, 1979.

Lewis, C.S. *A Preface to Paradise Lost*, London: Oxford University Press, 1960.

—*The Screwtape Letters*, Glasgow: Fount Paperbacks, 1977.

Lieb, Michael. 'Reading God: Milton and the Anthropopathetic Tradition', *MiltonS*, 25 (1989), 213-43.

Linville, Susan E. 'Contrary Faith: Poetic Closure and the Devotional Lyric', *Papers on Language and Literature*, 20 (1984), 141-53.

Low, Anthony. 'Milton's God: Authority in *Paradise Lost*', *MiltonS*, 4 (1972), 19-39.

Lyons, John. *Semantics*, 2 vols. Cambridge: Cambridge University Press, 1977.

MacCaffrey, Isabel, G. 'The Theme of *Paradise Lost* Book III', in *New Essays on Paradise Lost*, ed. Thomas Kranidas, Berkeley: University of California Press, 1969, pp.58-85.

Macovski, Michael, (ed.). *Dialogue and Critical Discourse: Language, Culture, Critical Theory*, New York and Oxford: Oxford University Press, 1997.

Macquarrie, John. *God-Talk*, London: SCM Press, 1967.

—*Principles of Christian Theology*, London: SCM Press, 1966.

—*The Humility of God*, London: SCM Press, 1978.

Mâle, Émile. *The Gothic Image: Religious Art in France of the Thirteenth Century*, London: Fontana, 1961.

Malpezzi, Frances. 'Donne's Transcendent Imagination: The Divine Poems as Hierophantic Experience', in Frontain and Malpezzi, pp.141-61.

Mann, Jill. 'The Power of the Alphabet: A Reassessment of the Relation between the A and the B Versions of *Piers Plowman*', *YLS*, 8 (1994), 21-50.

Martin, Catherine Gimelli. *The Ruins of Allegory: Paradise Lost and the Metamorphosis of Epic Convention*, Durham, NC, and London: Duke University Press, 1998.

Martz, Louis L. 'Donne and Herbert: Vehement Grief and Silent Tears', *JDJ*, 7 (1988), 21-34.

—*The Poetry of Meditation: A Study in English Religious Literature of the Seventeenth Century*, New Haven: Yale University Press, 1962.

Marx, C.W. *The Devil's Rights and the Redemption in the Literature of Medieval England*, Cambridge: Brewer, 1995.

Mazouer, Charles. 'Dieu, justice et miséricorde dans le *Mistére du Viel Testament*', *Moyen Age*, 91 (1985), 53-73.

McClendon, James Wm. Jr. *Doctrine: Systematic Theology Volume II*, Nashville: Abingdon Press, 1994.

McMahon, Robert. *The Two Poets of Paradise Lost*, Baton Rouge and London: Louisiana University Press, 1998.

Merback, Mitchell B. *The Thief, the Cross and the Wheel: Pain and the Spectacle of Punishment in Medieval and Renaissance Europe*, Chicago: University of Chicago Press, 1999.

Merrill, Thomas F. 'Miltonic God-Talk: The Creation in *Paradise Lost*,' *Language and Style*, 16:3 (1983), 296-312.

Mey, Jacob L. *Pragmatics: An Introduction*, Oxford and Cambridge Massachussetts: Blackwell, 1993.

Middleton, Anne. 'Acts of Vagrancy: The C Version "Autobiography" and the Statute of 1388', in Justice and Kerby-Fulton, pp.208-317

—'The Audience and Public of *Piers Plowman*', in *Middle English Alliterative Poetry and its Literary Background*, ed. David Lawton, Cambridge: Brewer, 1982, pp.101-23.

Miles, Josephine. 'Ifs, Ands, Buts for the Reader of John Donne', in *Just So Much Honour*, ed. Peter A. Fiore, University Park and London: The Pennsylvania State University Press, 1972, pp.273-91.

Miller, D.A. *Narrative and its Discontents: Problems of Closure in the Traditional Novel*, Princeton, New Jersey: Princeton University Press, 1981.

Miller, George. 'Stylistic Rhetoric and the Language of God in *Paradise Lost*, Book III', *Language and Style*, 8 (1975), 111-26.

Miller, Martyn J. 'Meed, Mercede, and Mercy: Langland's Grammatical Metaphor and Its Relation to *Piers Plowman* as a Whole', *Medieval Perspectives*, 9 (1994), 73-84.

Mills, David. 'The Role of the Dreamer', in Hussey, pp.180-212.

Milner, Andrew. *John Milton and the English Revolution: A Study in the Sociology of Literature*, London and Basingstoke: Macmillan, 1981.

Mitchell, J. Allan. 'Reading God Reading "Man": Hereditary Sin and the Narrativization of Deity in *Paradise Lost*, Book III', *MiltonQ*, 35 (May 2001), 72-86.

Moore, Peter G. 'Cross and Crucifixion in Christian Iconography: A Reply to E.J. Tinsley', *Religion*, IV (Autumn 1974), 104-13.

Murtaugh, Daniel Maher. *Piers Plowman and the Image of God*, Gainesville: University Presses of Florida, 1978.

Myers, Robert M. '"God Shall Be All in All": The Erasure of Hell in *Paradise Lost*', *Seventeenth Century*, 5 (1990), 43-53.

Oliver, P.M. *Donne's Religious Writing: A Discourse of Feigned Devotion*, London: Longman, 1997.

Patterson, David. *The Affirming Flame*, Norman: University of Oklahoma Press, 1988.

Payne, Craig. 'Donne's Holy sonnet XIV', *Explicator*, 54 (1996), 209-13.

Pearsall, Derek. 'Langland's London', in Justice and Kerby-Fulton, pp.185-207.

—'Poverty and Poor People in *Piers Plowman*', in Kennedy, pp.167-85.

Peter, John. *A Critique of Paradise Lost*, New York: Columbia University Press, 1960.

Phillips, Helen, (ed.) *Langland, The Mystics and the Medieval English Religious Tradition: Essays in Honour of S.S. Hussey*, Cambridge: Brewer, 1990.

Pickering, O.S. (ed.) *Individuality and Achievement in Middle English Poetry*, Cambridge: D.S. Brewer, 1997.

Pinka, Patricia Garland. *This Dialogue of One: The Songs and Sonnets of John Donne*, University, Alabama: University of Alabama Press, 1982.

Pollock, John J. 'Donne's "A Hymne to Christ"', *Explicator*, 38 (1980), 20-22.

Potter, Robert. 'Divine and Human Justice', in *Aspects of Early English Drama*, ed. Paula Neuss, Cambridge: Brewer, 1983, pp.129-41.

Pratt, Mary Louise. *Towards a Speech Act Theory of Literary Discourse*, Bloomington and London: Indiana University Press, 1977.

Radford, Richard. *A Linguistic History of English Poetry*, London: Routledge, 1993.

Raw, Barbara C. *Anglo-Saxon Crucifixion Iconography and the Art of the Monastic Revival*, Cambridge: Cambridge University Press, 1990.

Recanati, François. *Meaning and Force: The Pragmatics of Performative Utterances*, Cambridge: Cambridge University Press, 1987.

Reifelhoess, Paul. 'Milton's Pronomial Mating Dance: Paradise Lost 3.372-415', *MiltonQ*, 29 (1995), 106-11.

Reiss, Edmund. *The Art of the Middle English Lyric: Essays in Criticism*, Athens, Georgia: University of Georgia Press, 1972.

Rewak, William J. S.J. 'Book III of *Paradise Lost*: Milton's Satisfaction Theory of the Redemption', *MiltonQ*, 11 (1977), 97-102.

Richardson, Christine and Johnstone, Jackie. *Medieval Drama*, Houndmills and London: Macmillan, 1991.

Rickert, Margaret, *Painting in Britain: The Middle Ages* (2nd edn), Harmondsworth, Middlesex: Penguin, 1965.

Ricks, Christopher. *Milton's Grand Style*, Oxford: Oxford University Press, 1963.

Ricoeur, Paul. *History and Truth*, tr. Charles, A. Kelbley, Evanston, Illinois: Northwestern University Press, 1965.

—*The Symbolism of Evil*, tr. Emerson Buchanan, Boston: Beacon Paperbacks, 1969.

—*Time and Narrative*, tr. Kathleen McLaughlin and David Pellauer, Chicago and London: The University of Chicago Press, 1984.

Riggs, William, G. 'The Poet and Satan in *Paradise Lost*', *MiltonS* , 2 (1970), 59-82.

Romein, Tunis, 'Donne's "Holy Sonnet XIV"', *Explicator*, 42 (1984), 12-14.

Ross, Ellen M. *The Grief of God*, New York: Oxford University Press, 1997.

Rudd, Gillian. *Managing Language in Piers Plowman*, Cambridge: Brewer, 1994.

Ruffing, John. 'The Crucifixion Drink in *Piers Plowman* B.18 and C.20', *YLS* (1991), 99-109.

Russell, G.H. 'As They Read It: Some Notes on Early Responses to the C-Version of Piers Plowman', *Leeds Studies in English*, 20 (1989), 173-189.

—'Some Aspects of the Process of Revision in *Piers Plowman*', in Hussey, 1969, pp.27-49.

Samarin, William J. *Language in Religious Practice*, Rowley, Massachusetts: Newbury House, 1976.

Scase, Wendy. *Piers Plowman and the New Anticlericalism*, Cambridge: Cambridge University Press, 1989.

Schindler, Walter. *Voice and Crisis: Invocation in Milton's Poetry*, Hamden, Connecticut: Archon, 1984.

Schmidt, A.V.C. 'The Inner Dreams in *Piers Plowman*', *MÆ*, 55 (1986), 24-40.

—'Langland and the Mystical Tradition', in *The Medieval Mystical Tradition in England: Papers Read at the Exeter Symposium, July 1980*, ed. Marion Glasscoe, University of Exeter, 1980, pp.17-38.

—'Langland's Structural Imagery', *Essays in Criticism*, 30 (1986), 311-25.

—'*Lele Wordes* and *Bele Paroles*: Some Aspects of Langland's Word-Play', *RES*, 34 (1983), 137-50.

Scott, Anne M. '"Nevere noon so nedy ne poverer deide": *Piers Plowman* and the Value of Poverty', *YLS*, 15 (2001), 141-53.

Sellin, Paul. R. 'John Milton's *Paradise Lost* and *De Doctrina Christiana* on Predestination', *MiltonS*, 34 (1996), 45-60.

—'Satyre III No Satire: Postulates for Group Discussion', *JDJ*, 10 (1991), 85-9.

Shaw, William P. 'Milton's Choice of the Epic for *Paradise Lost*', *ELN*, 12 (1974), 15-20.

Shepherd, Geoffrey. 'Poverty in *Piers Plowman*', in *Social Relations and Ideas: Essays in Honour of R.H. Hilton*, ed. T.H. Aston, P.R. Cross, Christopher Dyer, and Joan Thirsk, Cambridge: Cambridge University Press, 1983, pp.169-89.

Sherry, Beverley. 'Speech in *Paradise Lost*', *MiltonS*, 8 (1975), 247-66.

Sherwood, Terry G. *Fulfilling the Circle: A Study of John Donne's Thought*, Toronto: University of Toronto Press, 1984.

Shoulson, Jeffrey S. 'The King and I: The Stance of Theodicy in Midrash and *Paradise Lost*', *MiltonS*, 36 (1998), pp.59-85.

Sicherman, Carol, M. 'Donne's Discoveries', *SEL*, 11 (1971), 69-88.

Simpson, James. *Piers Plowman: An Introduction to the B-text*, London and New York: Longman, 1990.

—'The Constraints of Satire in "Piers Plowman" and "Mum and the Sothsegger"', in Phillips, pp.11-30.

Smith, D. Vance. 'The Labors of Reward: Meed, Mercede, and the Beginning of Salvation', *YLS*, 8 (1995), 127-54.

Smith, Edward L. Jr. 'Achieving Impact through the Interpersonal Component', in Barbara Couture (ed.), *Functional Approaches to Writing: Research Perspectives*, London: Pinter, 1986, pp.108-19.

Smith, Julia J. 'Donne and the Crucifixion', *Modern Language Review*, 79 (1984), 513-25.

Southern, R.W. *The Making of the Middle Ages*, London: Hutchinson, 1967.

Spearing, A.C. 'The Development of a Theme in *Piers Plowman*', *RES*, n.s. 11 (1960), 241-53.

Spencer, T. J. B. '*Paradise Lost*: The Anti-Epic', in *Approaches to Paradise Lost: The York Tercentenary Lectures*, ed. C.A. Patrides, London: Arnold, 1968, pp.81-98.

Spurr, Barry. 'Salvation and Damnation in the *Divine Meditations* of John Donne', in *Changing Patterns of Salvation in 17th Century English Literature*, ed. William P. Shaw, New York: Lang, 1991, pp.165-74.

Stachniewski, John, 'John Donne: The Despair of the "Holy Sonnets"', *English Literary History*, 48 (1981), 677-705.

Steadman, John M. *Epic and Tragic Structure in Paradise Lost*, Chicago: The University of Chicago Press, 1976.

—'The God of *Paradise Lost* and the *Divina Commedia*', *Cithara*, 37 (1997), 22-39.

Stein, Arnold, *John Donne's Lyrics:The Eloquence of Action*, Minneapolis: University of Minnesota Press, 1962.

Steinberg, Theodore L. *Piers Plowman and Prophecy: An Approach to the C-Text*, New York and London: Garland, 1991.

Stiver, Dan R. *The Philosophy of Religious Language*, Cambridge Massachusetts and Oxford: Blackwell, 1996.

Stock, Lorraine Kochanske. 'Will, Actyf, Pacience, and *Liberum Arbitrium*: Two Recurring Quotations in Langland's Revisions of *Piers Plowman C Text*, Passus V, XV, XVI', *Texas Studies in Literature & Language*, 30 (1988), 461-77.

Stokes, Myra. *Justice and Mercy in Piers Plowman: A Reading of the B Text Visio*, London and Canberra: Croom Helm, 1984.

Strier, Richard, 'John Donne Awry and Squint: The "Holy Sonnets", 1608-10', *Modern Philology*, 86 (1989), 357-84.

Summers, Claude J. and Ted-Larry Pebworth (eds.), *"Bright Shootes of Everlastingnesse": The Seventeenth Century Religious Lyric*, Columbia: University of Missouri Press, 1987.

Sykes S.W. 'The Role of Story in the Christian Religion': An Hypothesis', *Literature and Theology*, 1 (1987), 16-26.

Thiselton, Anthony C. *New Horizons in Hermeneutics*, Grand Rapids, Michigan: Harper Collins, 1992.

Toolan, Michael. *Language in Literature: An Introduction to Stylistics*, London: Arnold, 1998.

Traver, Hope. *The Four Daughters of God: A Study of the Versions of this Allegory, with Special Reference to those in Latin, French, and English*, Philadelphia: Bryn Mawr College Monographs, 1907.

Ulreich, John C. 'Milton's Doctrine of the Incarnation', *MiltonS*, 39 (2000), 101-28.

Van Dijk, Teun A. *Handbook of Discourse Analysis: Volume 3 Discourse and Dialogue*, London: Academic Press, 1985.

Van Noppen, J.P. *Developing Pragmastylistic Competence*, Université Libre de Bruxelles, Senior Year Coursebook, Presses Universitaires de Bruxelles, 1995.

—*Transforming Words: The Early Methodist Revival from a Discourse Perspective*, Bern: Peter Lang (*Religion and Discourse*, 3), 1999.

Wall, John N. Jr. 'Donne's Wit of Redemption: The Drama of Prayer in the *Holy Sonnets*', *SP*, 73 (1976), 189-203.

Warner, Lawrence. 'Jesus the Jouster: The Christ-Knight and Medieval Theories of Atonement in *Piers Plowman* and the "Round Table" Sermons', *YLS*, 10 (1996), 129-43.

Wenzel, Siegfried. *Preachers, Poets, and the Early English Lyric*, Princeton: Princeton University Press, 1986.

—*The Sin of Sloth: Acedia in Medieval Thought and Literature*, Chapel Hill: University of California Press, 1967.

Werman, Golda. 'Repentance in *Paradise Lost*', *MiltonS*, 22 (1986), 121-39.

White, Hugh. *Nature and Salvation in Piers Plowman*, Cambridge: Brewer, 1988.

Wilding, Michael. *Dragon's Teeth: Literature in the English Revolution*, Oxford: Clarendon Press, 1987.

Wittig, Joseph. S. '"Culture Wars" and the Persona in *Piers Plowman*', *YLS*, 15 (2001), 167-95.

—'"Piers Plowman" B, Passus IX-XII: Elements in the Design of the Inward Journey', *Traditio*, 28 (1972), 211-80.

Wittreich, Joseph. 'Reading Milton: The Death (and Survival) of the Author', *MiltonS*, 38 (2000), 10-46.

Woolf, Rosemary. 'Doctrinal Influences on *The Dream of the Rood*', *MÆ*, 27 (1958), 137-53.

—*The English Mystery Plays*, London: Routledge and Kegan Paul, 1972.

—*The English Religious Lyric in the Middle Ages*, London: Oxford University Press, 1968.

— 'The Tearing of the Pardon', in Hussey, pp.50-75

— 'The Theme of Christ the Lover-Knight in Medieval English Literature', *RES*, 13 (1962), pp.1-16.

Wright, T.R. *Theology and Literature*, Oxford: Blackwell, 1988.

Yoder, R. Paul. 'Milton's *The Passion*', *MiltonS*, 27 (1991), 3-19.

Young, R.V. 'Donne's Sonnets and the Theology of Grace', in Summers and Pebworth, *"Bright shootes"*, pp.20-39.

Index

For Product Safety Concerns and Information please contact our EU
representative GPSR@taylorandfrancis.com Taylor & Francis Verlag GmbH,
Kaufingerstraße 24, 80331 München, Germany

Batch number: 08165901

Printed by Printforce, the Netherlands